THE KEY TO THE DOOR

THE
KEY
TO THE
DOOR

EXPERIENCES *of*
EARLY AFRICAN
AMERICAN STUDENTS
at the
UNIVERSITY OF VIRGINIA

Edited by

Maurice Apprey

and

Shelli M. Poe

University of Virginia Press

CHARLOTTESVILLE AND LONDON

University of Virginia Press
© 2017 by the Rector and Visitors of the University of Virginia
All rights reserved
Printed in the United States of America on acid-free paper

First published 2017
First paperback edition published 2024
ISBN 978-0-8139-5149-2

9 8 7 6 5 4 3 2 1

The Library of Congress has cataloged the hardcover edition as follows:

Names: Apprey, Maurice, 1947– editor. | Poe, Shelli M., editor.
Title: The key to the door : experiences of early African American students at the
    University of Virginia / edited by Maurice Apprey and Shelli M. Poe.
Description: Charlottesville ; London : University of Virginia Press, 2017. | Includes
    bibliographical references and index.
Identifiers: LCCN 2016051537 | ISBN 9780813939865 (cloth : alk. paper) |
    ISBN 9780813939872 (e-book)
Subjects: LCSH: University of Virginia—History—Sources. | University of Virginia—
    Alumni and alumnae—Interviews. | African Americans—Education (Higher)—
    Virginia.
Classification: LCC LD5678.8 .K49 2017 | DDC 378.1/9829960730755—dc23
LC record available at https://lccn.loc.gov/2016051537.

Cover art: Walter Nathaniel Ridley receives his doctorate of education from the
University of Virginia in 1953, becoming the first black graduate of the University.
(Albert and Shirley Small Special Collections Library, University of Virginia)

CONTENTS

Acknowledgments   vii

Preface   ix
Maurice Apprey

Foreword   xi
Teresa A. Sullivan

Introduction: Higher Education for the Public Good   1
Deborah E. McDowell

Perseverance and Resilience: African Americans at the
University of Virginia   9
Ervin L. Jordan, Jr.

The Only One in the Room: U.Va. Law School, 1955–1958   49
John F. Merchant

Becoming a Doctor in a Segregated World   83
William M. Womack

Life on Mr. Jefferson's Plantation   95
Aubrey Jones

Looking Back   111
Barbara S. Favazza

An Interview with Teresa Walker Price and Evelyn Yancey Jones   119
Maurice Apprey and Shelli M. Poe

A Son of the South: An African American Public Servant   125
David Temple, Jr.

CONTENTS

U.Va.—An Essential Experience   139
Willis B. McLeod

An Interview with Vivian W. Pinn   149
Maurice Apprey

Opening the Door: Reflection and a Call to Action for an
Inclusive Academic Community   159
*Shelli M. Poe, Patrice Preston-Grimes, Marcus L. Martin,
and Meghan S. Faulkner*

Addendum: Strategies for Creating a Sense of Place and
High Achievement   171
Maurice Apprey

Notes on Contributors   175

Index   181

Illustrations follow page 94.

ACKNOWLEDGMENTS

With grateful thanks, the editors and the authors acknowledge the Jefferson Trust, an initiative of the University of Virginia Alumni Association, for the substantive grant awarded to aid in the preparation and publication of this book.

Our thanks also go to all the African American graduates of the 1950s and 1960s for their courage and leadership in being among the first to desegregate the University of Virginia. We would also like to thank the alumni association for planning an extraordinary reunion event for these graduates. The committee—which included Jeffrey Moster, Norman Oliver, Marcus Martin, Judy Pointer, Carolyn Dillard, Daisy Lundy, and Timothy Lovelace—brought together many of our earliest African American graduates, some of whom had not returned to Charlottesville since their graduations. The event provided both a healing and a celebration. But more than that, it was a time for the University to show its gratitude to these remarkable pioneers.

The preparation of the manuscript could not have been completed without the able assistance of former Vice President for Media Affairs Carolyn S. Wood, who provided captions for the photographs featured in the volume. We also would like to thank Daniel K. Addison for the photographs, as well as Angela R. Comfort and Anne Bromley for their assistance in preparing the photographs.

PREFACE

Two fortuitous and uncanny situations account for this book's title, *The Key to the Door*. These events are still so vivid that I can recall them as though they were happening today. In the first, it is 1999 and I am in Kobe, Japan, to give a keynote speech on ethnonational conflict resolution at the World Health Organization Centre for Health Development. I am there to put forward the basic assumptions that subserve the understanding of determinants of violence and ethnic conflict. Before I can give my speech, something fortuitous happens. The person introducing me is an African American physician, a man who had qualified to attend the University of Virginia's medical school when he applied in the 1950s but because of the laws of the time, was barred from doing so. In fact, the Commonwealth of Virginia paid his tuition to go elsewhere.

In the second story, several years later, an uncanny parallel process takes place. James Trice, an engineering school graduate, is talking to a group of African American students about his experiences at the University, including the story of his first night on Grounds. He has closed the door to his room, he remembers, and is getting ready for bed, when white students begin to bang on his door to register their protest. His first night is, needless to say, a sleepless one. Much to his horror, he realizes the next morning that he had left his door key in the lock.

We cannot easily make amends to those African Americans whose education elsewhere was paid by the state. Nor can we erase the unnecessarily cruel treatment that those who attended the University at that time experienced. Like many others, I remain saddened, embarrassed, and even horrified by what happened to the University's first African American students at the very place—the very community—I have chosen for my own career.

In this book, seven of the University's pioneering African American students recreate for us, in exacting, sometimes heartbreaking, detail, what it took to break down the barriers and begin to lay the groundwork for a newly open and welcoming institution. In many ways, these stories chart the course of history for African Americans in our country who sought out higher education in the 1950s and 1960s, not just those who wished to or did attend the University of Virginia. Their stories foreshadow changes on the horizon, casting a dark shadow on the past while at the same time shining a bright light for future generations of students.

The Key to the Door serves as an apt metaphor for the courage of all the early graduates and for the efforts of those who provided the facilitating environment for them to succeed. Thanks to the success of these graduates, the University is now a different place: a top-ranked research university with an integrated student body, the highest graduation rates in multiple categories among its peer flagship state institutions, and graduates who have become leaders in multiple spheres of influence. *The Key to the Door* also speaks a note of caution. The University of Virginia cannot become complacent; a key that opens a door can also lock it.

Maurice Apprey

FOREWORD

The Reverend Martin Luther King, Jr., told us, "The arc of the moral universe is long, but it bends toward justice."

In *The Key to the Door*, we see that arc bending toward justice through firsthand accounts of the experiences of early African American graduates of the University of Virginia. Their contributions document their experiences before, during, and after their time at U.Va. Stories of persistence and transformation are threaded throughout their narratives.

This book was assembled when the University's rector, George K. Martin, was concluding his term as leader of the University's governing board. His colleagues on the Board of Visitors elected Mr. Martin, a 1975 graduate of the College of Arts and Sciences, to become the first African American in our history to hold this position. Mr. Martin's leadership is just one of the indicators showing us how far we have come since the days before desegregation, when the University was inaccessible to African Americans. At this university, where we cherish our history and our traditions, we must acknowledge that these harsh realities also are part of our history.

The President's Commission on Slavery and the University was formed in 2013 to provide advice and recommendations regarding commemoration of the University's historical relationship with slavery and enslaved people. The commission, this book, and other efforts in our community will help us create a full and candid account of the University's history while at the same time appropriately recognizing the contributions and achievements of many people who have gone unrecognized for so many years.

As we acknowledge our past, we can also celebrate our present. In many ways, U.Va. now leads the way in advancing the excellence of African American students, but work must continue.

The Key to the Door will resonate with many audiences—both within and beyond our University community—including historians and scholars in colleges and universities across the country. All of us can benefit from reading these stories and learning from them.

Teresa A. Sullivan
President of the University of Virginia

THE KEY TO THE DOOR

INTRODUCTION
Higher Education for the Public Good
Deborah E. McDowell

Education is a special, deeply political, almost sacred, civic activity. It is not a merely technical enterprise—providing facts to the untutored. Inescapably, it is a moral and aesthetic enterprise—expressing to impressionable minds a set of convictions about how most nobly to live in the world.
—GLENN LOURY

In 2014, "I, Too, Am Harvard," a multimedia project, took the Internet by storm, inspiring copycat versions at colleges and universities around the country. The project, which quickly dominated social media, is widely regarded as having flushed out into the open longstanding racial tensions festering on college campuses. Announcing the self-titled photographic component of the exhibition, the organizers wrote, "Our voices often go unheard on this campus . . . our experiences are devalued, our presence is questioned—this project is our way of speaking back, of claiming this campus, of standing up to say: We are here. This place is ours."[1]

It's hard to imagine any of the voices collected in *The Key to the Door* being so vocal, so boldly assertive either about their hard-won, and often controversial, presence at the University of Virginia or about the slights and insults, the slings and arrows they clearly endured while there. The point of my comparison is not at all invidious. After all, more than two generations separate these men and women from the roughly twenty-year-

1

olds enrolled at the Harvard of today, who put the world on notice when they declared, "This place is ours."

But to the extent that this current generation of students of color can claim ownership of/in Harvard, or any other institution for that matter, the ability to make that claim has depended greatly on those black students who dared decades ago to "explore strange new worlds," who dared to "boldly go" where no—or certainly few—black persons had gone before. At least John F. Merchant might not object to my appropriating the trademark introduction to the Star Trek series, for he readily likened his early days at U.Va. to being in a "foreign country."

In 1955, Merchant entered U.Va., not only on the threshold of a new era for the University but also for the nation; he arrived on Grounds (the term used to refer to the University's physical space in lieu of "campus") barely a year after the landmark *Brown v. Board of Education* Supreme Court decision. As he explains it, Merchant received his acceptance letter from U.Va.'s law school just prior to *Brown*, a ruling that, he acknowledges, would not likely eliminate the "practical issues of discrimination and racism." He was well-acquainted with such issues. Three years at Virginia Union University in Richmond, one of the historically black colleges and universities (HBCUs), may have represented an "island of safety" for him at one level, but it had shielded him neither from the attitudes, structures, and practices of Jim Crow nor from the threat of violence, especially from the looming presence of the Ku Klux Klan.

It seems right to begin these firsthand accounts with Merchant's narrative (following a historical overview by Ervin L. Jordan, Jr.), for it contains some of the most unvarnished revelations of the volume. Other contributors certainly acknowledge the isolation, racial friction, and bigotry of those early days, but Merchant's account does not gloss over his sleepless nights and frightened days at U.Va. Indeed, his narrative is punctuated by references to fear, to "trembl[ing] with fear," to being "scared, even terrified," for the entirety of his three years there.

These fears seemed fully justified. But if "fear was a constant companion," it walked side by side with a fierce determination to face it down. As Merchant put it, "I had no chance to give into my fears and go elsewhere."

Like others who tell the stories of their times at U.Va., Merchant also describes the sheer exhaustion that frequently comes with being a pioneer, the pressures of working to fulfill personal goals while simultaneously being expected to serve as a standard-bearer for the race, the pressure to take on the broader struggles against racial discrimination. With refreshing levity, he explains his decision not to participate in efforts in Charlottesville to bring diversity to public accommodations. As he puts it frankly, "I was tired, worn out emotionally, and not mentally prepared for expanding the battlefield."

Those who later joined him deemed it the better of both wisdom and self-preservation to adopt a similar approach. The academic rigors, to say nothing of the social pressures, demanded focus and a certain pragmatic— even stoical—approach to surviving a far-from-welcoming atmosphere.

To one extent or another, each of these narratives implies that slights and isolation—even the endless choruses of "Dixie" sung while students waved the Confederate flag—were a small price to pay for the advantages of education and the assurance of practicing a profession instead of languishing in what Merchant termed the "menial job brigade." The University of Virginia offered students a profession.

In an echoing statement, Willis B. McLeod writes, "It served its purpose and served it very well. U.Va. was an essential experience in my life." And for Merchant, "The U.Va. experience shaped me as a person and helped construct the foundation needed to direct my life."

Looked at from one angle, such statements—almost self-consciously flat and affectless—give the impression of the door to these memories being locked away in a vault. As a student of African American letters, I am reminded of the narrative strategies of those who penned the hundreds of fugitive slave narratives devoted, in part, to document the horrors of that "peculiar institution." In text after text, narrators offer up some variation on this passage from Henry Box Brown: "I am not about to harrow the feelings of my readers by a terrific representation of the untold horrors of that fearful system of oppression. . . . It is not my purpose to descend deeply into the dark and noisome caverns of the hell of slavery."[2] Again and again in these narratives, just at the point where the reader might expect to get a concrete description, the writers insert, "But let us drop a veil over these proceedings too terrible to relate."

I am not suggesting in the least that what these early U.Va. pioneers experienced could be likened to the brutalities of slavery, nor that their experiences were uniformly "too terrible to relate." Rather, I am concerned about what their reticence might suggest about the relationship between remembering and forgetting, or borrowing from Paul Ricouer, about the "pragmatics of forgetting," especially in representations of institutional histories and their largely commemorative functions.

Looked at from another angle, however, in choosing not to dwell on what many term "negative experiences," including, as notes Merchant, "racist attitudes and behavior, blatant discrimination, or scary episodes that involved more than one fistfight," these narratives speak to still other, nonliterary traditions. Here I think of what Ralph Ellison once described as that "American Negro tradition which teaches one to deflect racial provocation and to master and contain pain." Ellison goes on to say, "It is a tradition which abhors as obscene any trading on one's own anguish for gain or sympathy, which springs not from a desire to deny the harshness of existence, but from a will to deal with it as [people] at their best always do" ("The World and the Jug").[3]

The mastery that Ellison describes is everywhere apparent in the accounts collected here. More than one contributor admits to deciding to "forget" rather than "recite" certain difficult experiences: "It's not that I don't recall the negatives, because I do. It's just that I see no need to dwell on them." As David Temple acknowledges, "My response was to suck it up, to feed myself with false pride and chin up, and to keep moving." And keep moving he did, as did his counterparts, earning along the way the rewards not only of practicing their professions but also of living fulfilling lives.

It is striking, however, that more than one spoke of graduating from U.Va. and vowing never to return. Of course, time and the distance of years lessened the sting of exclusion, of un-belonging. For some, that return came decades after graduation, when the University invited them back to Grounds to honor and celebrate their achievements. "It was gratifying to receive official recognition," William Womack admitted. He found "forgiveness."

On the other hand, it is clear, even in the guarded descriptions, that the experiences of studying at U.Va. were trying; importantly, however, they were endurable largely because of the welcoming presence of the black— and very segregated—community of Charlottesville. There these early students could relax, be fed, and escape isolation and the stresses of being "alone but not unnoticed," the stresses of living in "the spotlight and under the microscope."

Generations later, Harvard students—in far greater numbers than these early African American pioneers at U.Va.—testify to vaguely similar feelings. The current sociological discourse has provided them a term for the recurrent hostilities they often face and feel: micro-aggressions. And while some of these students, much like these "firsts" at U.Va., put their heads down, deciding quietly to pursue their degrees, others have decided to voice their dissatisfactions out loud, even belligerently, "turning insult into art," to quote Patricia J. Williams.[4] But however powerful, resonant— and necessary—their campaign has been, it is important to note that the plight of minoritized students of color at predominantly white institutions of higher learning demands other, even more aggressive campaigns, which must transcend the virtual world of social media and move into arenas of social policy and legislation.

The experiences of these early pioneers unfolded during the highly charged years in the immediate aftermath of *Brown*, which, as Merchant observes, "trigger[ed] some of the darkest hours in our nation's history." The racial conflict unleashed in the wake of that monumental decision, particularly throughout—although not exclusively—the deep South, is rearing up again with new ferocity, no doubt because the stakes—as well as the price—of higher education have perhaps never been more fiercely contested than now as challenges to race-based admissions succeed in state after state. For this reason, we would do well to heed Maurice Apprey's observation that "a key that opens a door can also lock it."

The doors that swung open in the 1950s and since for the likes of John Merchant, David Temple, Willis McLeod, Barbara S. Favazza, and many other U.Va. alums are now swinging in the opposite direction, at least if we can trust the bellwethers of U.S. higher education. Although it is widely conceded that education is the bedrock of democracy, and that higher education is essential for the nation's economic development, the barriers to higher education, many of them economic, have become increasingly insurmountable for growing numbers of college aspirants, many of them students of color. It bears noting again that these early U.Va. graduates arrived in the aftermath of the *Brown* decision in 1954. As we marked the sixtieth anniversary of that decision in 2014, African American enrollment in flagship public institutions, as well as many privates, was in decline, particularly in those state colleges and universities where opposition to race-based admissions had taken effect. But even when the barriers to these students' enrollment are subtler in form, they are no less intransigent in fact. As Eugene Tobin, Martin Kurzweil, and William Bowen put it, "although explicit policies to keep certain people out on the basis of race, gender, and religions have been eliminated, more 'organic' barriers," including "outright financial hardship," remain.[5]

In a 1933 essay, "The Field and Function of the American Negro College," W. E. B. Du Bois recalled his application and admission to Harvard in 1890: "I had for the mere asking been granted a fellowship of $300, a sum so vast to my experience that I was surprised when it did not pay my first year's expenses." Du Bois readily attributed his successful completion of his studies at Harvard to "men [who] sought to make Harvard an expression of the United States," those men who committed themselves to "beating back the bars of ignorance and particularism and prejudice." While he wrote this essay to defend the need for separate schools for blacks in the face of caste and segregation, Du Bois simultaneously set himself the task of discussing the purpose of the university—any university—in a democracy. By then, he already understood that the most prestigious universities were established to narrow themselves to cater to a "sublimated elite of mankind," to "benefit . . . the privileged few." Such universities, he went on to say, tended to be "disembodied from flesh and action" and, as a result, fated to die "like a plant without room."[6]

Du Bois would likely shudder to see his early assessments born on the contemporary landscape of higher education. Although he imagined that university education could become the bedrock of democracy, the key to equal opportunity and upward mobility, how would he answer the likes of Peter Sacks and many others who now see the university as the "bastion of wealth and privilege that perpetuates inequality"?[7] I suspect that those early U.Va. graduates who recount their times in Thomas Jefferson's "Academical Village" would have much to say about these unsettling trends in higher education.[8] They might agree with Du Bois when he wrote: "A system of national education which tries to confine its benefits to preparing the few for the life of the few, dies of starvation. . . . It is only therefore, as the university lives up to its name and reaches down to the masses of universal men [and women] and makes the life of normal men [and women] the object of its training, it is only in this way that marvelous talent and diversity and emotion of all mankind pours up through this method of human training. . . . Herein lies the eternal logic of democracy."[9]

NOTES

1. Evette Dionne, "'I, Too, Am Harvard' Project Highlights Black Students' Stories, *Bustle,* March 6, 2014, http://www.bustle.com/articles/17376-i-too-am-harvard-project-highlights-black-students-stories.

2. Henry Box Brown and Charles Stearn, *Narrative of Henry Box Brown* (Boston: Brown and Stearns, 1849), 11.

3. Ralph Ellison, *Shadow and Act* (New York: Random House, 1964), 111.

4. Patricia J. Williams, "'I, Too, Am Harvard' Rocks the Ivory Tower," *The Nation,* March 12, 2014, https://www.thenation.com/article/i-too-am-harvard-rocks-ivory-tower/.

5. Eugene Tobin, Martin Kurzweil, and William Bowen, "Why It Pays to Factor Income into College Admission Policies," *Forward,* April 22, 2005, http://forward.com/news/3319/why-it-pays-to-factor-income-into-college-admissio/.

6. In *A W. E. B. Du Bois Reader,* ed. Andrew G. Paschal (New York: Macmillan, 1971), 51–69.

7. Peter Sacks, "How Colleges Perpetuate Inequality," *Chronicle of Higher Education,* January 12, 2007.

8. The Academical Village is the original space designed by Jefferson for living and learning. It includes the Lawn, adjacent pavilions, student rooms, and the Rotunda, which stands at the north end.

9. W. E. B. Du Bois, *The Education of Black People: 10 Critiques, 1906–1960,* ed. Herbert Aptheker (New York: Monthly Review Press, 2001), 115–16.

PERSEVERANCE AND RESILIENCE
African Americans at the
University of Virginia
Ervin L. Jordan, Jr.

There is no problem which the erosion of history cannot resolve. It is a question of time and generations.
—ALBERT MEMMI

WORKING WITHOUT WAGES

African Americans worked and resided at the University of Virginia before the granting of its charter (1819), before its first students and first day of classes (1825), before the conferring of its first degree (1828), before its first commencement (1829), and before the appointment of its first president (1904). During an 1817 meeting, the Board of Visitors of what was then called Central College (James Madison, James Monroe, and Thomas Jefferson) authorized the hiring of black laborers "for levelling the grounds and performing necessary services for the work or other purposes" and of overseers to supervise their work.

Central College became the University of Virginia when chartered by the Virginia General Assembly in 1819; soon afterward, hired African American slaves appeared in its ledgers (the preferred euphemism was "servant"). Its first neoclassical buildings of red brick with white trim were constructed by free blacks and slaves of local slaveholders, including Jefferson. Frustrated by what he considered a dawdling work pace, a watchful and impatient Jefferson often visited the construction site in hopes that his presence might pressure laborers to speed up their pace.

Chattel slavery was a relationship of submission and power between slave and master, and many faculty and administrators were unapologetic slaveholders. Some who began life enslaved at Jefferson's farms and plantations, including Monticello, subsequently toiled at the University. These included three Hern siblings: Thrimston, a stonemason who completed the Rotunda's stonework, and his sisters Lily and Fanny, purchased by faculty members. Other slaves worked as bricklayers, tinsmiths, painters, and carpenters.[1]

INVISIBLE FACES, FORGOTTEN VOICES

University officials prohibited private tutoring or schools for black children on the Grounds as state law banned the teaching of blacks "at any school house, church, meeting house or other place for teaching them." White violators of the law were subject to fines and imprisonment; black violators suffered twenty lashes.[2] A female British tourist hosted by the family of philosophy professor Robert Patterson recounted a conversation with the Patterson ladies: "Two facts struck me in the course of our feminine talk on the subject of housekeeping; that chickens are there to be had for a dollar a dozen ... and that Mrs. Patterson's coachman, a slave, could read." These remarkable violators are often invisible in U.Va.'s history. A University archaeologist once remarked, "The historical presence of African-Americans on land on and adjacent to the University has been largely missing from the university's institutional history." Even during their own time, they were relegated to the outskirts of the university. Many free black employees were residents of the "Canada" or "Little Canada" working-class neighborhood located across from the school's South Lawn, which was then open to view, as the faculty prohibited black people from residing on school property and in its buildings. The 1895 Rotunda fire provided justification for closing off the Lawn's south end for the controversial construction of Old Cabell Hall. This ended Jefferson's vision of an open vista but also blocked views of Little Canada.

More than this symbolism, distrustful and fearful whites demanded free blacks' expulsion from the University and the state. When a dining room employee named Monroe petitioned the General Assembly for permission to remain in Virginia during the 1850s, and several faculty attested to his "good character," Albemarle County residents objected. Fortunately for Monroe, the legislature granted his petition.[3]

While free blacks were unwelcome, slaveholding white male southern-ers comprised the student majority. The Board of Visitors, concerned that young men with the power of life and death over black human beings were increasingly disrespectful of faculty and administrators, prohibited their keeping slaves on the Grounds. Faculty and administrators were allowed unrestricted ownership or hire of slaves and housed them in cellars be-neath their Lawn residences or in kitchens and stables. One hired slave was assigned to every twenty dormitory students; daily and weekly responsi-bilities with scheduled deadlines included providing firewood, cleaning fireplaces and candlesticks, boot polishing, fetching ice and water, window washing, running afternoon errands to Charlottesville, and undertaking similar "menial offices." After death, slaves continued their service— medical faculty secretly employed professional grave robbers to steal black corpses for dissection as anatomical cadavers. Unmarked and forgotten slave cemeteries totaling nearly two hundred burials were discovered on University property during the 1980s and 2000s; a memorial plaque "in honor of . . . free and enslaved whose labor . . . helped to realize Thomas Jefferson's design for the University of Virginia" was unveiled in 2007.[4]

One slave, Lewis Commodore, became the first full-time African American employee. Later known as "Lewis the Bell-Ringer," he was pur-chased for $580 in 1832 and employed as a bell-ringer and janitor until the 1850s. His duties included ringing the Rotunda bell every morning at dawn, breakfast, lunch, dinner, and the beginning of lectures. Commodore took his duties seriously but students often made him the subject of pranks and beatings to keep him in his place. He was employed as a free man after slavery ended, and his descendants lived in Charlottesville well into the twentieth century.[5]

Another slave bell-ringer with a Jefferson connection, Henry Martin (1826–1915), began more than a half-century of service during the 1840s. He was born at Monticello, where his parents were enslaved, on the same day of Jefferson's death, July 4, 1826. At the 1827 estate sale of Jefferson's slaves, Martin, his twin brother, and their mother were purchased by a lo-cal resident who later sold Martin to the school. Between 1868 and 1909, he worked as the school's bell-ringer, first at the Rotunda until the 1895 fire and thereafter at the Chapel until his 1909 retirement. Like Commodore, Martin continued his University employment as a free man after the Civil War and his descendants, too, were Charlottesville residents. He was the subject of a 2012 commemorative plaque at the University Chapel: "Henry Martin rang the bell at dawn to awaken the students, and rang it during the day to mark the hours and the beginning and ending of class periods. He was beloved by generations of faculty, students, and alumni."[6]

WOMEN OF LABOR

Nameless African American women appeared in the University's earliest records as cooks, seamstresses, and laundresses, among them a slave cook assigned to the school's white overseer and the black laborers under his supervision. Most black women were gainfully employed as domestic workers. Catherine "Kitty" Foster (c. 1790s–1863), a laundress, purchased a homestead across from the school in 1833 in Little Canada. The property was owned by her descendants until 1906. The Foster family cemetery and homestead, rediscovered in 1993 during the preliminary construction for a parking lot, was dedicated as a park at the University's new South Lawn district in 2011. Isabella Gibbons (1833–89) was the slave cook of Professor Francis Smith during the 1850s while her husband, William (1826–86), was owned by Professor Henry Howard. Sally Cottrell Cole (c. early 1800s–1875), a former slave maid and nurse owned by one of Jefferson's granddaughters, was sold to mathematics professor Thomas Hewitt Key. Her life became a complicated legal matter after her marriage to a free black man named Reuben Cole. At the time, Sally was assumed to have been emancipated by Key, but under Virginia law freed slaves had to leave the state within twelve months or risk re-enslavement. She managed to maintain her freedom while remaining in Virginia and is among those African American slaves who worked for the Jefferson family and his University.[7]

There are unsubstantiated stories that Thomas Jefferson permitted a house of prostitution near the school staffed by black women to cater to white male students' sexual needs during the 1820s. Consensual or not, black women were considered sexual prey by many white males. After Maria, a maid owned by the family of a University administrator, gave birth to a mulatto son fathered by a law student, her owners sold her out of

Virginia and kept her child as their slave—undoubtedly to avert public embarrassment for the student.[8]

CONTINUITY AND DISRUPTION

Several instances of what the white community perceived as black insolence resulted in beatings and assaults. During the half-century before the Civil War, a low-level, surreptitious protest culture developed as individual African Americans' sullen compliance and frustrations over the stresses of slavery and racism intermittently boiled to the surface as passive-aggressive resistance, even though whites unhesitatingly resorted to legally sanctioned or extrajudicial violence as their racial privilege to discipline impertinence. The black night watchman of an African American cemetery shot and wounded a student trying to steal a corpse for anatomical classes. A slave named Thornton received several public whippings for gambling with students in their dormitories. A visiting female British abolitionist recollected how one professor's womenfolk sought to convince her and themselves that all was well: "These ladies, seeing apparently only domestic slaves kindly treated like their own, spoke lightly on the great subject, asking me if I did not think the slaves were happy; but their husbands used a very different tone, observing, with gloom, that it was a dark question every way." Other fearful faculty wives complained of increasingly insubordinate male slaves for whom whippings and threats of other punishments seemed ineffective.

Slaves were not always deferential to their self-styled racial superiors, and their behavior defied the ruling establishment's authority. The inability of round-the-clock close supervision worked to their advantage. One resident grumbled of a troublesome slave named Bob, a purported thief, habitual runaway, and curfew violator despite being shot at by town constables. Faculty slaveholders, though frustrated by their human property's escapes, also feared them. One professor claimed that "the disposition, character, and manners of the negroes in this Piedmont region are very distasteful to me; and the fortunes of [the] University . . . very uncertain." At the University, slavery was by and large business as usual during the Civil War, though free blacks and slaves in a variety of skilled and unskilled occupations earned higher wages and were trusted as healthcare workers for sick and wounded Confederate soldiers at the Charlottesville General Hospital, which consisted of several Charlottesville and University buildings. This did not prevent slaves' escapes from faculty owners; ten fled law professor James Holcombe's Bedford County estate during an invasion of Union soldiers.[9]

ECHOES OF AN ENSLAVED PAST

African Americans in the postwar South hoped Reconstruction would mean the dismantling of racial inequality but soon learned that in racial matters, many things remained the same. The 1870 Virginia General Assembly prohibited black and white students from attending the same public schools. A student minstrel troupe regularly performed in blackface. By the 1890s, blacks comprised 45 percent of all employees, mostly janitors, dormitory servants, groundskeepers, and laborers, who earned an average monthly wage of eight dollars. Several clandestinely resided on the Grounds to reduce housing expenses.[10] Racism continued at Mr. Jefferson's University. While on an American lecture tour during the 1890s, a British clergyman noted that University residents insisted blacks were happier during slavery and bemoaned the passing of the "faithful old time negro — respectful & respectable . . . of a kind the world will never see again."[11]

Yet there were occasions of racial tolerance and goodwill by some faculty and students. A philosophy professor publicly appealed to fellow whites for fair treatment of blacks as citizens. After the death of an unidentified black man who had fallen from scaffolding while cutting ice at the school pond, there were student-led calls for the establishment of a black hospital as none existed in the area.[12]

With the lukewarm support of local black clergymen, a nine-member board (which excluded blacks) of Charlottesville residents and University faculty attempted to build "a Hospital for colored people in this place." The chairman of the University's hospital building committee appealed to northern philanthropists for donations to help construct a segregated ward for black patients at the University Hospital. Local white physicians promised not to charge black patients for their services and to secure medicine for them at reduced costs. This effort failed, however, as local African Americans were understandably apprehensive they might become anatomical cadavers as a result of deliberate maltreatment by white physicians. Most families of the time, black and white, saw to the healthcare of loved ones at home.[13]

Traditionally, the University has been a major employer of black Charlottesvillians. One black Charlottesville teacher said of the University's black employees, "Their wages were low, but at least they had jobs."[14] Yet even low-paid African American employment was jeopardized by the Great Depression as blacks were displaced by whites desperate for menial and domestic jobs (maids, laborers, cooks, and janitors) previously reserved for blacks.

SCHOOL OF SEGREGATION

As the twentieth century began, white supremacists opposed high school and higher education for Virginia blacks. University of Virginia faculty chairman Paul Barringer contended blacks should remain little more than menials whose education "should be primarily a Sunday school education training. . . . Their moral training should be supplemented by the three R's, and such simple training in agriculture and the domestic arts as all will need." History professor and first dean of graduate education Richard Heath Dabney and state superintendent of public instruction Joseph W. Southall echoed Barringer's and other whites' hostility to black education. Dabney opposed the use of public taxes to educate blacks, while Southall declared "Negro education . . . a failure."[15]

Even though African Americans were the subjects of academic studies, they were not permitted to enroll or teach at the University. The Phelps-Stokes Fund awarded $12,500 for the creation of fellowships for the study of Negroes, which resulted in the publication of several racially derogatory works between 1915 and 1950. Likewise, the library received an endowment from industrialist Arthur Curtiss James for the acquisition of books and materials on Negroes. Many members of the University faculty were among the nation's leading eugenicists and advocates of the theory of Negro inferiority and their sterilization, along with Jews and the so-called feeble-minded. Student chapters of white supremacist groups such as the Ku Klux Klan and the Anglo Saxon Clubs of America were founded.[16]

FIRST APPLICANT: ALICE JACKSON

The 1902 Virginia General Assembly revoked the 1882 charter of the state's only black public institution of higher education, Virginia Normal and Collegiate Institute. They renamed it Virginia Normal and Industrial Institute and terminated its authority to confer undergraduate degrees, in effect reducing it to a high school–level vocational training institution for the manual arts during 1902–22. Virginia Union University, a private school in Richmond, was the only black institution of higher education to confer bachelor's degrees during this period. Virginia Normal's baccalaureate program was restored in 1923, but its first students to graduate with bachelor's degrees were not until 1925. The school was later renamed Virginia State College for Negroes (1930), Virginia State College (1946), and Virginia State University (1979). Hampton Normal and Agricultural Institute (renamed Hampton Institute in 1930), whose original mission was analogous to that of a trade school with instruction in farming, carpentry, choral music, tailoring, and housekeeping, also expanded its collegiate offerings and undergraduate degrees during the 1920s. By 1930, Virginia ranked third, after Texas and the District of Columbia, in the number of black college graduates.[17]

In August 1935, in response to appeals from the National Association for the Advancement of Colored People (NAACP) for academically qualified graduate school candidates, Alice Jackson (1913–2001) of Richmond, Virginia, became the first African American applicant at U.Va. This twenty-two-year-old Virginia Union University teacher and daughter of a Richmond pharmacist had earned a bachelor's degree in English from Virginia Union (1934), attended Smith College in Northampton, Massachusetts, on an English literature scholarship during 1934–35, and had completed preliminary graduate work in French at Smith. During her admission attempt, Thurgood Marshall (later the first black associate justice of the U.S. Supreme Court) was one of the NAACP lawyers who prepared a brief on her behalf.

Jackson's application to the University's graduate School of Romance Languages was rejected at a September 1935 meeting of the Board of Visitors in accordance with the state's racial laws. In her handwritten reply, Jackson wrote, "Gentlemen: In rejecting my application for admission to the graduate department of the University of Virginia, you issued a public statement to the effect that I was a Negro and 'for other good and sufficient reasons not necessary to be herein enumerated.' . . . I wish to know in full, the reasons why my application was rejected. So far as your rejecting my application because I am a Negro is concerned, I will discuss that further with you when you have itemized the 'other good and sufficient reasons' upon which it was rejected." Her attempt made state and national headlines, and the NAACP considered hers a valid test case and hinted a lawsuit was forthcoming.

The Virginia General Assembly averted this by enacting a 1936 act "to provide equal educational facilities for certain persons denied admission to Virginia state colleges, universities, and institutions of higher learning," and to carefully avoid legal challenges by specifying the eligibility of any "bona fide resident and citizen of this state, regardless of race, possessing the qualifications of health, character, ability and preparatory education." This so-called Dovell Act required an admissions shell game: a black student first had to apply and formally be denied admission to the University (or any white college) in order to qualify for out-of-state tuition assistance for graduate degrees not available at Virginia's public and private black institutions of higher education.

Hundreds of black students received this state funding and enrolled at nearly thirty colleges and universities between 1936 and 1940—so many that the University frequently appealed to the legislature for additional funding. Jackson, having dropped her legal challenge on the advice of the NAACP, graduated from Columbia University in 1939 with a master of arts degree in English and comparative literature and became a distinguished educator. Alice Jackson Houston Stuart died in 2001 in Massachusetts shortly after her eighty-eighth birthday. The Virginia General Assembly passed a joint resolution: "Alice Jackson Stuart was the first known African-American to seek admission into a state graduate or professional school; and ... leaves behind a legacy that has impacted thousands of Virginians in the most positive of ways."[18]

FIRST ADMISSION: GREGORY SWANSON

The postwar period of 1945–65 saw the development of national liberation movements and the decline of colonialism, the independence of African and Third World nations, and their increased global influence during the Cold War. In the United States, a resurgent and politicized black American middle class resolved to secure equal citizenship, voting rights, and access to public facilities including formerly all-white, state-supported educational institutions.

Attitudes began to change as a result. In a 1948 poll of U.Va. students, 40 percent of white graduate students favored admission of black graduate students. In a later poll, 73 percent favored blacks' admission to graduate and professional schools. The *Cavalier Daily,* U.Va.'s student newspaper, also called for the admission of academically qualified blacks. Academia began to recognize and appreciate African American scholars and studies. Luther Porter Jackson (1892–1950), a Virginia State College history professor and pioneering civil rights activist, became the first black scholar to lecture at the University when he delivered a 1949 conference paper defending the NAACP's legal challenges against school segregation. Twenty-eight years later, the University named the Office of African-American Affairs' Luther P. Jackson House in his honor. As the posthumous subject of a Virginia State University art professor's oil painting, displayed at the University's special collections library, Jackson is among the few African Americans with portraits in University buildings.

In 1949, before the 1954 *Brown v. Board of Education* decision, Virginian Gregory Hayes Swanson (1924–92) applied to the University's law school and later enrolled as its first black student, the result of *Swanson v. Rector and Visitors of the University of Virginia* (1950). A federal district court ordered his admission under the Equal Protection Clause of the Fourteenth Amendment to the U.S. Constitution and ruled that the university must pay his attorneys' fees. Swanson's NAACP legal team again included Thurgood Marshall. Swanson's first day of law classes was September 20, 1950, but his hopes to earn a graduate law degree ended with his 1951 withdrawal following death threats and racial shunning. Swanson transferred to Howard University Law School and went on to practice law in Virginia and Washington, D.C., as an Internal Revenue Service attorney. In 1958, John F. Merchant became the first African American to earn a law degree. Twelve years later, Elaine R. Jones became the University's first black female law graduate.[19]

FIRST GRADUATE: WALTER RIDLEY

Postwar Virginia anticipated that thousands of black military veterans under the age of twenty-five would take advantage of the educational benefits offered under the federal G.I. Bill of Rights, but they assumed none would seek admission to predominately white schools. That assumption was incorrect. Four-year colleges and universities offering courses leading to the master's degree included the College of William and Mary, Hampton Institute, the University of Richmond, the University of Virginia, Virginia Polytechnic Institute, and Virginia State College for Negroes. Only predominately white schools offered law and medical degrees: the College of William and Mary, the Medical College of Virginia, the University of Richmond, and Washington and Lee University.

The first individual admissions of black students began during the 1950s. Admitted in the fall of 1951 based on his academic credentials, Walter Nathaniel Ridley (1910–96) became the first African American graduate of U.Va. in June 1953, receiving his doctorate in education. He was also the first black student initiated into a University honor society (Kappa Delta Pi, a professional education society) and was later named president of Elizabeth City State Teachers College, North Carolina (1958–68). After an absence of thirty-four years, Ridley was formally invited to return to the University for its first annual Black Alumni Weekend (1987), during which a privately funded scholarship was established in his honor to provide tuition assistance for black students.

Edward Wood became the School of Medicine's first black graduate in 1957. Also during this period, Randolph L. White (1896–1991), a University hospital employee since the 1930s, became its first black department supervisor in 1950 and four years later founded the *Charlottesville Tribune*, one of Virginia's most significant black weekly newspapers.

Even though qualified blacks were admitted on a case-by-case basis, many were either not admitted or did not graduate for a variety of racial, financial, and academic reasons. Black women had an especially hard road to travel throughout the decade. Public school teachers seeking graduate and summer school admission to earn credits toward license renewal were routinely directed to supposedly equal course offerings at Virginia State College for Negroes. But one of that school's professors, Louise Stokes Hunter, received an education doctorate in August 1953, making her the University's first black female and second black graduate.[20]

DESEGREGATION DECADES: THE 1960S AND 1970S

School segregation was an embodiment of white American racism. Dr. Martin Luther King, Jr., and other integrationists believed "integration is an opportunity to participate in the beauty of diversity," but skeptics were unconvinced it could conclusively enhance blacks' quality of education. "Integration and education are not synonymous," James Baldwin observed, "though Americans appear to think so." Robert A. Bland was the first to receive an undergraduate degree (bachelor of science, electrical engineering, 1959), and chemistry major Amos Leroy Willis was the first College of Arts and Sciences graduate (1962) and first black student Lawn resident (1961–62). Wesley L. Harris, Sr., the second black student assigned a Lawn room (1963–64), acted as an unofficial bodyguard for King during a 1963 speech at the University. (Harris later recalled King's privately predicting his eventual assassination.) Harris graduated with honors in 1964 with a bachelor of science degree in aerospace engineering and eventually became a professor in the School of Aerospace Engineering and Engineering Physics. His brother William became the University's first dean of its Office of African-American Affairs (1976–81) and an architecture professor.[21]

Several whites affiliated with the University risked their lives, reputations, and careers during the civil rights movement of the 1950s–70s. A Ku Klux Klan cross was burned on the lawn of Sarah Patton Boyle (1906–94), a civil rights activist and wife of a drama professor. History professor Paul Gaston, who publicly supported "the historical quest for equality by the American Negro" during a Jefferson Society speech, was severely beaten while participating in a 1963 desegregation sit-in at a Charlottesville restaurant. English professor William Elwood (1932–2002), who helped recruit black students, was among the first white faculty to incorporate black authors into his curriculum and advised the Charlottesville black community on secondary public school desegregation. (Elwood and Gaston were 1999 and 2013 recipients of Charlottesville's Martin Luther King, Jr., Community Award.) Board of Visitors member S. Buford Scott (class of 1955) resigned in 1994 in protest over the lack of an African American member. Virginia governor George Allen appointed Richmond educator Elsie Goodwyn Holland (1935–2008), an African American, to serve the final year of Scott's term and reappointed her to a full term in her own right; Governor Jim Gilmore reappointed her to a second four-year term that ended in 2003.[22]

FIRST FACULTY AND ADMINISTRATORS

An African American faculty member once described the black experience in America as "sugar-coated arsenic . . . just because Time passes does not mean you will have progress." As African Americans entered predominately white institutions of higher education during the 1960s, 1970s, and 1980s, they were confronted by the deeply embedded racism of campus conservatives who, for all intents and purposes, said, "We'll enroll a few of you as students, but won't help you graduate, and you'll be obstructed by the condescension of white students, faculty, and administrators. We'll hire a few of you as faculty, but regardless of your credentials and abilities won't grant you tenure, and you'll always be subordinated to whites of equal or lesser qualifications." Academic relations often devolved into outright racial friction.

To address the University's discriminatory past, early internal studies on black faculty recruitment and retention were conducted. These studies predicted that black faculty would be more effective counselors for black students than whites, and the development of a black academic and administrative presence might offset institutional racism. A 1972 report indicated that black enrollment stood at just 2 percent. Foot-dragging on increasing the African American presence and hiring, however, did not extend to entertainers such as James Brown, the Coasters, the Four Tops, the Harlem Globetrotters, Dionne Warwick and others who regularly performed at University venues throughout the 1950s, 1960s, and 1970s.

Black professional and administrative staff were first hired on a regular basis during the late 1960s and early 1970s, usually as the result of black student demands: Fred Stokes, an education graduate student, was hired for black recruitment (1968); Caesar Hackney, police officer (1968); Elizabeth Johnson, assistant dean of admissions and the University's first full-time African American admissions officer (1969); Linwood Jacobs (1969), associate dean of students and coauthor of one of the first reports on black University students; Donald W. Jones, presidential advisor on minority affairs (1973); Howard "Hank" Webster Allen (1919–2012), who began as a director for the federally funded Consultative Resource Center for School Desegregation (1969) and later became the center's director (1973–80) and a School of Education professor until his 1986 retirement.

In 1967, Nathan Edward Johnson, Sr. (1909–80), an authority on school desegregation, became the University's first black faculty member (School of Education) and received a doctorate from the school in educational administration that same year. He was the associate director (1967–73) of the Consultative Resource Center on School Desegregation and the first black tenured faculty member (1970). He retired in 1979; a student residence hall was named in his honor in 1992. Joan C. Franks, appointed in 1973 as the first full-time black female faculty member (assistant professor of education), retired as associate professor in 2000. Charlotte H. Scott (1925–2010) was a University professor of commerce and education from 1976 to 1998; her husband, Nathan A. Scott, Jr. (1925–2006), was a faculty member from 1976 to 1990 who chaired the Department of Religious Studies. The Scotts were the first tenured African American faculty couple. Vivian Verdell Gordon (1934–95), who received her Ph.D. in sociology from the University (1974) for her dissertation "The Self-Concept of Black Americans," became the chair of the Department of Sociology and director of an undergraduate Afro-American studies program during the 1970s and 1980s.

Other notable faculty include Matthew Holden, Jr., Henry L. and Grace M. Doherty Professor of Politics (from 1981 until his 2002 retirement), and award-winning public administration scholar; Lincoln Lewis, the first affirmative action and equal opportunity officer (1987–94); and Bonnie Guiton Hill, first African American dean of an academic department (McIntire School of Commerce, 1992–97). At the law school, Larry Wilson was its first full-time black professor (1972). Alex M. Johnson, Jr., joined the law school faculty in 1984, and in 1995 became the University's first vice-provost for faculty recruitment and retention, a position he held until 2002, when he was appointed dean of the University of Minnesota Law School. In 2007, he returned to U.Va.'s law school faculty, where he continues to teach.[23]

The number of faculty increased from one during 1967–68 (and only thirty black students) to six black faculty and administrators during 1969–70, eleven in 1971, and sixteen in 1972. By the fall of 1975 there were 1,368 administrative and teaching faculty positions at the University—only 21 were held by blacks, and an Office of Institutional Analysis report identified a typical faculty member as a thirty-something white male who had received his doctorate from the University. By April 1978, of 1,455 full- and part-time faculty members, fewer than 30 were black. A black faculty advisory committee was appointed by Provost David Shannon in 1980 (there were only eight tenured black faculty that year) to identify prospective black faculty members and persuade them to accept appointments to the University. Other officials attributed the diminishing of potential available black faculty candidates to cyclical national factors beyond the University's control such as blacks not choosing academic careers. By 1982, there were thirty-two full-time black professors, and fifty-five in 1985, of which thirteen (23 percent) were tenured. Traditionally, most black University employees are in nonacademic positions; during the 1990s blacks averaged 52 percent of maintenance-janitorial employees and 3 percent of faculty while African American students were 9 percent of the student population. Of 2,724 faculty reported by the Office of Institutional Assessment and Studies a generation later (May 2015), 91 were black and of these, 59 (65 percent) were tenured, mostly in the College of Arts and Sciences and the schools of medicine, education, and engineering.[24]

The University's small African American professoriate could not fully support black students or aggressively push for faculty recruitment because of their own low numbers coupled with concerns about tenure vulnerabilities. However, during the 1980s a few bravely established organizations such as the Afro-American Faculty-Staff Forum to lobby for black faculty recruitment and retention, and fair treatment of classified staff. Unfortunately, this group became defunct within two years because of internal disputes over tactics and goals.

As their numbers swelled black students continued their campaigns for the recruitment and tenure of black faculty. Yet by the 1990s some frustrated students publicly characterized black faculty as "apathetic, self-absorbed and neglectful of [them] and [unwilling] to invest time and energy in black students." Such comments troubled black faculty; drama professor Ishmail Conway responded by summing up their experience as being in a "world of invisibility" and racial and academic isolation that made it an everyday struggle to teach, publish, and serve on University and national committees and be effective full-time advocates for students. Increases in the number of black faculty throughout the 1980s and 1990s were inherently the result of pressure from black students and alumni. Students occupied academic departments' offices, held silent protests on the Lawn during Founder's Day activities, and engaged in demonstrations at the University president's Carr's Hill residence in protest of institutional and cultural racism, demanding increased student financial aid and the re-cruitment and retention of black students and faculty. Nearly two decades into a new millennium the University's low percentage of black faculty and administrators remains a point of campus contention; as the school grapples with the issue it hopes that faculty recruitment and hiring could be the keys to attracting more African American students. It is a concur-rent goal that remains unmet and will require more than mere numerical changes.[25]

The Board of Visitors is responsible for general policies, tuition and other fees, the annual budget, administrative and faculty appointments, and the purchase of real estate. Visitors are appointed by Virginia's gover-nor to four-year terms and are eligible for reappointment to a second four-year term. Ten African Americans have served. The first was Dr. Frank S. Royal of Richmond, Virginia, for a single term (1978–82). African Amer-ican women members include Elise Goodwyn Holland (1994–2003); Su-san Y. Dorsey (2003–11; College, class of 1982, M.B.A., 1987); Glynn D. Key (2004–12; College, class of 1986, law, class of 1989); and Sheila C. Johnson (2010–11).[26]

ORGANIZATIONS AND PUBLICATIONS

In the 1980s, there were nearly twenty-five black academic and social or-ganizations. The first and most influential, Black Students for Freedom, founded in 1969, changed its name to the Black Student Alliance (BSA) in 1971 and sponsored annual Black Culture Week celebrations in February. Among the BSA's goals was "cultural and educational awareness, to rep-resent the social and political concerns of the African-American student body, and to establish a more perfect union between various components of the African-American community."[27] One of its first presidents, John Charles Thomas (b. 1950), later became the Virginia Supreme Court's first black chief justice.

The BSA was followed by Black Voices (1972), a student choir that performed African American gospel music, and three Greek organizations during 1973–74: Delta Sigma Theta and Alpha Kappa Alpha sororities and Omega Psi Phi fraternity. There were eleven such organizations by 2005. From 1992 to 1996, Concerned Black Students (CBS) publicly denounced faculty racism, unfair grading practices, and reprisals against students who wore African Kente clothing to class. The CBS, which occasionally held joint protests with the BSA, never publicly identified its members or officers, and during public protests wore black gags taped across their mouths, symbolizing their lack of voice in University governance and decision making, and of African Americans' oppression.[28]

Varying in quality and themes, black-related publications first appeared during the 1970s, though most were short-lived. Among these were the BSA's *Habari Gani* (1985–86) and *Pride: A Cultural Magazine at the University of Virginia* (1975–present). The Office of African-American Affairs (OAAA) issued several publications, including *Ujamaa* (1982–84), *Profiles in Excellence: The Newsletter of the Walter N. Ridley Scholarship Fund* (1990s), *Visions: A Newsletter for Parents of African-American Students* (1990–2005), and, *Orphée Noir: Expressions of the Black Experience on Grounds and Beyond* (2015), an illustrated black student online monthly news magazine. Of noteworthy interest is *Still I Rise: Thirty Years of Success*, published for the OAAA's thirtieth anniversary as a collection of photographs and essays describing the experiences of African American students in the classes of 2007 to 2010.

University-wide faculty-staff organizations have been short-lived (with the exception of two email groups) and ineffectual compared to student organizations. Those that existed included the Afro-American Faculty-Staff Forum (1980s), the Black Faculty and Staff Council (2000s), and the Black Faculty and Staff Organization (2000s). Minor squabbles, personal and professional jealousies, and apathy too often impaired whatever usefulness these organizations might have achieved.[29]

JEFFERSON'S GLADIATORS: ATHLETES AND COACHES

African Americans participated among themselves in a variety of sports activities after work and at certain holidays during the University's first century, though whites opposed the concept of slave leisure time and saw such activities as disguised combat training of would-be rebels. Typical pastimes included ball games, bare-fisted contests, cockfights, foot races, horseshoes, marbles, wrestling, and games of chance.

Given the racial customs of the times, white students and blacks most likely did not play together, at least not publicly; two gymnasia were constructed in the 1820s only for the former's use. Not until an assenting majority vote by students did a black collegiate athlete, Harvard football player Chester Pierce, compete at the University. The occasion was the 1947 homecoming game. At first, the University requested that Harvard not bring Pierce but retreated when Harvard threatened to cancel the game. The NAACP issued an advisory to Charlottesville's black community: "We are certain Pierce will do nothing to embarrass [himself and us], and we can help both the University and Pierce to make it easier for others of our race in the educational and athletic world." In compliance with a 1926 state law, 200 blacks in a segregated seating section were among Scott Stadium's 25,000 spectators.[30]

Between the 1950s and early 1970s, the athletic department had an unspoken and unwritten policy against recruiting and offering scholarships to black athletes, allegedly because none met the school's athletic and academic requirements or because of the belief that academically qualified black athletes preferred historically black colleges and universities. The first black student-athlete joined the wrestling and lacrosse teams between 1964 and 1966 as a walk-on (there were only eighteen enrolled full-time black students at the time). By 1969 only four blacks were on sports teams, two basketball players, one football player, and one track squad member. The first athletic scholarships were issued to black men and women basketball players during the early 1970s. Since then, African Americans have participated on basketball, football, lacrosse, soccer, swimming and diving, tennis, and track and field teams. Many went on to successful careers as professional athletes and, as alumni, generously donated to the school's fund-raising campaigns.

Basketball players Ralph L. Sampson and Dawn M. Staley are among the school's greatest athletes. Between 1979 and 1983, Sampson, a seven-foot, four-inch center, led his team to Atlantic Coast Conference (ACC) titles, National Collegiate Athletic Association (NCAA) tournament appearances, and a National Invitational Tournament championship. Staley, a point guard on the women's basketball team from 1988 to 1992, was ACC Player of the Year in 1991 and 1992, and led her team to NCAA Final Four appearances in 1990–92 as well as ACC regular season and tournament titles. Staley also led the U.S. women's basketball team to gold medals during the 1996, 2000, and 2004 Olympics. Staley, who is currently head women's coach at the University of South Carolina, was invited to be the

University's valediction speaker in 2009. In 2006, she received the University's Distinguished Alumna Award.

Craig K. Littlepage was appointed the University's first black athletic director, a position he continues to hold, in 2001. He joined the University's athletic department in 1976 and served in a variety of positions, including assistant basketball coach, assistant athletic director, and senior associate director. Previously, he had coached at Villanova, Yale, and the University Pennsylvania. *Sports Illustrated* named him one of the nation's most influential minorities in sports in 2003. Dave Leitao was hired by Littlepage in 2005 to coach men's basketball, the University's first black head coach of any University sports team.

Four years later, Littlepage hired Mike London as the University's ninth head football coach—and its second black head coach of a sports team. London's extensive football experience since 1979 as a player and coach includes the National Football League, the University of Richmond, the College of William and Mary, and Boston College.[31]

"EDUCATE, MOTIVATE, LIBERATE":
UPWARD BOUND, THE OFFICE OF AFRICAN-AMERICAN AFFAIRS,
AND THE CARTER G. WOODSON INSTITUTE

Student demonstrations in the 1970s led to the creation of new programs. Several black and white student organizations formed a "Student Coalition" in 1969 that articulated these concerns, held rallies to demand the resignation of what they termed racist members of the Board of Visitors, and pressured the University to fully commit itself to integration and the establishment of a black studies department. In February 1969, Virginia State College history professor Edgar A. Toppin offered two black history courses in the form of taped replays of his Virginia State lectures. The Board of Visitors approved an undergraduate Afro-American studies program in June 1970 and appointed Joseph R. Washington, Jr., a U.Va. professor of religious studies, as its first director. He taught an introductory course and occasionally invited nationally prominent guest lecturers, such as NAACP executive secretary Roy A. Wilkins (1901–81). This program, hampered by the lack of a regular budget because it was not a degree-granting academic department, experienced uncertainty by students and disparagement by white administrators. Still, Washington's efforts enabled the University Library to receive supplementary funding for increased purchases of black-related books and periodicals. Sociology professor Vivian Verdell Gordon served as director of Afro-American studies from 1975 to 1980 until she resigned to return to full-time U.Va. teaching because of what she described a hostile environment against black studies.[32]

Upward Bound, among the University's earliest black academic-based organizations, was established in 1968 as a federally funded program for educational assistance to disadvantaged students. It offered intensive college preparatory training at the University for select local black high school students based on their financial need and potential to achieve in higher education. Of the first Upward Bound students, four were eventually offered University admission. Leah Wilson-Puryear, who joined the program in 1980, became its first African American female director in 1982.

In 1969, Black Students for Freedom and "members of the Black Academic Community" submitted a detailed written proposal for a "balanced and integrated program of undergraduate and graduate teaching and research." It called for an interdisciplinary Afro-American studies program as a means "to meet a debt owed to the black community." A month later, contending that the history department "is the strongest authority on the [American Negro]," administrators rejected the proposal, adding, "It is quite impossible for the administration to force any department to offer a course for any program that it does not wish to do. This is an essential part of the University structure."[33]

The Black Student Alliance's 1975 "Proposal for the Establishment of an Office of Minority Affairs at the University of Virginia" called for the office's creation by 1976 and was endorsed by nearly all of the University's five hundred black students, but the administration responded with vague promises and minimal pseudo-solutions. Several similar internal reports—from 1969 to 1974—were ignored or shelved. The following year's "Farmington incident" proved a catalyst for tangible change. Several University officials, including members of the Board of Visitors and the school's president, were members of the Farmington County Club, a racially exclusive private club in Albemarle County. Following a series of student protests beginning in February 1976 led by future Virginia Supreme Court Chief Justice Leroy R. Hassell, Sr. (1955–2011), most of the board resigned their club memberships, especially after Farmington's president publicly reaffirmed its racial restrictions. By the spring of 1976, a nine-member planning committee of students, faculty, and administrators made recommendations for the proposed office's authority and functions, including its most important responsibility to combat insensitivity to black students' concerns.[34]

The establishment of the Office of Afro-American Affairs (OAAA, also known colloquially on Grounds as "O Triple-A," and later the Office of African-American Affairs) began with the July 1976 appointment of William L. Harris, Sr., who was recruited from Portland State University, as its first dean and assistant provost. Perhaps the foremost historical irony of the office is its location in an area that once consisted of slave quarters. Martin Dawson (1772–1835), commissioner of accounts, bequeathed to the school his farm where his sixty slaves were housed while employed in the construction of the school's original buildings. This five-hundred-acre tract with "two negro quarters" was sold at public auction for twenty thousand dollars in 1859 and the proceeds used to construct seven brick, two-story dormitories (later faculty and staff residences).[35] The OAAA officially opened in March 1977 at 4 Dawson's Row and was dedicated as the Luther P. Jackson House the following October. No. 3 Dawson's Row eventually housed the Luther P. Jackson Black Cultural Center.

Luther Porter Jackson, a Virginia State College history professor and civil rights activist, risked his life and career to promote African American studies and to urge African Americans to become registered voters despite poll taxes and other obstacles. Known as "Mr. Civil Rights of Virginia," Jackson was secretary of the state chapter of the NAACP and a founder of the Virginia Voters League.

For much of its administrative history, the OAAA was under the vice president for student affairs (formerly the dean of students); currently, the vice president and chief student affairs officer oversee OAAA. Five African American men have served as its dean: William M. Harris, Sr., a professor of architecture (1976–81); Paul L. Puryear, a professor of government and politics (1981–86); Rev. Joseph A. Brown, a Jesuit priest and professor of English and religious studies (1986–88); M. Rick Turner, a career college administrator, who taught higher education administration, sociology, and African American history (1988–2006); and Dr. Maurice Apprey, a professor of psychiatric medicine (2006–present).

An historical overview of their times and tenure is instructive. Among the OAAA's greatest challenges under its first dean were external actions and decisions that demeaned and stifled its initial growth and development. Administrators publicly questioned its necessity and called for cuts or the ending of its funding. William Harris issued annual "State of Race" reports that more often than not concluded that, despite the University's stated commitment to affirmative action, there were pointed failures in improving the number of black faculty and professional staff and students, and in offering social and cultural events. He also cited examples of violence and harassment against not only himself and OAAA (the office was often vandalized with racial slurs) but also other blacks by white members of the University community. Another obstacle was faculty obstructionism and discouragement of black graduate students from pursuing scholarly research on African American studies.[36]

In spite of these obstacles, Harris's annual reports proudly documented OAAA's successes in academic advising, tutoring, career counseling, and social and cultural programming. It also monitored students' mental and physical health, and assisted with on- and off-Grounds housing. The Luther P. Jackson House became a meeting place for black student organizations and events, and its Nat Turner Library held nearly three thousand volumes. Of the nearly 900 blacks annually enrolled during this period, the number of graduates increased from 94 in 1978 to 158 in 1981, mostly from the College of Arts and Sciences. Moreover, OAAA staff enhanced its visibility by serving on University-wide committees and participating in state, regional, and national conferences.[37]

In the wake of Harris's 1981 resignation as dean to resume teaching as an associate professor of urban planning and community development, he was succeeded by Paul L. Puryear (1930–2010) of the University's Institute of Government (later the Weldon Cooper Center for Public Service). His efforts and accomplishments notwithstanding, Puryear was criticized by a highly vocal BSA despite his estimable career at Norfolk State University, Tuskegee University, Fisk University, Florida State University, and the University of Massachusetts at Amherst. OAAA expanded its services during his tenure despite bureaucratic obstructions of his authority and the office's activities by conservative elements. Puryear resigned in April 1986 and returned to full-time teaching, claiming to have achieved his goal of improving African American students' academic performance.[38]

Father Joseph Brown was OAAA's third (interim) dean from 1986 to 1988. He had the wide support of black students and staff, and made significant accomplishments, though he had the shortest tenure of any dean. OAAA buildings were remodeled and completely wired for computers, and a Black Alumni Association and a Parents' Advisory Program were established. Nevertheless, after what Brown characterized as "some very ugly fights," his budget was reduced. He later recalled his greatest challenge as dean was "maintaining any degree of optimism . . . [of] my integrity as an educator, administrator, and priest in an environment that was too often buffeted by concerns that were parochial, short-sighted and divisive." Shortly after his 1988 resignation he became director of the Institute for Black Catholic Studies at Xavier University in New Orleans.[39]

The fourth dean, M. Rick Turner, former director of a tutorial assistance program at the University of California, was appointed in August 1988. His professional work at the University of Connecticut, the University of California–Irvine, and Stanford University focused on African American students at predominantly white institutions, and particularly recruitment, admission, retention, and graduation. Yet the African American community worried his role would merely be that of a caretaker since some University officials had discussed the possible downgrading of OAAA. Turner's tenure (the longest to date at eighteen years) included bureaucratic battles. He outlined his goals and challenges as "the building [of] the image of our office as one which delivers quality services to African-American students in a timely manner. I want the University to recognize the OAAA as an integral part of Student Affairs and as an asset to both the University and Charlottesville communities." Turner delivered "State of African-American Affairs at the University of Virginia" addresses that in part confronted white faculty and students who took exception to his insistence on the continued need for affirmative action and the OAAA. In 1990, the OAAA began publication of *Visions: A Newsletter for Parents of African-American Students,* dedicated to their "hard work, sacrifice, [and] love to their children."

In spite of Turner's repeated assertion that African American faculty and administrators should not be at the University except as advocates of African American students, at times OAAA seemed underappreciated by its constituency. Its twentieth anniversary celebration in 1996 was poorly attended, notwithstanding a series of public events and special guests, including former deans Harris and Brown. One University task force's 1997 proposal for the office's restructuring into a multiethnic cultural affairs center of academic and support services for African American, Hispanic/Latino, Asian, and Native American students met with sustained opposition from Harris and African American students who denounced it as a betrayal, despite the University's insistence that the new center's budget and resources would be substantially increased. The proposal was eventually scrapped as unfeasible, and Turner assured the University community that OAAA would continue and even expand the scope of it services.

Turner later recalled being the only African American present during high-level administrative meetings and considered this as proof of the lack of commitment in the hiring and promotion of African Americans to major leadership positions. When two white University fraternities insisted on the right of their guests to wear blackface at private events and claimed the posting of such images on the internet was constitutionally protected speech during the early 2000s, Turner slammed this racist mockery of African Americans. School administrators joined in denouncing this incident. Still, citing student self-governance, the administration did not punish the fraternities, who later issued public apologies. When Turner told a local newspaper he was calling for "the transformation of the prevailing political and economic system . . . facilitated by [courses] on multiculturalism," editorial letters demanded his dismissal and characterized him as a "liberal socialist" with a "Communist agenda" under the guise of multiculturalism. Turner retired in July 2006. His parting OAAA newsletter article noted that the African American graduation rate of 87 percent was among the highest of any public institution of higher education. Subsequently, as president of the Charlottesville-Albemarle branch of the NAACP, he has continued to champion the African American community.[40]

Turner was succeeded in August 2006 by then-interim dean Maurice Apprey, former associate dean for diversity at the School of Medicine. A member of the faculty since 1980, Apprey had extensive experience in minority student recruitment and retention. A psychoanalyst and internationally recognized expert on conflict resolution, Apprey's low-profile approach to problem solving, as well as his empathy and good humor, were in contrast to some of his predecessors yet keenly appreciated. Named permanent dean in 2007, Apprey (the fifth and current dean) announced goals of increasing black graduate school enrollment by encouraging undergraduates to maintain high grade point averages and improving the University's internal racial climate and diversity. He also hoped to see more African American students in prominent roles as honors students and Lawn residents. Delivered in the Rotunda's Dome Room, Apprey's first "State of Race" address urged the University to increase its support for African American students, especially those seeking careers in business, international affairs, and medicine. He added that he did not see his role as that of the spokesman on racial matters and that everyone's top priority should be academic achievement.

An OAAA Black History Month poster summarizes the organization's history, purpose, and services: "Educate, Motivate, Liberate." Events for the OAAA's thirtieth anniversary celebration, "Still I Rise: Thirty Years of Success" (2006), were well-attended. One keynote speaker traced the University's history of slavery and segregation while speculating on OAAA's future: "Will OAAA celebrate its 50th anniversary 20 years from now in 2026? Can it continue to overcome every challenge to its survival and progress? ... Fate and history have chosen OAAA as a link during one of the most challenging times in the University's history, and it must not be the weakest link. If this link breaks, the entire chain will shatter."[41]

On the eve of its fortieth anniversary in 2016, the OAAA is the University's most successful and influential black-themed institution. During the 2000s its deans and staff implemented mentoring programs, published collaborative articles in the *Peabody Journal of Education*, and, in the spring of 2005, founded an annual "Donning of the Kente" ceremony to annually recognize fourth-year graduating African Americans and faculty for their individual "contributions and dedication to the students of the University community." Each student received a customized West African Kente cloth stole as a symbol of appreciation and achievement.[42]

Responding to increased criticism from the BSA, the Student Council, and the University chapter of the NAACP regarding the need for an undergraduate and graduate degree-granting Afro-American studies department, the Institute for Afro-American and African Studies was established by the Board of Visitors in 1981 to attract and enhance minority faculty and promote systematic academic study of peoples of African descent. A year later the board formally named it in honor of Carter G. Woodson (1875–1950), "the Father of Black History," and established fellowship programs. The Woodson Institute has since conducted oral history interviews of civil rights movement participants and similar interdisciplinary research initiatives.

Armstead Louis Robinson (1947–95), a nationally renowned black studies pioneer, joined the faculty in 1980 as an associate professor of history and became the Institute's first director. Robinson co-chaired the Venable Lane Burial Site Task Force, which examined the cemetery and history of a nineteenth-century free black family discovered on University property. Armstead and his wife, Mildred W. Robinson, a University law professor and legal scholar, were included in a landmark study of African American intellectuals.

Having survived budget cuts and closure threats in the 1990s, the Institute has published nearly forty volumes in its *Woodson Series in Black Studies,* hosted a national symposium commemorating the NAACP's centennial, and celebrated its own thirtieth anniversary (2011) with a two-day multidisciplinary symposium. Since 2008, the Woodson Institute has been directed by English professor Deborah McDowell, a faculty member since 1987 and a nationally renowned African American literature scholar. Today the Carter G. Woodson Institute for African-American and African Studies administers an undergraduate major and minor in African American and African Studies.[43]

ENHANCING THE COMMUNITY OF TRUST:
THE HONOR SYSTEM AND MULTICULTURALISM

The University's student-run Honor System (established in 1842) is the oldest among American colleges. As a "community of trust," under its precepts no student, academically or personally, may lie, cheat, or steal, nor tolerate those who do, on or off University Grounds. The single sanction for violations after admission of guilt or conviction by the honor court is permanent expulsion and revocation of any degrees already received. Black students have long asserted that the Honor System disproportionately impacts them, even with regular elections of blacks to the Honor Committee including its first black chairman, Ken Easley (1976), whose tenure provoked a simmering racial climate with Watergate-like allegations concerning his mental capacity, forged medical documents, and secret tapings of telephone conversations, which contributed to his being stripped of many of his administrative powers by a mostly white male eleven-member committee. The BSA and the Virginia NAACP accused his critics of being racists as Easley lost his seat as honor chairman after an earlier than usual election the following year and was accused of several honor offenses, but these charges were soon dropped. Easley, who graduated in 1977, filed charges of racial discrimination, but a 1978 investigation by the federal Office for Civil Rights cleared U.Va. of any wrongdoing.[44]

Some faculty are said to have resorted to the Honor System as a means to remove black students from their classes for no other reason than racial prejudice. The earliest known honor case involved a doctoral candidate dismissed from the University by the committee during the late 1950s. Throughout the 1980s and 1990s the BSA complained that eight of every ten black students tried were convicted. By 1987, nearly 30 percent of all honor accusations were against African American students, a number significantly higher than their 8 percent representation in the student population. Although the Honor Committee statistics suggested whites and Asians were twice as likely to be tried and convicted in honor trials as blacks and Hispanics, the Council of Black Student Leaders accused the system of "raping our black peers every day.... These white students ... spend ... four years here trying their hardest to get rid of us." By the early 2000s African Americans were demanding that racism be declared an honor offense.[45]

Ostensibly, the University promoted multiculturalism during the 1980s, defined by the Student Council as "a social condition where members of different ethnic, racial, religious, sexual orientation, gender and other groups coexist as a pluralistic community, yet maintain their individual identities and perspectives." A multicultural journal, *Seasons,* appeared between 1987 and 1991. Deans in OAAA often recommended that the University community be required to attend multicultural seminars. Multiculturalism was not warmly embraced by all; two 1993 polls indicated that students discouraged fellow students' participation in multicultural activities, and black students continued to feel racially alienated and isolated. These were partly addressed by the following: the class of 1996's $150,000 gift for the creation of a multicultural center at the University; a 2003 announcement of a new $100,000 online undergraduate multiculturalism course; and, in response to a series of ugly racial incidents, the appointment of the University's first vice president and chief officer for diversity and equity in 2005.

Affirmative action and racial quotas were demonized by political and cultural conservatives as reverse discrimination, and the term "diversity" generally replaced "multiculturalism." By the 1990s and early 2000s, as far as most African Americans were concerned, the problems of new and old-fashioned racism were embedded at Mr. Jefferson's University despite its pronouncements of "equal respect" and "an inclusive and welcoming environment that embraces the full spectrum of human attributes, perspectives, and disciplines . . . and broaden the horizons for us all." From the black perspective, more often than not, the University—and America— retreated from racial equality and diversity instead of advancing it.[46]

OF TIMES AND GENERATIONS: THE TWENTY-FIRST CENTURY

At the beginning of the twenty-first century, lingering issues of racial inequality and cultural bias hung like a pall across an American landscape of angst. Two June 23, 2003, U.S. Supreme Court decisions, both concerning the University of Michigan's admissions programs, typified societal incongruities. In *Gratz v. Bollinger* the Court held that the use of racial preferences in undergraduate admissions violated the Constitution's equal protection clause and the Civil Rights Act of 1964's Title VI ban against discrimination on the grounds of race, color, or national origin in programs and activities receiving federal financial assistance. Conversely, the Court ruled in *Grutter v. Bollinger* that the equal protection clause did not prohibit the use of race in graduate admissions decisions to promote a diverse student body.

Nationally, Hispanics became the largest minority group in 2004 while African Americans remained the largest racial group. At the University, Asian students became its fastest growing minority, and between 2000 and 2003 surpassed African Americans in the number of students and faculty. In 2016, Asian American students remained the largest racial minority at 14 percent, followed by African Americans at 7 percent and Hispanics at 6 percent. As African American University and community leaders worried about the implications of this (as a potential death knell for OAAA or the transmuting of its name and mission), a leading education journal speculated that the University's national leadership role for racial diversity in higher education was at risk.[47]

Statistics cannot substitute for the onerous realities of actual human experience, particularly where race is concerned. Even so, numbers can be instructive. In 2003, for the tenth year in a row, the University led major public universities with an 87 percent black graduation rate, compared to a 39 percent average for other predominately white institutions of higher education. The Office of African-American Affairs dean reported in 2005 that of 1,500 African American students at the University, nearly 300 were enrolled in graduate schools, a continuation of a five-year decline. African Americans barely comprised 6 percent of approximately 4,000 University faculty positions but, as usual, were the majority (53 percent) of maintenance positions. Between 2000 and 2011, African American undergraduates averaged 8.4 percent among enrolled students; their peak enrollment years were 1990–93, at 12 percent. As of the 2011–12 academic years, the African American undergraduate population was 7.2 percent and the total black student enrollment, 8.5 percent, down from 11 percent in 2004. Black undergraduates were 6.5 percent of students during the 2012–13 academic year, a proportion not seen since the 1980s.[48]

Plato's aphorism, "Never discourage anyone who continually makes progress, no matter how slow," is applicable to race relations. On the 264th anniversary of the birth of the school's founder (April 2007), the Board of Visitors issued "a formal statement of regret for the slavery that helped build Thomas Jefferson's university." At year's end, the University received the Council of Graduate Schools/Peterson's Award for Innovation in Promoting an Inclusive Graduate Community for its "innovative institutional programmatic efforts in the identification, recruitment, retention, and graduation of minority graduate students . . . as models for other institutions." This offered little consolation to African Americans wearied of the sugarcoating of anonymous racist actions as constitutionally protected free speech (for example, the May 2013 racist graffiti incident on Beta Bridge) and ineffective, repetitive discussion forums and belittled indignation meetings. (Citing "school traditions," academic freedom, and concerns over possible violations of students' First Amendment rights, some University officials ignored or declined to take action against fraternities for their blackface parodies and nonviolent racist actions. White students and alumni objected to any punishment for such activities as an infringement of free-speech rights that would possibly subject U.Va. to lawsuits, leading one black professor to observe that while the school usually "reaffirmed its commitment to racial diversity and inclusiveness, especially where people of African descent are concerned . . . not all Cavaliers and Wahoos got the memo.")

The full implications of a declining African American faculty and student population, welcomed by some and feared by others, remains to be seen, but the problem has been publicized and well-meaning efforts are purportedly underway to find constructive solutions. The University has presumably pursued this imperative since the 1970s, yet its track record on the whole reflects the views and attitudes of its often-indifferent traditionalist majority and those of often contrarian white moderates and liberals.[49]

BICENTENNIAL CODA: 1819 AND 2019

More than eleven thousand African Americans now comprise 6 percent of University alumni.[50] As often as not, the state's flagship university's goal of diversifying seems to mean increasing the number of out-of-state students, not increasing diversity for race or ethnicity. The University has too few African American faculty members, and on the face of it, has demonstrated varying levels of urgency about its need to change by welcoming efforts that diversify its faculty.

The end of slavery and legalized state-sponsored segregation has not meant African Americans were or will always be welcomed as equals and colleagues. Much remains to be done toward the dual challenges of checking de facto re-segregation while fostering a culturally diverse and inclusive academic community of equality and dignity; such efforts will require sustained and sincere long-term efforts. On the eve of the bicentennial of Mr. Jefferson's University, the African American community's incalculable legacy is of struggle and success, resilience and potential, and of having left the University better than they found it.

NOTES

1. Ervin L. Jordan, Jr., "Blacks and the University of Virginia: An Overview 1819–1987" (unpublished manuscript, 1987–2015, in author's possession), 2–4; University of Virginia, Board of Visitors, Minute Book, 1817–28, October 1817, RG-1/1/1.381, Albert and Shirley Small Special Collections Library, University of Virginia, Charlottesville (hereafter U.Va.); Proctor's Journal, 1819–28, RG-5/3/1.961, U.Va.; Philip Alexander Bruce, *History of the University of Virginia: 1819–1919,* 5 vols. (New York: Macmillan, 1920–22), 2:190–91 (impatient Jefferson), 231; Lucia C. Stanton, *Free Some Day:*

The African-American Families of Monticello (Charlottesville, Va.: Thomas Jefferson Foundation, 2000), 58–67; Petrina Jackson and Ervin L. Jordan, Jr., "Working without Wages: Enslaved Laborers at the University of Virginia, 1819–1865," exhibition, Albert and Shirley Small Special Collections Library, January 2012. The Rotunda, a half-scale interpretation of the Pantheon in Rome, is the University's signature landmark. It was designed as the University library but today houses special study, meeting, and event space, as well as the offices of the Board of Visitors and the vice president for student affairs. Pendleton Hogan, *The Lawn: A Guide to Jefferson's University* (Charlottesville: University Press of Virginia, 1987), 2, 10–13.

2. June Purcell Guild, *Black Laws of Virginia: A Summary of the Legislative Acts of Virginia Concerning Negroes from Earliest Times to the Present* (Richmond: Whittet and Shepperson, 1936; reprint, New York: Negro Universities Press, 1969), 176–77, 179. In keeping with Jefferson's preferences, "Grounds" is the term used to refer to the University's physical space in lieu of "campus."

3. Ervin L. Jordan, Jr., "A Just and True Account: Two 1833 Parish Censuses of Albemarle County Free Blacks," *Magazine of Albemarle County History* 53 (1995): 114–39; [University of Virginia Proctor], Receipt Book, RG-5/3/2.101, U.Va; Bruce, *History of the University*, 2:56–57, 163–64; University of Virginia General Faculty, 1828, RG-19/1/1.461, U.Va.; Journals of the Chairman of the Faculty, RG-19/1/2.041, U.Va.; Jordan, "Blacks and the University," 38, 56; M. Drake Patten, "Report on the 1994 Summer Excavation Season at Venable Lane" (Charlottesville: Department of Anthropology, University of Virginia, November 1994, in author's possession), 2 ("historical presence"); Amy E. Grey, M. Drake Patten, and Mark S. Warner, "A Preliminary Assessment of the Venable Lane Site" (Charlottesville: Department of Anthropology, University of Virginia, June 4, 1993, in author's possession), fig. 5 (between pp. 7 and 8); Coy Barefoot, "Digging in the Dirt: A Tour of Local Archaeological Sites," *C-VILLE Weekly*, April 2–8, 1996, 8–9; Harriet Martineau, *Retrospect of Western Travel*, 2 vols. (New York: Harper and Brothers, 1838), 1:206. Designed by Thomas Jefferson, the Lawn was intended to be the center of daily academic life. It is a rectangular, terraced green space framed by ten Pavilion faculty residences and fifty-four student Lawn Rooms, as well as a number of academic buildings. Hogan, *The Lawn*, 28–70.

4. Board of Visitors, Minutes, vol. 1, box 1, October 4, 1824, RG-1/1/1.383, U.Va.; Minutes of the General Faculty, vol. 6, October 1, 1842, Accession 2328, U.Va.; Board of Visitors, Minutes, vol. 3, July 7, 1840, RG-1/1/1.382, U.Va.; Resolutions and Enactments of the Board of Visitors, faculty volume 1827–45, RG-1/1/1.461, U.Va.; Charles Coleman Wall, Jr., "Students and Student Life at the University of Virginia, 1825 to 1861" (Ph.D. diss., University of Virginia, 1978), 43–86; "U.Va.'s Lost Pond," *The Hook* (Charlottesville), August 14, 2003, 24; James Jetwin Thomas, "Slaves at the University," 2, Accession 8103, U.Va. ("menial offices"); James O. Breeden, "Body Snatchers and Anatomy Professors: Medical Education in Nineteenth-Century Virginia," *Virginia Magazine of History and Biography* 83 (July 1975): 321–45; Ervin L. Jordan, Jr., *Black Confederates and Afro-Yankees in Civil War Virginia* (Char-

lottesville: University Press of Virginia, 1995), 94, 209; "Graves Remain at Housing Site," *Cavalier Daily* (Charlottesville), July 21, 1983, 1; "Graves Found at U.Va. Site," *Richmond Times-Dispatch*, March 31, 1983, n.p.; Brendan Wolfe, "Unearthing Slavery at the University of Virginia: Recent Discoveries Raise New Questions about the Past," *University of Virginia Magazine,* Spring 2013, 24–26, 30.

5. Board of Visitors, Minutes, vol. 2, RG-1/1/1.382; Journals of the Chairman of the Faculty, vol. 3, January 2, 1832; D. C. T. Davis, "Old Times at the University," *Alumni Bulletin of the University of Virginia,* old series, 4, no. 4 (February 1898): 115.

6. "Henry Martin, 1826–1915," *Alumni Bulletin of the University of Virginia,* 3rd series, 8, no. 5 (October 1915): 597–601; Virginius Dabney, *Mr. Jefferson's University: A History* (Charlottesville: University Press of Virginia, 1981), 47–48, 71, 268; Cecile Wendover Clover and F. T. Heblich, Jr., *Holsinger's Charlottesville: A Collection of Photographs by Rufus W. Holsinger,* 2nd edn. (Charlottesville, Va.: Art Restoration Services, 1995), 60–61; Jackson and Jordan, "Working without Wages"; "The Enduring Legacy of Henry Martin: Explorations in African American Life in Charlottesville and the U.Va. Community," panel discussion, January 25, 2012, Albert and Shirley Small Special Collections Library, University of Virginia.

7. Jordan, "Blacks and the University," 3–5, 20–21; Wall, "Students and Student Life at the University," 276–78; "The Recollections of Richard Thomas Walker Duke, Jr., Transcribed by Gayle M. Schulman for the Albemarle County Historical Society, 2001," Richard Thomas Walker Duke, Jr., Recollections, 1899–1926, I-22–23, Accession 9521-O, U.Va.; Grey, Patten, and Warner, "Preliminary Assessment of Venable Lane," 3–9; "Graves Found during U.VA. Construction Are Thought to Belong to a 19th Century Free Black Family," press release, June 5, 1993, University of Virginia News Office, Charlottesville; "Catherine's Ghost," *Washington Post,* October 10, 1993, F1, F5; Ervin L. Jordan, Jr., "The Catherine Foster Family: Free Blacks in the Slavery Era," *Charlottesville Tribune,* June 10, 1993, 1, 4; Kathleen Kennedy Manzo, "Unearthing the African American Past" and "What History Books Don't Tell," *Black Issues in Higher Education* 11, no. 4 (April 21, 1994): 14–19; "Foster Family and Canada Community Park Dedication," April 8, 2011, program, in author's possession; Gayle Mueser Schulman, "Slaves at the University of Virginia," September 2004, folder "19th [century]," 1–2, 6, 8, 17, 20–22, 23–24, 32–33, Accession 13201, U.Va.; Wolfe, "Unearthing Slavery," 27.

8. Duke Family Papers, 1845–1983, box 1, volume 1, "Recollections of My Early Life," pp. 11,13 17–27, 29–30, 39, 89–90, 122, 130, 153–154, 165, 185–86, 213, 215, 217, Accession 9521-H, 9521-I, U.Va,

9. Bruce, *History of the University,* 2:111; Jordan, "Blacks and the University," 21, 24, 41–42, 44–48; Wall, "Students and Student Life at the University," 148–96, 266–76; Martineau, *Retrospect of Western Travel,* 1:206–7; Bedford County, Va., slave lists, 1865, Accession 11839, U.Va.; Ervin L. Jordan, Jr., *Charlottesville and the University of Virginia in the Civil War* (Lynchburg, Va.: H. E. Howard, 1988), chaps. 3–6; Faculty Minutes, vol. 9, p. 163, March 3, 1865, RG-19/1/1.461, U.Va.

10. Guild, *Black Laws of Virginia,* 180; Jordan, "Blacks and the University," 50, 53, 56.
11. Samuel Reynolds Hole, *A Little Tour in America* (London and New York: Edward Arnold, 1895), 282; "Recollections of Richard Thomas Walker Duke, Jr.," IV-180.
12. Jordan, "Blacks and the University," 287.
13. Charles W. Wynes, *Race Relations in Virginia, 1870–1902* (Charlottesville: University Press of Virginia, 1961), 87; "Collegiana," *Virginia University Magazine* 15, no. 4 (January 1877): 222; "An Appeal for Aid in Establishing a Hospital for Colored Persons in the Town of Charlottesville, VA," Papers of Eugene Davis, Accession 2483, U.Va.
14. Phelps-Stokes Fellowship Papers, *Publications of the University of Virginia,* Alderman Library, U.Va.; University of Virginia Scholarship Funds Report, folder "1962 September 13 Report of University of Virginia Scholarship Funds," unnumbered page "Phelps-Stokes," RG-18/2/1.061, U.Va.; George Michael Dorr, *Segregation's Science: Eugenics and Society in Virginia* (Charlottesville: University of Virginia Press, 2008), 18, 53–65, 83–85; *Corks and Curls* (University of Virginia student yearbook), 1926, 374; Jordan, "Blacks and the University," 65, 151–58; Fred M. Alexander, *Education for the Needs of the Negro in Virginia* (Washington, D.C.: Southern Education Foundation, 1943), 87, 94, 97 (tables XII, XIX, XXI); Florence Coleman Bryant, *Rebecca Fuller McGinness: A Lifetime, 1892–2000* (Charlottesville, Va.: Van Doren, 2001), 94.
15. Louis R. Harlan, *Separate and Unequal: Public School Campaigns and Racism in the Southern Seaboard States, 1901–1915* (Chapel Hill: University of North Carolina Press, 1958), 138–39; Margaret L. Watson, ed., "A History of Public Education in Virginia" (Richmond: Department of Education, Commonwealth of Virginia, 2003), 8–9, http://www.cteresource.org/TFTfinalWebFiles/OtherDocuments/history _public_ed.pdf.
16. Jordan, "Blacks and the University," 188, 205; "New Books on Negro Question," *Alumni Bulletin of the University of Virginia,* 3rd series, 6, no. 2 (April 1913): 260–61; Harry Clemons, *The University of Virginia Library, 1825–1950: Story of a Jeffersonian Foundation* (Charlottesville: University of Virginia Library, 1954), 83, 169.
17. Edgar A. Toppin, "V S U Centennial Chronology," in *Virginia State University Centennial Celebration and Annual Founder's Day Observance Sunday, the Seventh of March Nineteen Hundred and Eighty-Two Two O'Clock the Virginia Auditorium* (Petersburg: Virginia State University, 1982); Sarah S. Hughes, "The Twentieth Century," in *"Don't Grieve after Me": The Black Experience in Virginia, 1619–1986,* ed. Philip Morgan (Hampton, Va.: Hampton University, 1986), 71; Charles S. Johnson, *The Negro College Graduate* (Chapel Hill: University of North Carolina Press, 1938), 28, 293.
18. Alice Jackson Stuart, interview with author, September 8, 1987; "Biographical Information Concerning Alice Jackson Stuart—Resumes and Personal Data Sheets, ca. 1950–1980," box 11, Alice Jackson Houston Stuart Papers, Accession 12512, U.Va.; Alice C. Jackson to Rector and Board of Visitors, September 28, 1935, subseries 2, box 18, folder "1935–1936 Negro Admissions and Scholarships," Papers of the President, RG-2/1/2.491, U.Va.; Ervin L. Jordan, Jr,. "To Go Boldly: Alice Jackson, African-

American Women, and the Desegregation of the University of Virginia," lecture at "NAACP 100: Advancing Civil Rights and Social Justice for a Century: A Symposium," University of Virginia, October 29, 2009.

19. Jordan, "Blacks and the University," 84, 87–89, 107; Box 31, folder "Segregation 1950," Papers of the President, RG-2/1/2.581, U.Va.; "Correspondence with Gregory H. Swanson, University of Virginia's First Negro Student," box 7, Papers of Sarah Patton Boyle, Accession 8003-A, U.Va.; John F. Merchant, interview with author, July 20, 1987; Kathleen Valenzi, "A Voice for Justice," *U.Va. Alumni News,* July–August 1994, 27–31.

20. Virginia Department of Education, *Educational Opportunities in Virginia: A Handbook for Veterans and Their Advisers* (Richmond: Department of Education, 1945), 9–14, 16–17, 40; Papers of Walter Nathaniel Ridley, RG-22/2/65.781, U.Va.; Dr. Walter Nathaniel Ridley, interview with author, April 24, 1987; Yolanda Ridley Scheunemann (daughter of Walter Ridley), interview with author, October 2, 1996; Yolanda Ridley Scheunemann, "Walter Nathaniel Ridley (1910–1996)," obituary/ eulogy, October 2, 1996, in author's possession; Ervin L. Jordan, Jr., "Walter N. Ridley: U.Va.'s First Black Graduate," *Charlottesville-Albemarle Tribune,* October 3, 1996, 1, 6; *Ridley: It Takes a Special Man to Be the First* (Silverthorn Films, Media Studies Program, Media Studies Department, University of Virginia, 2007), DVD; David Maurer, "Randolph Louis White Did It All during His Life: Bridgewater Native Founded Charlottesville-Albemarle *Tribune,"* Charlottesville *Daily Progress,* July 29, 2012, D5, D8; Jordan, "Blacks and the University," 84, 97–104, 110–12, 114.

21. Martin Luther King, Jr., *Where Do We Go from Here: Chaos or Community?* (Boston: Beacon Press, 1967), 123; James Baldwin, *No Name in the Street* (New York: Dial Press, 1972), 59; Jordan, "Blacks and the University," 125–27; Dabney, *Mr. Jefferson's University,* 480; "Failure's Brink: How MLK Snatched Success in Charlottesville," *The Hook* (Charlottesville), April 3–9, 2008, 35, 36, 39; Fredson Bowers, dean, Faculty of Arts and Sciences, to Professor Wesley L. Harris, Sr., School of Aerospace Engineering and Engineering Physics, April 28, 1969, Paul M. Gaston Papers Pertaining to Black Students for Freedom, Accession 12966-A, U.Va.

22. Sarah Patton Boyle, *The Desegregated Heart: A Virginian's Stand in Time of Transition* (New York: William Morrow, 1962), 253–55; "Sarah Patton Boyle Is Dead at 87," Charlottesville *Daily Progress,* March 5, 1994; "Negro's Quest," Charlottesville *Daily Progress,* April 2, 1962, 13; "*Brown's* Birthday: The Road to Equality in Charlottesville," *The Hook* (Charlottesville), May 6, 2004, 26; "Minority to Serve on BOV," *University Journal,* March 22, 1994; S. Buford Scott, "Explanation," *Cavalier Daily* (Charlottesville), March 25, 1994, 2; Jordan, "Blacks and the University," 174–75; "University of Virginia Professor William Elwood's Assessment of the Impact of the Civil Rights Act of 1964 for a Charlottesville Public Meeting, May 1964," in Ervin L. Jordan, Jr., "Embracing Equality: Before and Beyond *Brown v. Board of Education,* 1950–1969: An American Civil Rights Exhibition," Albert and Shirley Small Special Collections Library, University of Virginia, January 21–March 8, 2013.

23. Jordan, "Blacks and the University," 125–27, 184–85, 262, 313–414 *passim;* "Report on Attracting Black Faculty Results in Special Committee, Advisor," *University Register,*

October 5, 1971, 1–3; "President's Annual Report Outlines Recent Advances by University," *University Register,* November 9, 1972, 1; Laura Hughes, "Black Progress: As Enrollment Drops, African-American Faculty and Students Try to Preserve Culture," *C-VILLE Weekly,* May 14–20, 2013, 25, 27; Ervin L. Jordan, Jr., "Invisible Mirrors: Two Centuries of African-Americans at the University of Virginia," lecture at Osher Lifelong Learning Institute at the University of Virginia, March 2, 2011; Dr. Joan C. Franks, interview with author, April 16, 1994, February 15, 1999; Matthew Holden, *Continuity and Disruption: Essays in Public Administration* (Pittsburgh: University of Pittsburgh Press, 1996).

24. Jordan, "Blacks and the University," 504–7, 511, 521–22, 530, 546, 781–82; "Black Retrospectives," *The Declaration,* March 4, 1982; "Board of Visitors Acts on Budget, Affirmative Action, Elections," *Inside UVA,* June 15, 1980, 1, 3; "Board Asked to Address Issues Contributing to Low Faculty Morale," *Inside UVA,* April 15, 1992, 1, 4; "A Brief History of African Americans at U. Va. from Its Founding in 1819 to the Present," *Inside UVA,* February 27, 1998, 6–7; "University Plans Minority Affairs Office; Students, Faculty Express Goals at Forum," *University Register,* November 1, 1975, 1, 4; "Report Details Faculty Characteristics for 1974–75 Academic Year at U.Va.," *University Register,* December 1, 1975, 2; "University of Virginia Black Faculty—Fall 1993," Office of Institutional Planning and Studies, October 26, 1993, in author's possession; Ervin L. Jordan, Jr., "A Great Light: The Office of African-American Affairs at the University of Virginia, 2006–2015," September 2015, 2–3, http://oaaa.virginia.edu/great-light.

25. John Townes, "Intellectual Racism: The Plight of Blacks in Academia," *Thoughtlines,* Fall 1984, 21–22; "Demonstration on Carr's Hill" and "Casteen Addresses African-American Concerns," *Skandaline,* March 1994, 6, 12; "And Still We Rise: Rafiq and Jeremiah Jeffries Graduate from UVA," *Charlottesville-Albemarle Tribune,* May 8, 1997; "Professor Profile" column, "Dr. Ishmail Conway," *Cavalier Daily* (Charlottesville), March 11, 2003, B5, B6; Ervin Jordan, Jr., "An Overview of the UVA Afro-American Faculty-Staff Forum (1982–1984), Prepared for the First Meeting of the Black Faculty and Staff Forum, 17 April 2003," in author's possession.

26. Jordan, "Blacks and the University," 475–76.

27. Black Student Alliance of the University of Virginia, statement of purpose, February 19, 2009, in author's possession.

28. "Two Service Groups to Celebrate 20th Anniversaries," *University Journal,* September 3, 1993; "Listing for African-American Fraternities and Sororities at the University of Virginia," Reading Room, U.Va.; "Black Students State Grievances" and "The Revolving Door of Dialogue," *University Journal,* April 8, 1994; "CBS Statement," *University Journal,* April 21, 1994; "CBS Requests More Minority Faculty," *University Journal,* April 22, 1994.

29. William M. Harris, "Annual Report for the Period July 1, 1979–June 30, 1980," box 2, folder 9, p. 29; "Annual Report for the Period July 1, 1980–August 31, 1981," box 2, folder 10, p. 32, both Papers of the Office of the Vice President for Student Affairs, RG-18/2/1.031, U.Va.; "Proposed Revision of the Constitution of the Black Students

for Freedom/University of Virginia," April 24, 1969, Gaston Papers; Jordan, "Blacks
and the University," 167, 179–80, 183, 199, 276–77, 280–81, 293–96; Office of
African-American Affairs, University of Virginia, *Still I Rise: Thirty Years of Success*
(Charlottesville: Office of African-American Affairs, University of Virginia, 2007),
v, 1. The two African American email group sites are blakfacstaf@virginia.edu and
Sistah Circle (sistah-circle@list.mail.virginia.edu, sistah-circle@virginia.edu), which
is for African American women at the University.

30. Bruce, *History of the University*, 2:336–37; Arthur R. Ashe, Jr., *A Hard Road to Glory:
A History of the African American Athlete, 1619–1918* (New York: Warner Books,
1988), 9–11; Ashe, *A Hard Road to Glory: A History of the African American Athlete
since 1946* (New York: Warner Books, 1988), 115–16; Guild, *Black Laws of Virginia*,
148–49; Jordan, "Blacks and the University," 90–91.

31. Jordan, "Blacks and the University," 156–58, 174, 212, 244, 265–66, 397–99, 419,
446–47; Don Aduba, "Top 15 Athletes of the Past," *Pride Magazine*, Spring 2007, 21;
Ervin L. Jordan, Jr., "Jefferson Gladiators: Sixty Years of African-American Athletes
at the University of Virginia," *Pride Magazine*, Spring 2008.

32. "Two Black History Courses Set to Begin This Semester," *Cavalier Daily* (Char-
lottesville), February 5, 1969, 1; "Wallowing Whiteness," *Cavalier Daily*, February 5,
1969, 2; "Education Center Offers Films on Desegregation Problems," *Cavalier
Daily*, February 6, 1969, 1; "Large Response Incited by Black History Course,"
Cavalier Daily, February 7, 1969, 1; "SAC Blasts Student Booing of Scott," *Cavalier
Daily*, February 11, 1969, 3; "SAC Reasoning Questioned, Protested," *Cavalier Daily*,
February 12, 1969, 2; "Williams Explains University Difficulties with Increased Black
Student Enrollment," *Cavalier Daily*, February 13, 1969, 1; "Not the Real Problem,"
Cavalier Daily, February 14, 1987, 2; "SDS-SSOC Seek Resignation of Visitor
C. Stuart Wheatley," *Cavalier Daily*, February 17, 1969, 1, 2; "Students to Present
Proposals for Ending Racist Atmosphere," *Cavalier Daily*, February 18, 1969, 1, 4;
"Black Student Group Promises More Than Verbal Expressions," *Cavalier Daily*,
February 28, 1969, 1; "200 Students Walk out of Founder's Day Ceremony," *Cavalier
Daily*, April 15, 1969, 1, 4; "Wheatley Retraction Accepted by Council," *Cavalier
Daily*, April 16, 1969, 1; "Afro-American Studies Offered," *Cavalier Daily*, February 8,
1971, 1; "Student Demonstrations in 1970s Led to Creation of New Programs,"
University Journal, April 15, 1994; "A Brief History of African Americans at U. Va.,"
6–7; The Carter G. Woodson Institute for African-American and African Studies at
the University of Virginia, http://woodson.virginia.edu/about-the-institute.

33. Jordan, "Blacks and the University," 168, 417; "Proposal for an Afro-American Studies
Program," March 1969, 1–2, and Bowers to Harris, April 28, 1969, 1–2, Gaston Papers.

34. Ervin L. Jordan, Jr., "The First Generation: Thirty Years of the Office of African-
American Affairs at the University of Virginia," lecture at Office of African-
American Affairs' 30th Anniversary Kickoff Celebration, University of Virginia,
November 7, 2006, http://oaaa.virginia.edu/first-generation.

35. John S. Patton, *Jefferson, Cabell and the University of Virginia* (New York: Neale,
1906), 194–95; Bruce, *History of the University*, 2:389–95; Michael Plunkett, Ervin

Jordan, Jr., and Jeanne C. Pardee, "A Report on the Building Identified as #3 Dawson's Row," May 1991, 3–4, Special Collections, University Archives, University of Virginia; Jordan, "Blacks and the University," 47.

36. "Mr. Hereford Answers BSA Questions, Sets July 1 for Minority Affairs Office," *University Register,* November 15, 1975, 3; "No Twelve Gauge Solutions or Panaceas from New Afro-American Affairs Dean," *Cavalier Daily* (Charlottesville), August 5, 1976, 4; William M. Harris, "Annual Report for the Period July 1, 1979–June 30, 1980," box 2, folder 9, pp. 21–22, 36–37; "Annual Report for the Period July 1, 1980–August 31, 1981," box 2, folder 10, p. 26, both Papers of the Office of the Vice President for Student Affairs; "Vice President & Chief Students Affair Officer," http://www.virginia .edu/vpsa/; Jordan, "Blacks and the University," 194–96.

37. William M. Harris, "Annual Report for the Period July 1, 1979–June 30, 1980," box 2, folder 9, pp. 5, 8, 12, 18–19, 21–24, 26–29, 31, 36–37; "Annual Report for the Period July 1, 1980–August 31, 1981," box 2, folder 10, pp. 1, 12, 20–23, 25–26, 32, both Papers of the Office of the Vice President for Student Affairs.

38. See Paul Puryear's "day I resigned" quote in "Implementation of a Dream: Focus on the Deans," *Visions,* Spring 1996, 3; Jordan, "Blacks and the University," 234–36.

39. Father Joseph A. Brown, correspondence with author, October 23, 2009; Jordan, "Blacks and the University," 237–39.

40. "What's in a Name?" and "Name Change Reflects Identity," *University Journal,* July 1, 1993; "Dream Keepers: Office of African-American Affairs Twentieth Year Celebration 1976–1996 / University of Virginia / April 17–20, 1996" (Charlottesville: University of Virginia Printing and Copying Services, 1996, in author's possession); "Office of African-American Affairs Turns 20," *Cavalier Daily* (Charlottesville), April 17, 1996; "Funding Uncertain for Minority Program," Charlottesville *Daily Progress,* November 29, 1997; John T. Casteen III et al., "An Open Letter to the University Community: A Final Report," *Visions,* Spring 1998, 4; "UVa Honors 25 Years of Black Affairs: Former, Current African-American Affairs Deans Encourage Racial Pride," Charlottesville *Daily Progress,* November 10, 2001, A1, A9; M. Rick Turner, "Just a Reminder," *Visions,* Fall 2006, 1–2; Jordan, "First Generation"; Jordan, "Blacks and the University," 258–59, 268–87, 332–36, 350, 360–65, 370, 411–15.

41. University of Virginia, Office of African-American Affairs, "Black History Month: Educate, Motivate, Liberate" (Charlottesville: Office of African-American Affairs, University of Virginia, 2007), U.Va.; Jordan, "Blacks and the University," 411–15; "Dean: Black Students Need More Support," Charlottesville *Daily Progress,* February 2, 2007, A2; "Après Turner: Apprey Takes Quiet Command," *Hook* (Charlottesville), February 1–7, 2007, 23; "Changing of the Guard: Key University Positions Filled," *University of Virginia Magazine,* Fall 2007, http://uvamagazine.org /university_digest/article/changing_of_the_guard/; Jordan, "First Generation."

42. Jordan, "A Great Light," 1, 3, 5–6.

43. Box 5, folder "1981–1995 University of Virginia: Carter G. Woodson Institute for Afro-American and African Studies," Armstead Robinson Papers, Accession 12836, U.Va.; University of Virginia, *University of Virginia's President's Report 1980–81*

(Charlottesville: University of Virginia, 1981), 9; Ervin L. Jordan, Jr., "Armstead L. Robinson: In Memoriam, 1947–1995," *Charlottesville-Albemarle Tribune*, August 31, 1995, 1; Susan Tyler Hitchcock, *The University of Virginia: A Pictorial History* (Charlottesville: University Press of Virginia and University of Virginia Bookstore, 1999), 212; Ervin L. Jordan, Jr., "Changing History: The Armstead Robinson Papers," *Carter G. Woodson Institute Newsletter*, April 2, 2009, in author's possession; William M. Banks, *Black Intellectuals: Race and Responsibility in American Life* (New York: Norton, 1996), 162, 245, 289; Woodson Institute, "NAACP 100: Advancing Civil Rights and Social Justice for a Century: A Symposium," University of Virginia, October 29, 2009; Deborah E. McDowell, *Leaving Pipe Shop: Memoirs of Kin* (New York: Scribner, 1996); Lucy Whittle Goldstein, "Carter G. Woodson Institute," *Arts and Sciences* 28, no. 1 (Spring 2010): 24–27; Jordan, "Blacks and the University," 211–12, 223, 239, 282, 299, 266, 345, 449.

44. Jordan, "Blacks and the University," 577–79.

45. William M. Harris, "Annual Report for the Period July 1, 1980–August 31, 1981," box 2, folder 10, p. 26, Papers of the Office of the Vice President for Student Affairs; Jordan, "Blacks and the University," 111–12, 177, 195, 223, 224, 230–31, 243, 246, 252, 278, 351–52, 401–8; Coy Barefoot, "The Evolution of Honor: Enduring Principle, Changing Times," *University of Virginia Magazine*, Spring 2008, 27; "The Honor System: Is Race an Issue?" *University Journal*, September 30, 1992, 2; "Honor System Needs Major Reformation," *Cavalier Daily* (Charlottesville), September 30, 1992, 3.

46. Jordan, "Blacks and the University," 242, 243, 248n312, 319, 378, 404–8; "Coalition Plans Presentation for Board Meeting," *Cavalier Daily* (Charlottesville), March 21, 1990, 1, 6; "Council Defines Multiculturalism," *Cavalier Daily,* March 21, 1990, 1; "Poll Reflects Ailing Racial Relationships," *Cavalier Daily* (Charlottesville), November 17, 1993, 1; "Study Suggests Racial Isolation," *University Journal,* November 18, 1993; "Statement on Racial Incidents at the University of Virginia from University President John T. Casteen III," August 29, 2005 ("President's Statement on Racial Incidents," August 28, 2005, email, in author's possession); President's Commission on Diversity and Equity, University of Virginia, "Embracing Diversity in Pursuit of Excellence: Report of the President's Commission on Diversity and Equity," submitted by commission co-chairs Angela M. Davis and Michael J. Smith, September 10, 2004 (Charlottesville: University of Virginia, 2004), RG-20/86/1.041, UVa; "The University of Virginia's Commitment to Diversity," Vice President and Chief Student Affairs Officer, http://www.virginia.edu/vpsa/.

47. *Gratz v. Bollinger,* 539 U.S. 244 (2003); *Grutter v. Bollinger,* 539 U.S. 306 (2003); Jordan, "First Generation"; Jordan, "Blacks and the University," 347–48, 392, 427; "University of Virginia: Will America's Great Cheerleader for Racial Diversity in Higher Education Lose Its Leadership Position?" *Journal of Blacks in Higher Education* 26 (Winter 1999/2000): 45–46, 65; "Class of 2020," *C-VILLE Weekly*, August 24–30, 2016, 9.

48. "M. Rick Turner Cites Optimism, Continuing Challenges in Annual Address," *Charlottesville-Albemarle Tribune*, February 9, 2006, A1, A6; Jordan, "Blacks and the

University," 236, 395, 412; Ervin L. Jordan, Jr., private notes of Black Faculty and Staff Organization (BFSO) first meeting, June 22, 2012, Minor Hall, University of Virginia, Charlottesville, in author's possession; Claudrena N. Harold, history professor, to BFSO, June 29, 2012, "African American Participation in AccessUVa," in author's possession; Camisha Jones, UCARE Project Director [University and Community Action for Racial Equity, "a grassroots community organization with a mission to understand and remedy the University's legacy of slavery, segregation and discrimination within and outside of the University," ucareva.org], email, April 24, 2013, "Forum on Declining Enrollment of African American Students at UVa," in author's possession; Ted Strong, "Diversity in UVa Admissions Questioned," Charlottesville *Daily Progress*, April 30, 2013, A5; Hughes, "Black Progress," 25. Created in 2004, AccessUVa is a multimillion-dollar student financial aid program of grants and loans; by 2013, 33 percent of students qualified for this aid. "As Need Rises, Costs Does, Too: Growing Need Drives up Expense of UVa's Financial Aid Program," Charlottesville *Daily Progress*, April 28, 2013, A1, A7.

49. Jordan, "Blacks and the University," 432–34; "Accolade Recognizes Minority Recruitment," Charlottesville *Daily Progress,* December 12, 2007, A3; Black Student Alliance, untitled statement in response to Beta Bridge racist graffiti incident of May 1, 2013, May 2, 2013, http://www.virginia.edu/president/documents/BSAResponse20130501 .pdf; Teresa Sullivan, president, Marcus L. Martin, vice president and chief officer for diversity and equity, and Patricia M. Lampkin, vice president and chief student affairs officer, email, May 2, 2013, "Statement Regarding Hateful Speech on Beta Bridge," in author's possession; Jordan, "A Great Light," 1, 3, 4, 5–6. See also "National Chapters Suspend Two Fraternities: Kappa Alpha, Zeta Psi Punished for a Jointly Sponsored Halloween Party in Which Several People Dressed in Blackface," *Cavalier Daily* (Charlottesville), November 19, 2002, A1, A3; "2 U-Va. Fraternities Suspended over Photos Images of Halloween Party Guests in Blackface Were Posted on Web Site," *Washington Post,* November 20, 2002, B1; "U-Frats Cleared in Blackface Incident," *Washington Post,* December 3, 2002, A15; "University President to Give Lessons about the University's Racial Past: Says Halloween Costume Controversy Not an 'Isolated Incident,'" Charlottesville *Daily Progress,* November 24, 2002, A1, A9; "Council Clears Fraternity Members in Racial Controversy," Charlottesville *Daily Progress,* December 4, 2002, A1, A10; "Freedom to Be Wrong, and to Correct Error," Charlottesville *Daily Progress,* December 4, 2002, A8; "4 Better or Worse: Worst Sorority Hijinks" and "Blackface: Offending Costumes Roil UVA," *The Hook* (Charlottesville), November 28–December 12, 2002, 5, 7–8.

50. Jordan, "Blacks and the University," 441–42; "HoosOnline Re-examines Posting Rules: Anti-Catholic Messages Upset Some on UVa. Site," Charlottesville *Daily Progress,* March 20, 2008, A1; Rita Dove, quoted in *Ridley.*

THE ONLY ONE IN THE ROOM
U.Va. Law School, 1955–1958

John F. Merchant

Fear is a strange thing. It can arrive unexpectedly, though, more often, it is preceded by some period of apprehension. Then fear appears, heightens, becomes real, and, too frequently, lingers long. It is difficult to describe fear to someone who has had little or no experience with it. Also, if one lacks a real understanding of the circumstances giving rise to the fear, it can be easily misunderstood, even passed over as trivial. But if the experience is personal, it cannot be forgotten. Conceivably, one must "walk a mile in your (my) shoes" to fully appreciate my experience. Yes, I have known fear, preceded by apprehension, and am not ashamed to admit it.

It started fifty-five years ago, in the Commonwealth of Virginia, and lingered for an extended period of time, three years. I was alone the entire time. In September 1955, approximately one year after the U.S. Supreme Court decided *Brown v. Board of Education,* I arrived at the University of Virginia in Charlottesville to attend its law school, one of the country's best law schools then and now, and the state's sacred cow. I had applied earlier in the year, honestly believing that I would not be accepted. A letter of acceptance was received just prior to the release of the *Brown* decision, creating a serious dilemma for me, namely, what do I do now? Looking back, I recall wondering how, and why, I was accepted.

Perhaps it helped that on the face of my application I was a Virginian, having used my dad's address in my application. He lived in Buena Vista, Virginia, a town I claimed as my residence and, in a sense, it was. When I applied for admission, I knew that *Brown* was pending and that a decision was expected at any time. I spent little or no time contemplating potential reactions to a plaintiff's decision because, after all, I would not be accepted. My thoughts were focused on graduating from Virginia Union University in Richmond, hoping that New York University or Michigan would admit me to their law schools, and worrying about paying for a law-school education. If admitted anywhere, paying would be a real challenge. Hell, I still owed for college. I saw no point in analyzing potential ramifications beyond clinging to a naive belief that if the plaintiff prevailed in *Brown,* it would simply mean that segregation in public education, as practiced by many states including Virginia, would be deemed unconstitutional and prohibited. We are a law-abiding nation, aren't we? Also, it was about time and the right thing to have happen.

My naiveté was inexcusable. Reactions to a potential plaintiff's decision had begun, and the violence had already started. Still, as best I can recall, in my mind I was headed back North and had no conscious concern about something that would not involve me directly. No time was spent thinking about the fact that if the plaintiff prevailed, the decision could not eliminate the practical issues of discrimination and racism. No thought was given to the Ku Klux Klan's potential for enormous growth in its active membership and activities as a direct response to the decision.

Yes, I should have known better since the signs were clear, and I was keenly aware of the country's racial issues, especially in Virginia. Three years at one of the nation's historically black universities, Virginia Union University in Richmond, had provided me with a personal exposure to southern attitudes toward persons with an African heritage or any semblance thereof. That knowledge and experience were the major reasons I was going home to the North, where things were better—not great but better. In my mind, there was no need to continue an exposure to southern attitudes and actions by Virginia's government and its citizenry. Staying did not enter my mind. My clear choice was to leave my island of safety at Virginia Union and return to a northern refuge where I knew how to cope. Three years of "whites only" signs were enough for me, or so I thought.

The arrival of the acceptance letter changed all that. I was honor-bound to share that letter with those who had encouraged me to apply in the first place, notably Dr. Samuel D. Proctor, Union's vice president, and Dr. John M. Ellison, Union's president. Reluctantly, I showed them the letter. They were pleased and said so. Two pleased out of three ain't bad, unless you are the third, as I was.

Who knew that the decision in *Brown* would trigger some of the darkest hours in our nation's history? Who knew that Virginia's leadership, political and otherwise, was unalterably opposed to the decision and would take immediate steps to disobey a decision of the U.S. Supreme Court? I didn't. Unbelievable, when you think about it. Would secession follow? I soon learned that the darkness of those hours had neither streetlights nor paved roads to follow. My fears arose before ever setting foot on Grounds, and they turned out to be reasonable and justifiable.

After conversations with Dr. Proctor and my parents, I agreed to enroll at U.Va.'s law school. The summer of 1955, then, became a time to consider the ramifications I deliberately ignored before the acceptance letter arrived. It was impossible to overlook the racial unrest caused by the decision. Acts of violence and hatred kept springing up around the nation. The lion's den loomed and the lions were roaring. Common sense dictated that they should be feared. Too quickly, September arrived and I was on my way. Honestly, I literally trembled with fear as I traveled to Charlottesville alone, captured by thoughts about what might await me, afraid of the known and the unknown. My arrival marked the beginning of a three-year experience during which I cannot recall being unafraid for any extended period of time. For many different reasons, some level of fear was a constant companion, in and out of the classroom, starting with the Confederate flag hoisted high outside someone's dormitory window on my first day on Grounds. This was September 1955.

Fast forward to May 1956, approximately nine months after my arrival. Classes at the law school had ended; only final exams remained. Unbelievably to me, I had completed almost a full school year at this prestigious southern law school. I had endured, adjusted reasonably well, made some friends, and somehow managed to deal with the many racially inspired negatives that existed, on and off Grounds.

Actually, the law school's student body was not a primary or major source of any problems. That distinction was held by the university's all-male student body and the majority community's leaders and citizens. Being ignored by many of my peers was not a problem since it was expected. The required courses and the process of learning were a problem and a real struggle for me. They were the law school's major contributions to my personal difficulties. On the other hand, it was somewhat reassuring to receive and accept the hands of friendship offered by those classmates who did not ignore me. Although mostly silent, many seemed pleased and supportive of the effort at diversity my presence represented. To the extent practical, they sought to ease the difficulties they knew existed for me in that situation. But now, in May 1956, the schedule provided two days to prepare for final exams, covering almost all coursework during the full school year. Twenty-seven of the year's thirty credits were at risk. Final exam results would determine whether or not a first-year law school student would become a second-year student.

As far as I knew, all first-year students were preparing for finals. Me? I was admitted to the university's segregated hospital. The diagnosis was mononucleosis. If timing is everything, my timing seemed educationally fatal. A fear of failure now merged with other fears I had lived with daily, and it both consumed and motivated me. Then it won the competition with the host of other fears and dominated. I was overwhelmed, depressed, and alone, with no one to talk to or with. Would I be physically able to take my exams? If I did take them, and if my illness led to poor results, what then? If I failed to achieve the grades needed to return as a second-year student, then my time would have been wasted. Frankly, given my physical condition, I could easily flunk out. Could the exams be postponed? Add to this the fact that hospitals were unfamiliar to me. I had never spent a night in one except, perhaps, at birth. I had been feeling ill, listless, tired, and unable to eat for several days. Paying attention in class the weeks before had been a real chore; studying for finals was out of the question. The medical help I finally sought led to the hospital admission, an event that exacerbated the real possibility of failing. Failure dominated my thinking, overriding the painful discomfort of the illness.

ALONE IN MY BLACKNESS:
FEAR AND ISOLATION PERMEATE FIRST YEAR

It had been a long and difficult year, starting with my first day at the law school. Shortly after arriving on Grounds, an eerie feeling of being in a "foreign country" appeared and would not go away. Certain facts made it clear to me that I was being watched. By whom, how many, and why were, to me, serious questions without answers. The legitimate concerns I had pondered over the summer became real. My active mind raged out of control. I was not acquainted with a single human being in Charlottesville, on or off campus. Advice was not available. A support system didn't exist, and creating one seemed out of the question. I was alone with my blackness, and the dark clouds surrounding me allowed no beacon of light to poke through and point a way.

It was the real beginning of a period of loneliness and fear. The eerie feeling of being in a foreign country rarely left me. Too often, the question I pondered was whether this was the America the history books talked about. The books and teachers I was exposed to from kindergarten through high school had misled me, unfairly. My three years at Virginia Union taught me that. There, I learned firsthand that the teachings and teachers in the Greenwich, Connecticut, school system had failed to tell me and others the whole truth. Do not fertile minds deserve the whole truth? Of course they do, but it wasn't provided by one of the best public school systems in America. Virginia Union required, among other things, that all students take a course in Negro history. Carter G. Woodson's history book was the Bible and provided me with an awareness of American history, in stark and scholarly detail, that Greenwich schools had overlooked. Truth entered my fertile mind at last, and was welcomed.

Fortunately, in time, Charlottesville's black community provided the respite needed to maintain a sense of mission, direction, and courage. It gave me time to be and feel normal around friends—wonderful people who went out of their way to ease the burdens. I could not have endured without their help and friendship. Three families named Jackson including Punjab, the dentist, and his wife, Mae; Edward and Eunice; and Teresa and her two sons, Bo and Frankie, were for me a refuge and a haven to which I could escape and refuel. Frankie and Bo were special little boys who grew to be good men. They called me "Superman" because they watched me lift a heavy couch for some reason and had seen it done just once . . . on TV, watching cartoons! Young minds are often the soothing balm needed.

In a real sense, Charlottesville's black community provided a refuge and a haven for all of the black pioneers enrolled in the university's engineering, medical, and law schools. The difference for me was that the engineering and medical schools had other blacks enrolled—three in the medical school, two or three in the engineering school, then me alone in law school. I was told that one year before my arrival, in September 1954, a black student had entered the law school as a full-time first year but had flunked out. No help for me there. In fact, no other black students enrolled in or attended the law school during my entire three years, nor did I ever have a roommate.

Talking the law makes learning it easier, but I had no one to talk to or with, not in that setting. Of course, my parents and friends had been supportive during the preceding summer. Their support was welcomed and appreciated but did little to ease my concerns. It was verbal and not strengthened by any personal experiences that remotely resembled what I was about to face. Sure, my parents knew about the Commonwealth of Virginia. They were raised in Lexington, Virginia. They left in the 1930s, ending up in Greenwich, where they found work: Mom as a domestic, Dad as a gardener, something he knew little or nothing about.

A FATHER'S DREAM REALIZED; A SON'S COURAGE TESTED

Almost all blacks in Greenwich had similar employment, working for wealthy white folks. Many lived in the homes of their employers and got very little time off during a normal seven-day period. It mirrored slavery, although they were paid a pittance, along with free room and board, for their sixty- to ninety-hour-work weeks. Mom and Dad knew about southern attitudes and traditions. They knew about racism. They knew about the need to stay in your place or suffer consequences that could be fatal. However, talking with them did little more than increase my fears. Their support for what I was about to do contained constant references to those negatives and warned about the potential consequences if I failed to conform. Could I conform? Nonsensical conformance was not a habit I had ever acquired, nor do I have such a habit today.

Meaningful advice or counsel of an encouraging and positive nature didn't exist. I did get a lot of what I called "don't dos." You know, "don't do this, don't go there, don't do that or bad things will happen, keep your chin up" stuff. These warnings foretold nothing but danger and added to my concerns. My dad, Garrett McKinley Merchant, despite having only a sixth grade education, was excited and proud. No surprise there since he is the reason why I ever even considered becoming a lawyer. It's what he wanted to be but couldn't. So he was bent on living his dream through his son, spending a lot of time discussing such an ambition with me.

I had no such dreams but loved and respected my dad to such an extent that following his dream was a good thing. He tried to be positive in his talks with me about the South and Virginia, and the attitudes and dangers that existed. He talked about the negatives that were increasing and predicted. He believed that the *Brown* decision signaled the start of a more serious conflict between the races in America, especially in the South where too many folks seemed to want a second chance at winning the Civil War. They simply ignored the fact that they had lost and it was over. Majority community Christians packed the churches for a short time on Sundays then forgot the teachings the rest of the week, especially as they related to those with an African heritage.

Dad scared me when he made it clear that danger lurked for any blacks involved in making changes that threatened the southern way of life. He advised that I was going into what could be a lion's den, unarmed, except with his conviction that I was doing the right thing. He believed that I had the intellectual capacity to achieve and helped give me the courage to try. How did I know that he knew these things? He discussed them all at length with me. He convinced me that I must attend and deal with whatever occurred. To him, attending U.Va.'s law school was simply something that had to be done. He apologized for his inability to help financially but promised to do what he could, and did. Between Dad and Dr. Proctor, I had no chance to give in to my fears and go elsewhere. Dad and I were friends. He was my rock to lean on, a man who loved and parented his children in admirable ways, helping me to grow, understand and expand my outlook, and make my mind work objectively.

Growing up, I had the good fortune to spend quality time with him, especially from age eleven to sixteen, despite his being separated from Mom when I was two. We talked a lot, or I should say he talked and answered my questions. I listened, asked questions, and learned a lot. He had a good mind and used it. I still believe he was one of the most intelligent people I have ever met, unlettered but wise. His focus was on looking ahead, not simply seeking immediate gratification. He believed that in time things could and would change among the races, and he firmly believed that my getting a law degree from U.Va. would be an important part of the changes that were inevitable. He could not, and would not, even guess at a timetable. He did stress that it would take a long time.

Dad had always wanted to be a lawyer. As stated, he spent many hours talking to me about why being a lawyer was a desirable thing. In that way, his goal became mine. He also talked about being an elected official, a legislator who helped to make the laws rather than just a citizen who had to obey them. I never had any real interest in being a legislator, so I never tried to be one. He talked about the need to be educated and prepared, and the importance of being a real part of one's community, not just a resident. He discussed doing the right thing and doing a job right the first time. He talked about the dire need for justice for all who appeared in the courts, without regard to race, color, or creed. He gave me a strong philosophical basis for existing, one that clearly embraced the teachings of Christianity. I learned, even as I struggled to understand fully. I accepted and cherished his wisdom but was still afraid. There is no substitute for a father who cares and spends time helping a child to grow and develop. I was fortunate.

Unfortunately, Dad died before he had a chance to watch me practice law. He would have liked that. I can see him finding excuses to hang around my office, attending any trials I was involved in and critiquing my performance. I litigated a lot, civil and criminal; he would have liked being there for that. On reflection, I must admit that I did not truly share his dream of being a lawyer. Life's circumstances, my immaturity, and a lack of knowledge and money made it difficult for me to even dream about being a lawyer. Also, I wasn't really convinced that being a lawyer was what I wanted, but, then again, I really didn't know what I wanted to be or what I could be. I did know that I wanted to be like my father—good, strong, wise, smart, caring, courageous.

So why did I apply to U.Va. in the first place? Actually, it was not my idea. It was a request from Dr. Proctor, who also promised to try to help. He said that if I agreed to enroll in the law school, he would try to raise money to help defray the expenses. He kept his word and raised 25 to 30 percent of my expenses in keeping that promise. Dr. Proctor was a special human being, and I owed him. He took me off the streets and was enormously helpful to me during my time at Virginia Union. I applied to U.Va. only because he asked me to. Doing so was a way to pay back my debt to him, and he insisted on payment without ever voicing it in those terms. I honestly didn't fully understand Dr. Proctor's all-consuming interest in my attending U.Va.'s law school. Why me? Some insight was obtained years later when I read his explanation in a book that he wrote, *The Substance of Things Hoped For.* In short, he wanted the first black graduate to be a Virginia Union man. As for why me, he wrote: "At a conference in Greenwich, Connecticut, a woman came up to me and begged me to take her son off the streets. She was terrified he was going to wind up in jail. I persuaded him to enroll in our college. John Merchant went down with me, played basketball, waited tables in the hotels, took campus jobs, and made an outstanding record. He had a kind of Yankee audacity about him and a never-give-up tenacity that made him an excellent candidate to break down barriers" (80).

Dad firmly believed I could do it and encouraged me to be positive and unafraid. I tried. Dad's advice and counsel, along with Mom's firm but unsubstantiated belief that it would be okay, were major sources of strength. Each was absolutely certain that God would make a way. I leaned on God; my parents; my two sisters, Barbara and Elizabeth; and some friends. Then, I journeyed to Charlottesville, alone, except for the unanswerable questions and persistent fears that traveled with me. Unknown to me, that "Yankee audacity" also went with me, and apparently I latched on to that "never give up tenacity" Dr. Proctor believed I had. Frankly, I never knew that I had those things. All I knew about myself was that I didn't know how to quit, but this could be a first. Somehow, the tuition was gathered and sent, and I was on my way.

FINALLY EQUAL BUT STILL A WIDE SEPARATION

Upon arrival, I carried my meager but adequate belongings into the law-school dorms, located directly across the street from the law school. The accommodations were comfortably designed for gentlemen: two-room suites containing a bedroom and a combination study and living room, complete with fireplace. The furnishings and furniture were more than adequate, newer and better than those in the attic room I called home. A bathroom was shared with two occupants of an adjoining suite. While awaiting a roommate's arrival, I met the men in the adjoining suite: two New Yorkers, both second-year students. That was when the confederate flag loomed large, and the questions began immediately: Why were two northerners, New Yorkers, to share a bathroom with a black student at this southern university? Where was I going to eat dinner tonight? Or lunch? Or breakfast? In an effort to think positively, it occurred to me that perhaps the administration was taking steps to make me comfortable, avoid some issues, and ease the transition. I didn't really believe that. I awaited my roommate, but a roommate never appeared. I did say hello to a student as he was moving into his room directly above me. I learned later that he was from Georgia and, as best I could surmise, not at all thrilled to see me. It didn't take long to realize that I was alone but not unnoticed. My presence was known though not heralded.

I believed, and knew, that I was being watched. My hope was that the surveillance was protective in nature, but that could not be confirmed. I prayed; why not? I also hoped that the Ku Klux Klan was not watching, a scary thought. The 1954 *Brown* decision had led to enormous unrest and racial violence throughout America, especially in the South. While at Virginia Union, I was privy to events that led to *Brown*.

Oliver Hill, a courageous and extraordinary lawyer, was representing a group of black students from the Prince Edward County, Virginia, school system in an effort to eliminate the separate-but-equal nonsense that was Virginia's educational guidepost for public schools. His efforts were a constant subject of discussion at Union, as were other aspects of the struggle that led to *Brown*. The timing seemed bad, or given my first-day experiences, I thought it was bad. The Klan had been active in Virginia during my three years at Virginia Union University in Richmond. I had no personal encounters with the Klan at Union but was fully aware of its presence and mission. Virginia's governor, John S. Battle, was soon leading the South in a plan of "massive resistance" to *Brown,* designed and fully supported by Harry F. Byrd's political machine, the media, and Virginia's majority population. Virginia's entire white population seemingly bought into Byrd's approach and flaunted their opposition to the Supreme Court's decision.

Civil disobedience demonstrations brought out the worst in people. Too many seemed to believe that slavery was the only way to deal with people who possessed an African slave heritage. Second-class status, evidenced by the treatment received from the majority community, even seemed too high a classification to bestow on those who arrived, or rather were brought here, on the wrong boat from the wrong place. That boat did not dock at Ellis Island in New York.

Some behavior required of blacks simply defied belief. Among those were stepping into the gutter so that a white person could use the sidewalk; being dragged away at night and flogged or lynched by the Klan for simply being accused of looking at a white woman; not being allowed to use a public bathroom when traveling through the South, or buying food, when traveling, at a window in the back of the restaurant near the garbage cans; being referred to by your first name only, never Mr. or Mrs. Brown, or being addressed as "nigger" or "boy" with no recourse; drinking from a water fountain for "Colored," if you could find one, or facing a bathroom door where a sign said, "Whites Only," knowing the sign meant what it said; traveling from the country into town to register to vote only to be told by the person at the voting registration window that it was closed at 10:15 a.m. and would not reopen that day; or trying to explain to your children why these things occurred and why this was the way it was.

Incredibly, in the twenty-first century, many still harbor the belief that the above examples are the best way to deal with the black population. In the 1950s, Governor George Wallace of Alabama soon became a loud voice against both desegregation and integration of the public schools. His negative and provocative behavior deliberately fanned the flames of racial unrest and led to increased violence throughout the South and elsewhere. Young black children and their parents showed enormous courage as they integrated many public schools in the South, usually accompanied by the National Guard. The firehose was a weapon of choice in Alabama and elsewhere, along with clubs and other tools of violence. Local police protection for blacks disappeared as the entire country took sides, often in support of Senator Byrd, Governor Wallace, and their ilk, causing more unrest and incredible violence.

It was not a time for Americans to be proud of their country, their neighbors, and, too often, themselves—their personal thoughts and behavior. Clearly, the struggle for civil rights had taken on new dimensions. More explosions were inevitable; everyone knew that.

For me, a twenty-two-year-old black male, born and raised in the North, in Connecticut, with parents who had fled Virginia, it was a scary time. I admit to being scared, even terrified, and that is truth, not an overstatement. I wondered if I would be involved in any incidents, or even cause one. Either, or both, possibilities existed. The U.Va. administration knew I was here; did the Klan? What would be the attitudes of the mostly southern student body and the faculty? Would I be alone without friends? How would I deal, presumably alone, with what lay ahead? Where could I eat dinner? The questions were further complicated by the fact that my personality and general attitude had never been conducive to turning the other cheek. I have always had a basic and fundamental belief in freedom of speech and the need for it. My preference was, and is, for meaningful discussions of issues and differences. Would this become a problem for me? If so, how would I handle it in this foreign country, with no known source of help if problems appeared?

AT TIMES, QUITTING SEEMED LIKE A GOOD IDEA

I was very concerned, and very afraid, to put it mildly. Still, I forced myself to look into the bathroom mirror where a 5-foot, 11-inch, 158-pound person, totally unprepared for any physical violence that might erupt, looked back at me. I shrugged, unpacked, and sat down. Fear grumbled in my belly and rose rapidly to my brain. It was frightening. What am I doing here? How did I allow it to happen? Yes, I thought seriously about leaving, spelled quitting, and was tempted. Should I?

The answers came slowly, but they came. Somehow, I had to find a way to change my urge to quit into a commitment to stay and a plan to endure and advance. Could I? Not unless you get to work right now, John. I answered those questions that day, telling myself: "You are the reason you are here. You agreed to apply, and you were accepted. You clearly promised your parents and Dr. Proctor that you would matriculate in an attempt to ensure that the first black graduate of this law school was a Virginia Union University man."

"Face it, John," I said to myself, "or start your future as an unreliable failure. If you quit, everyone will know that you quit, an embarrassing thought." I had never quit anything in my life, but it seemed like a good idea at that time.

I talked myself into staying, asking God for courage, strength, help, and support. My thoughts then shifted a bit as I tried to imagine what might lay ahead of me and how I would respond to and cope with whatever had to be faced, in and out of class. Would I manage to survive unscarred, physically or mentally? Would I earn the law degree Dr. Proctor wanted a Virginia Union man to have? Did I really want to be a lawyer? Where would I eat dinner tonight?

I made a short list of rules for survival. One self-imposed rule I never failed to obey was that I would not complain about treatment in class or my grades unless they threatened my qualifying for and receiving the law degree I was sent there to get. I never violated that rule. I still don't complain about things. My approach is to try to clearly identify the problem, then, if possible, discuss it with the relevant people, roll up my sleeves, and work to figure out a way to solve it. It occurred to me that this was just the first day; presumably, three years lay ahead, a seemingly impossible eternity to ponder. A long, long time to be alone in a "foreign country" filled with turmoil, racial unrest, and violence, and surrounded by a horde of potential perpetrators of those negatives. I told myself, "Take it one day at a time, John, and please don't let the media make you a public person and exacerbate your situation."

The hospital admission at the end of my first year triggered thoughts of my only other experience with a southern hospital. At the age of nine, while visiting grandparents in Lexington, I fell out of a tree and dislocated my right wrist. Mom took me to the hospital where I was required to wait three or four hours before the only black doctor in the area arrived to treat me. White hospital staff did nothing except ignore me. They left me alone with my pain and tears until a very competent black doctor finally arrived and treated me, and I was released. My recovery was complete but would that treatment be repeated here? Virginia was not like Greenwich.

On the other hand, Greenwich, in terms of race relations and its attitude toward blacks, was no Garden of Eden. Its black population consisted primarily of charter members of the "menial job brigade," most jobs just one small step above the tasks performed during slavery. Most were domestics who worked for wealthy white folks. Some recollections of growing up there were as bad as I imagined and believed U.Va. would be.

AND WHERE WOULD I EAT DINNER?
NOT AN UNIMPORTANT QUESTION

I tried to think positively but it was a struggle. In my search for positives, the thought occurred that perhaps after this first year, another black student would enroll and make the task easier by his or her presence. I could certainly hope for that; however, that did not happen. Would I be alone for three consecutive years? Would I have any friends, later if not sooner? Would the media get involved and how would I handle that if they did? Would I be able to learn two new languages: the language of the law and the languages of specific subjects such as torts, contracts, real property, and others, all first-year required subjects? I was a total stranger to those languages, though many of my classmates were not. The competition had an edge. Where could I eat dinner? This was not an irrelevant question, especially since wherever food existed I had to walk to get it. In what direction? How far? In the dark? Simple questions, tough to answer.

At that time, and still, the law school was ranked as one of the top ten law schools in the United States, thus it was reasonable to assume that my class would include many who were among the best and brightest in the country. I expected that most of them would be southerners with southern attitudes and biases—sons of the wealthy and powerful, preparing to carry on southern traditions, most of which were decidedly unfriendly to black citizens. I was wrong about that. The students came from many states, although the South and the Commonwealth of Virginia were clearly well-represented. Ironically, I did not really fear competing with whites in the classroom. I had learned to do that throughout my life in the Greenwich public school system. Admittedly, I wasn't sure why I was going to school, but I enjoyed learning and was good at both learning and remembering things. I did realize that I needed to apply myself, develop and maintain good study habits, and learn those skills quickly. Good study habits were a real challenge since I had none. In truth, I have no recollection of ever carrying a book home from high school or of doing homework at home. I entered high school at age twelve, was four-feet, eleven-inches tall, and weighed eighty-eight pounds.

My entire high school time and my summers involved leaving Greenwich High School at the end of each school day and catching a bus to Stamford, where I swept floors at the B and S Coat Company on Stillwater Avenue. Dad had a room there, and as part of his living arrangement, he was to sweep the floors in the building and around the sewing machines each day, a chore he did not relish after working all day. So he hired me to do it, and I did, for five consecutive years. He paid me a dollar a day. Bus fare was a dollar a week, school lunch the same, one dollar went to Mom, another dollar was my allowance, and a dollar was put in savings each week. I saw and talked with Dad almost every day. After cleaning the factory, I caught a bus back to Greenwich, arriving there around 7 p.m. For two to three years, I got off the bus on Greenwich Avenue and went to a bowling alley where I set up pins each night until around 9 or 10 p.m. and then walked home to save the ten cents bus fare. This schedule didn't leave much time for studying.

My homework was done at school during study periods. At the time, the public school system in Greenwich was considered one of the best in the country. I did well there but would have done better if I had studied or believed that I was preparing for college. I never had a black classmate in high school. The only other black student that I know of, a female, chose the college curriculum, so we never shared a classroom together. For me, the idea of going to college didn't exist. It was neither economically feasible nor seemingly worthwhile. The "menial job brigade" was assumed to be in our futures. We all understood the dominance of the majority community and did not believe that opportunities would be made available because of a college education.

The few college-educated blacks in Greenwich, and there were a couple, were simply not allowed to use their college-acquired skills because the majority community denied them employment opportunities. Alver W. Napper, a graduate of Albany State University in Georgia, finally found somewhat suitable employment when he was hired as the director of the Crispus Attucks Community Center in Greenwich, the only black community center in the state, if not in all of New England. (Crispus Attucks [1723–70], a black man, became the first casualty of the American Revolution when he was shot and killed in what became known as the Boston Massacre.) After earning his degree, Mr. Napper returned to Connecticut, but the only work he could find initially was as a toll collector on the Merritt Parkway, a state job that required a fight to get. Other toll collectors resented his presence and the presence of the very few blacks ultimately hired to perform what can only be described as a simple job, one requiring little educational achievement.

I had graduated high school at age sixteen with only white classmates. I had learned quickly that they were no more capable of learning than I was. As I recall, not many performed better than I did. Thus, my concern upon entering law school was learning languages while coping with the pressures, real and imagined, that existed.

Early on, the entire first-year law class was convened and told, among other things, that we should "look at the students to our left and right; one of you will not be here three years from now." There is nothing like receiving a morale booster on the first day of the "gathering of the clan."

I remember thinking that the professor was slyly talking only to me, a thought that both annoyed and challenged me. The men on my left and right kept staring at me, so I stared back, asking myself which one of them would disappear. False bravado at work, for sure, but often it's the little things that drive and sustain us.

REMEMBERING OTHER PIONEERS AND BOURBON WITH A PROFESSOR

I had graduated from Virginia Union University, a historically black college. It was there that I first attended a class with other blacks. I was certain that no other person in the building had ever sat in a class with a black student, or not many had. My tenure at Union was truly an uplifting experience. I watched young men and women enter from southern segregated school systems into a college where they were exposed to a nurturing and educational experience that I believed, and still believe, was phenomenal. They soaked up learning, graduated as well-educated people, quenching a thirst to learn, and left prepared to face a world of work that fundamentally did not want them. They produced and achieved, many in meaningful and dramatic ways.

Union's student body included others of note, such as Rev. Wyatt T. Walker, who became Dr. Martin Luther King's right-hand man; Rev. Walter Fauntroy, who served as a minister in Washington, D.C., and who became the first elected congressional representative from the District of Columbia; Leroy Vaughan, a great athlete, hampered by bad knees, who received a tryout with the Baltimore Colts; and Howie Jones and Ronnie Bressant, two New Yorkers who manned Union's championship backcourt, both All City out of Boys High in New York City but with no chance to play in the NBA because it wasn't scouting or drafting from historically black colleges then. That would happen later and change the face of college sports. Mo Vaughan, Leroy's son with his wife Shirley, was the beneficiary of an earlier generation's hard work. He became an outstanding baseball player with a successful career with the Boston Red Sox and New York Mets. Leroy himself went on to earn a Ph.D. in education.

There were many others who made their mark after leaving Union, a clear tribute to the effectiveness of the historically black colleges and their ability to inspire and produce well-educated, productive men and women who positively impacted a culture and a world of work that did not want them. I feel compelled to mention two others, though I leave out too many. Douglas Wilder had graduated from Union a year or two before me. He was elected lieutenant governor of Virginia in 1985, and in 1990 became the first African American elected governor of any state in America. Sure we are tired, but we've come a long way; America has come a long way. Let's take some deep breaths, rest a bit, and continue the journey. There is a light at the end of the tunnel. To me, Wilder was the proof that Barack Obama could be elected president of the United States.

Henry Marsh graduated from Virginia Union in 1956, a year after I did. He earned a law degree from Howard University in 1959 and joined the law firm of Hill, Tucker, and Marsh, becoming a partner in 1966. Henry has successfully litigated more than fifty cases against school boards in Virginia and more than twenty employment discrimination cases during a distinguished legal career that is still ongoing. A brilliant lawyer and a gentleman, his reputation as one of the leading trial and appellate attorneys in Virginia is well-deserved. In addition, he became Richmond's first black mayor in 1977 and later served as a senator in the Virginia State Senate from 1991 to 2014.

Three years at Virginia Union allowed me to be a witness to the racial prejudices and attitudes that prevailed and dominated in the South—and to study them. Now, at U.Va., it seemed that I was to be completely surrounded by those prejudices and attitudes; expecting the worst was not unreasonable. The arrival experience did nothing to discourage those negative thoughts. Then, after enduring those first-year classes and a full year of fear, I found myself in the hospital, still very much alone, awaiting final exams but not physically able to prepare for them. My confidence level was not high. In fact, it was very low, almost nonexistent. Yes, after about nine months as the only black student at this prestigious law school, in a setting where I was surrounded by southerners and taught by a faculty that had never conferred a law degree on a black student, legitimate concerns abounded. Many of that faculty were U.Va. law school graduates themselves, so who could tell what they thought about my being there?

A word about the faculty. Notably, there were those who were sensitive about my situation, supportive of my being there, and helpful in large and small ways. Of course, there were others as well who had different feelings. Dean F. D. G. Ribble was a gem. He understood and cared. Hardy C. Dillard, who taught contracts in my first year, is a legend at the law school. I recall that he was the first to call on me to discuss a case and be questioned about it in front of the whole class. That happened to everyone, but I was pretty nervous when my turn came, afraid that I would humiliate myself. However, Professor Dillard very adroitly and skillfully guided me through the experience in a manner that ensured a solid performance at my first speaking engagement at the law school. I was, and am, grateful for that.

Professor Charles O. Gregory taught torts and labor law. He was a nationally acclaimed expert and taught from books he authored on both subjects. We became friends. He spent his summers in New Hampshire, as did I, and once invited me to dinner at his New Hampshire home. During that night, I recall that he and I shared the better part of a fifth of bourbon, talked about a variety of subjects, and consumed several loin lamb chops prepared by his wife, a wonderful woman. I remember well that I learned to enjoy bourbon from Charley Gregory, a good man.

Before that, though, I also remember thinking that my illness was totally unfair, especially after what I had been through during the past several months. Or, I asked myself, "was this just another challenge laid before me?" I voted for unfair but accepted the challenge and somehow was not deterred. Dad had taught me that you are always in charge of your attitude, regardless of the situation or circumstances. "Stay positive and never give less than your best" was his credo. He taught me that failure should be the result of one's inability, not the result of giving less than your best. He believed that you could do almost anything if you applied yourself properly to the task.

Admittedly, I had serious reservations about Dad's teachings throughout the year, but not enough to convince me that he was wrong. I continued to give my best and was willing to accept whatever result prevailed. Mononucleosis prevented any studying; it also prevented swallowing food and drinking water without serious pain in my throat. I lost weight and was thoroughly exhausted and weak. I was terrified that I would fail and that my tenure at the law school would end. I struggled with sickness, depression, and loneliness. I thought back on the school year spent as the only black law student at this prestigious school, trying to learn and remember new languages, along with the law that applied. Frankly, I was not really confident that I had mastered the languages, let alone the relevant legal concepts that pertained.

Real property? What is a mortgage or a deed? What does it mean to record either one on the land records? Fee simple, fee tail, life estates, tenancies, the Rule in Shelley's Case, bailor, bailee, landlord and tenant rights and responsibilities, the statute of frauds, unenforceable covenants, and a lot more since September. All these were either new words or new concepts to me, none of which I had ever heard mentioned, let alone discussed, prior to entering law school. We did not speak about such things in the rat-infested attic on Charles Street in Greenwich where my mother, two sisters, and I spent most of my growing-up years. In fact, my parents never had a checking account or a share of stock, and we would never have been mistaken for middle-class folks.

After my parents separated, my dad moved to Stamford where he started a house-painting business that was not a smashing success but provided work and some income. As far as I know, he contributed child support to my mom regularly, more when he had more, without a court order. He came every Sunday and spent time with his children, always taking us for a ride in his car where we enjoyed singing and harmonizing. For years he also gave us a weekly allowance of one dollar—for the three of us, not a dollar apiece. With that money, we joined other young people at the movies at the Pickwick Theater most Sundays, a veritable ritual for us. At one point, the movies cost seventeen cents per person. The forty-nine cents remaining was used for candy and popcorn, split three ways. There were weekly discussions over who got the odd penny, actually more like arguments among siblings. Bobbie usually argued that being the oldest, she should get it. My position was that as the only male in the group I deserved it, a chauvinistic approach soon abolished by a failure to gather the votes. Liz was creative in her arguments but didn't have the votes either, so rarely won. It just happened that Bobbie sang soprano, Liz was an alto, Dad sang bass, and I was a baritone. The components for harmony were there, and we loved using them. The songs we sang came from three sources: church hymns and gospel, current hit-parade numbers, and songs Dad taught us from his youth. Bobbie, Liz, and I sang in the junior choir at First Baptist Church. We attended church every Sunday.

My parents each had an admirable work ethic that they passed on to their children. Receiving welfare was out of the question, but doing well in school was a priority rigidly enforced, as was attending church and staying out of trouble. Ours were really tremendous parents we were fortunate to have.

Contracts and torts, like real property, were six-credit courses that also contained strange words, combinations of words, and unfamiliar concepts. I believe that most law students will agree that learning the law is made easier when one is able to talk to other students about the law, its applicability, nuances, and twists and turns as you study it. I did not have that opportunity, though others did. I missed the advantage of having a roommate or other students to talk with about the law. In truth, learning was a real struggle.

FINAL EXAMS, SOME MAC AND CHEESE, AND A RECIPE FOR FAILURE

So how in the world would I pass these courses, especially with mononucleosis on hand? Visions of disappointing Dr. Proctor, my family, my friends, and myself dominated and left me depressed. The fact that my hospital room was in the "colored" section of the hospital did not help either. I asked about postponing my exams until I had recovered. The answer was yes, I could postpone them until next year, May 1957. Not a very good option to me. Trying to remember after nine months was tough enough. Waiting twenty-one months impressed me as an excellent recipe for failure.

So there I was, hospitalized in a segregated hospital, concerned about the level of care that could be expected—and facing final exams. A skinny kid who could not eat and maintain weight, now faced his greatest challenge alone, except for my God. I prayed and asked for help; it came.

As I think back, it occurs to me that the hospital administrators probably had their own concerns. If so, they did not share them with me. I thought: a segregated hospital had admitted a black student who was integrating the university's law school. Would integrating the hospital be his next target? To the hospital, that could mean a lawsuit if the administration and staff failed to provide proper care. Also, please don't let Merchant die because of inattention or any form of malpractice. The ensuing lawsuit could possibly do harm to the hospital's budget and bring totally unwanted national attention to a university and its hospital, both striving to achieve, maintain, and elevate their status as one of the South's leading educational institutions, including in the field of medicine. If they thought along those lines, they had my total support. I didn't want to die either. Equally as important, I thought, could be their fear that this law student might later sue to desegregate and integrate the hospital.

Little did they know that my thoughts focused only on being able to eat a good meal, gain some weight, feel better, get well, take my exams, pass them, return home to Connecticut for the summer, then, maybe, even return to Charlottesville as a second-year student. The problem was that there was no known cure for mononucleosis. In fact, there was little anyone could do to ease the discomfort though, in fairness, the hospital tried. They tried in many ways to treat me and make me happy and contented. Seemingly every doctor in the hospital visited me and tried every approach they had ever heard of anywhere to cure me or at least make me more comfortable. In a sense, I felt like an experiment, and probably was, for whatever reason. In my opinion, there was never any indication of the hospital providing me with less than the best care they could. Their interest and efforts were appreciated, but through no fault of theirs, the immediate medical results left a lot to be desired.

The head nutritionist took time to visit me. She told me that I could order any food on the planet and it would be served to me. The condition was that I must eat everything I ordered or that particular food would not again be served. Seizing this unexpected opportunity, I tried steaks and chops but had to quit and go to milkshakes. The pain in swallowing was simply too great to bear. The milkshakes hurt going down but, in sliding down, hurt less and were bearable. I lost weight but at least did not die.

The exam issue was resolved by my leaving the hospital on the morning of an exam, walking to and taking the exam, then returning to the hospital. All exams were taken except for one I simply did not have the strength to take: the contracts exam. My physical condition was such that I was not upbeat about what the results would be. I received permission to delay the contracts exam until May 1957. I took it then and was amazed when I passed with a reasonably good grade.

My grades at law school probably merit some discussion, but I will limit it. It didn't matter to me what my grades were anyway as long as I stayed on the right road leading to a degree. No recruiters were ever going to interview me for a possible position—and they didn't. Even the federal government was uninterested. I believe that some professors cheated me on my grades, but no clear evidence of that exists or existed, nor did I pursue the issue. Frankly, I honored my rule that I would not contest any grade I received as long as it didn't prevent me from graduating with a law degree.

In my third year, an incident unrelated to grades did trouble me a bit, although I laugh about it now. It involved money. Shortly before my last semester, I had figured out that I was broke and needed money in order to eat—at all—during that last semester. I met with the professor in charge of making loans to students and was initially denied the loan. He told me that existing policy prevented him from lending money to a student receiving financial aid. I told him that the policy did not apply because I was not receiving aid. He insisted, without disclosing any evidence to support his position, that my application for financial help had been approved and that I had received financial aid. No loan could now be made. I stood up before him and meekly and politely, with hat in hand, convinced him that I had never received any scholarship dollars and, at this late stage, had no interest in fighting about it. Please, just lend me money so that I can eat. Ultimately, he did. That loan was needed to cover the cost of one meal a day for a full semester.

The meal consisted of elbow macaroni cooked in a pot on a hot plate in my room. To the macaroni was added Cheez Whiz and B&M Baked Beans right out of the can. The beans were warmed by the elbows and eaten out of the pot with a spoon "borrowed" from the cafeteria. I returned the spoon before graduation. Incidentally, that is a meal I enjoy to this day and eat often. To the elbows and cheese in one bowl, add some broiled chopped sirloin mixed with onions, green peppers, and carefully selected seasonings. Stir until mixed well, then serve with a salad on a separate plate and a glass of pinot grigio. Delicious! One caution: only B&M Baked Beans will make it the culinary delight that it is. Friends have enjoyed this dish over the years; some have even raved about it. They call it "Merchant Goulash."

Soon after first-year exams ended, I was released from the hospital, somewhat improved but weak and depressed. I returned home to Connecticut, thence to Winchester, New Hampshire, to work as a camp counselor, as I had done for several summers. The mononucleosis went away, then recurred, but ultimately disappeared with the help of Dr. John Houpis in Brattleboro, Vermont, the camp's doctor.

STAYING THE COURSE DESPITE FEAR OF FAILING, CONSTANT FRUSTRATIONS, AND ISOLATION

While awaiting results, the fear of failing never left me. More time was spent thinking about how I had happened to attend U.Va.'s law school and why I had agreed to go there in the first place. More than one private self-pity party was sponsored by me, for me, and attended only by me, until grades arrived. The parties ended when the results arrived and I learned that I had passed all the exams and could return in September as a second-year student. But the self-reflection continued and did not ease up. The wait for exam results gave me time to think seriously about the experience. I found it hard to discuss the U.Va. experience with anyone. Actually, until exam results arrived, there was little to discuss. I guess you had to be there, sharing the experience, to fully understand my unwillingness to talk about it. Also, not many folks really cared to listen and understand. When grades finally arrived, I could now talk about returning. Mom and Dad were pleased; I was amazed and pleased. The challenge had been successfully met, and my confidence level rose regarding the education I was receiving.

The issue for me was whether or not I wanted to return, transfer, or quit. Not an easy question, but answered after several serious discussions with Dad, Mom, George Twine from Greenwich, Dr. Proctor, and a few others. George Twine, a black man, was the person who hired me to work at the camps in New Hampshire, Rabbit Hollow and Forest Lake. He was a graduate of Lincoln University, a journalism major, born before his time. Very talented and energetic, he never found employment in his field as should have been the case. Many highly capable black college graduates experienced that problem; some still do but not nearly as many. The discussions leading to my return were with men who had a vision that exceeded mine. They argued long and hard for returning. When those arguments seemed doomed to fail, they demanded it.

They taught me the value of having a vision, the need for courage and fortitude, and the value of patience while working toward an important and desirable goal. They pointed out that apprehensions about returning had to be significantly less than those concerning attending in the first place. The first year's experience should have eased my fears since I now knew what to expect and how to deal with it. The real or imagined negatives had been endured without major damage. The university and the city of Charlottesville had become somewhat familiar territory. Supportive friends in the community had been made, thus providing an escape, a respite if you will, from the stress and fears of being alone and lonely. Law students had generally accepted me, or my presence, and were not a source of serious problems.

These men argued persuasively that returning should be an easier scenario to contemplate. I knew where to eat and what stores not to enter, even though I refused to step off the sidewalk to make room for white pedestrians, be they students or others. They recognized that racial conflicts had heightened in Virginia and in the South generally. Thus, they understood that danger still lurked, and given the Byrd-inspired legislation championing "massive resistance," conflict could be expected to continue and accelerate. They argued that these things were not and could never be a reason to quit. Easy for them to say!

In response, I pointed out that I was physically, emotionally, and mentally exhausted. Also, I was still afraid and alone. The aloneness and the loneliness were more serious issues for me than I could convey to those with whom I spoke, as was the fear. It was as if no one cared about those critical items except me. They were unimpressed by them. I was stressed out and at or near my limits, when I needed to be strong. My reluctance was fueled by a clear belief that there must be a better way or a better person to get the job done. Why me, Lord?

They postulated that there would be a better way, down the road, for others who followed in my footsteps. "You have proven that you can handle the assignment by your first year's performance and can't quit now. Besides," they argued, "other black students may enroll in September and that would help tremendously. In any event, you have to finish the job. You can and must. Also, you now know where to eat dinner!"

They were wrong about additional black enrollment but nothing else. The right decision was made; I returned to Charlottesville. My second year did see a change in my comfort level, downward. Unfortunately, during my uncertainty about returning, I failed to send a deposit for a room in the law-school dorms, and now none was available. I was assigned to an undergraduate dorm where noise, disrespect, racist attitudes, and continuous conflict characterized my time there.

REGULAR THREATS, SOME TUSSLES,
BUT THEN AN UNEXPECTED APOLOGY

Conflict was never-ending, leading to experiences I would rather forget and will not recite, except for one. It started as a verbal disagreement with three undergraduate students. It escalated to the point where the biggest of the three grabbed me by the neck, backed me up against the wall, and threatened to "whip my negro butt." He could have done so, with or without help from the other two. He balled up his fist and was about to punch my lights out when I looked him in the eye and told him, in effect, that he had better kill me or never walk around another corner without looking first. A failure to look would lead to a meeting with a tire iron that he would not enjoy. He did not punch me. Later, as I sat in my room shaking, I was surprised by the calm way in which I had delivered my threat. I was even more surprised to realize that I had meant what I threatened and would have carried it out. Apparently, nonviolence, thy name is not John Merchant, a scary realization for a skinny guy alone in this foreign country. Not very smart either.

I began to examine the depth of my feelings regarding being at law school and the racial issues that appeared daily in this dormitory. This examination took place as I left the scene of the incident, then went to my room, then left the room and walked downtown, accompanied by a stout stick and levels of anger and frustration that were unfamiliar to me. I took that walk in the dark in order to cool off and hopefully find a friend in the community with whom I could vent my rage. I did that and provided an opportunity for a serious common-sense talk with myself, a talk focused on developing better control over these emerging and deeply held feelings. I needed a better attitude, one that enabled me to walk away from, not confront, potential or actual conflict, if that was possible. After all, I reminded myself, I was in charge of my attitude and could change it. You know the one: the "sticks and stones can break my bones but names can never hurt me" attitude, thus avoiding some violent encounters.

But even these sensible thoughts did not eradicate the constant fear that prevailed and consumed me, nor did they help me learn the lessons in the classroom. The experiences were changing me into someone I didn't know and didn't want to be. And there was no one with whom I could discuss these things as the need arose. I did realize that survival would be impossible without an attitude change. I'm no fighter and would be hopelessly outnumbered even if I were. I threw away my stick and struggled to find new directions.

It is difficult to recall in honest detail all that occurred during my three years at the law school, so I will not try. However, a few things are worthy of mention. Not all the students were southerners, and many, including some of the southerners, became friends over time. My class, as well as the entire student body at the law school, had men from different parts of the country, including many graduates of the Ivy League schools—Yale, Harvard, Princeton, and others. Three women were part of the class of 1958 as well, including Barbara Coppeto from Waterbury, Connecticut, who later became a Connecticut Superior Court judge.

No racial incidents involving any of the law-school students ever occurred. In fact, many went out of their way to extend a hand of friendship, especially during my second and third years when it became clear that I was there to stay and would do whatever was needed to earn my degree.

One measure of my experiences at law school involves the social life there. The school had its own social events a few times each year, off campus at privately owned facilities. In my first year, invitations to the dining and dancing were extended to all students except me. No big deal and hardly unexpected. In my second year, a committee of class officers, all third-year students, requested a meeting with me at which they apologized for not sending me an invitation to these social occasions. They explained that the privately owned sites of the dance or other events would not permit me to mingle with other students as a guest. Happily, they didn't say that I could come and be a waiter, dishwasher, or busboy, and I was grateful for that.

The truth is that I was very surprised and pleased by what I viewed as a positive attitude and an important step for diversity. I could only imagine the discussions that took place and led to the apology: an utterly amazing but positive sign to me. In my third year, members of my class were now the officers with whom I met, at their request. Their agenda was short and had a narrow focus, a focus that humbled me at the time and still does. Simply stated, they spent considerable time to convince me that I must participate in law-school social events off Grounds, no exceptions, no excuses. In return, if I agreed to participate, they would find a public place that would permit me and a date to be part of any activity scheduled.

Hmm, I thought, a date? In Charlottesville? What is that? In truth, there were few, if any, places in or near Charlottesville that could conveniently accommodate the number of people reasonably expected to attend. Finding such a place would be difficult, probably impossible in the area, but their commitment to the effort was genuine. The intensity of their commitment was impressive. Less than four years after *Brown* and despite continuing unrest, multiple lawsuits pending against school boards, and massive resistance legislation, the leadership of this southern law school was adamant about its willingness to help break down existing social barriers, even if it meant incurring the wrath of law-school student dissenters who would be inconvenienced by the change of venue.

I declined for many different reasons but still get emotional when I recall the meetings. My tenure at U.Va. had not become an issue deserving of major public scrutiny or attention. The only media coverage had been short-lived. The timing for any involvement by me in attacking social barriers seemed bad. Let's finish the diversity effort first, then move into other areas. Besides, Dr. King's efforts had a public accommodations focus that was not being generally accepted, although it was slowly making serious inroads, despite taking on casualties. I didn't believe that I should be at the center of an effort to bring diversity to public accommodations as well as fighting the separate-but-equal battle. On a more personal basis, I was afraid about the potential fallout if I agreed to participate. Acceptance had the potential to elevate and disclose my presence to a level I did not need, a level that could mean more intense unrest and violence than Virginia was presently experiencing. It occurred to me that an invitation to me was also an invitation to the Klan and could have undesirable results that I could live without. Also, I was tired, worn out emotionally, and not mentally prepared for expanding the battlefield.

My interests were simple, my goal even simpler. Earn the degree and get out of Tombstone before the Earps and Clantons converged. I could get nailed by a wayward gunshot, or even worse, provide the Klan with an additional focus.

On reflection, I am not sure that I made the right decision. My decision had the effect of preventing a leadership group from actively participating in helping Dr. King's dream become a reality and being intimately involved in further pursuit of the promise of *Brown*. But I did decline to participate. Any serious evaluation of my three years at U.Va. must consider the actions just mentioned. The law school's student leadership totally ignored me in my first year, despite my status as a legitimate, paid-up member of the group. In my second year, leadership felt a need to apologize for excluding me from participating socially in law-school activities. They cited existing values as being immovable barriers, ones that they were unwilling to challenge for many different reasons that were not detailed at our meeting. Then in my third year, leadership acted to correct an unsupportable community value. They practically begged me to join in their effort knowing that it could not be done without my agreement.

I declined but have never been certain that mine was the correct decision. Was it? It is not totally clear to me what lessons should be drawn from the leadership's actions over a three-year period. However, it is absolutely clear to me that my personal evaluation of the time spent at U.Va. has to be positive partially because of this progression, if for no other reason. Other reasons existed, less dramatic perhaps, but clearly they existed.

LAYING THE GROUNDWORK FOR VALUABLE LESSONS

In a real way, those meetings justify my lifelong search for bridges. They support my commitment to building bridges wherever and whenever circumstances permit. Happily, circumstances during my journey through life have allowed me to exercise my commitment to building bridges. In many important ways, the U.Va. experience shaped me as a person and helped construct the foundation needed to direct my life. Many positives occurred to impact my thinking and my attitude. These positives outweigh the negatives by a large amount. It's not that I don't recall the negatives, because I do. It's just that I see no need to dwell on them, or even mention most of them, considering what I believe the experience really involved and led to, namely, a significant step in the right direction. Among other things, it confirmed a need to judge people by the "content of their character" and not the "color of their skin" or their heritage. I don't use the term "whitey" when discussing the majority community nor do I use the "N" word. Each is equally abhorrent to me and should be to everyone.

Throughout my life, America has been intimately involved in a never-ending search for fairness, parity, and equality. Frankly, believe it or not, that search is moving forward at a more rapid rate than I might have imagined. It was and is being aided and supported by untold numbers of white Americans without whom progress would not exist. I firmly believe that continued progress requires finding ways for the different races to actively relate better with each other. Integrating areas of life, where all humans have identical concerns, can provide the arena for better relations among the races. Is there a better way? I don't think so. Clearly, for me, there is a need to focus on what unites us as human beings, rather than relying on the superficiality of race, color, or creed as the means for judging others. U.Va.'s law-school population came to accept me for a lot of reasons. Among them was the fact that I was doing something, getting an education, helping myself, and not looking for a handout. I was doing something positive, not just complaining about the negatives that confront too many of us on a daily basis and were certainly confronting me in Charlottesville at that time.

Additionally, some law-school students just didn't care to be involved. Their focus was on their personal lives, concerns, dreams, and issues, a perfectly normal way to act. Obviously, I spent little time drawing attention to racial issues, and no one ever heard me complain. I did not make fiery speeches that dealt with the race issue that was being discussed rationally and irrationally throughout the country. Not complaining has always been my style. It would be difficult for anyone to recall an instance where they heard me complain about anything. The act of building bridges leaves no room for throwing stones and identifying culprits. In essence, I believe that if we cannot sensibly discuss issues and resolve them, we can always fight or go to war. But if that happens, people get hurt and even die. Who needs that?

Athletics played an important part in creating positive relationships with other law-school students. I had played varsity basketball at Virginia Union and played intramural basketball and softball for law-school teams. Sports are often a great outlet. The issue is, "Can you play and help us win?" not where did your parents come from, although sports can have their rough edges also. Intramural basketball involved mostly undergraduate teams, many of which had players who apparently were neither appreciative of my being in the league nor happy about the fact that I could play. Consequently, I got beat up pretty good during games, and often. I did become pretty good at giving back.

A fellow law-school student learned about the punishment I was taking and decided he would join the team. I call him Hammurabi. He sat with me and explained that I couldn't afford a physical encounter with a college student and said he would handle things when they got rough. He did just that. Using the five fouls each player is allotted, he saw to it that any punishments were equal, but separate. When I became a taker of unnecessary physical abuse, he became the giver who equalized things. A serious physical incident involving me was thereby avoided, and I enjoyed having him substitute for me so that I could watch as he gave true meaning to "separate but equal." At last, the concept made some sense to me, but only in this narrow application.

In softball, our law-school team, the Barristers, won the university championship in 1957. The win earned us an invitation to participate in an American Athletic Union tournament involving champions from all colleges and universities in Virginia to be played in Richmond at Byrd Park. Yup, the park is named after the Byrd family whose son, the U.S. senator, was at the time leading the cause of massive resistance to integration. A few minutes before our scheduled game at Byrd Park, we were told that a mistake had been made and our game was to be played at Parker Field, located literally across the tracks. It was a lesser facility out of sight of the majority community; obviously, separate but not equal. We lost to William and Mary, two to one, in extra innings and returned to U.Va. I thought nothing more about it although we did discuss the relocation on the ride back to Charlottesville.

The next week, the May 9, 1957, edition of the *Virginia Law Weekly* ran a front-page story entitled "Negro's Presence Causes Transfer of Softball Game." In addition, an editorial was printed criticizing the racial discrimination inherent in the relocation order. Recently, I reread the article and had a good laugh when I read the following: "Mr. Reynolds (Director of Recreation and Parks) noted also that the lighting at Parker Field was better, in his opinion, and therefore the team was not required to use inferior facilities." The game was played entirely in daylight without the need for, or use of, lights. I had no idea that the relocation matter would become a media matter. Happily, no other newspapers I know of covered the story, and I put it out of my mind. We got beat: end of story.

Yet I could not help but consider it an act of courage for the staff at the *Weekly* to have taken it up and announced it to their constituency. I often wonder what might have happened if we had gone deeper into the tournament. The two stories recounted here are important memories for me since they describe unexpected and very positive actions by people who cared and were willing to let their feelings be known.

The events taught me very valuable lessons that I have retained. The major lesson was that the cause of right has more friends than many in the black community know about or seek out. Looking back, they exemplify signs of change that were catching on in America. The obvious more recent highlight, of course, was Barack Obama's election as president of the United States.

Since receiving my degree, I have chosen not to dwell on most of my negative experiences at U.Va., including racist attitudes and behavior, blatant discrimination, or scary episodes that involved more than one fistfight. Doing so would have no value and would lead us down the road to nowhere. It doesn't mean that I have forgotten the episodes, including those on the Corner, the site of retail establishments and restaurants adjacent to the University and popular with students.

A black person could not spend money on the Corner. Food, clothing, U.Va. memorabilia, whatever, carried a "whites only" tag, unwritten but highly visible. Owners would not allow a black to enter their stores or remain there if you did enter. Any effort made to sit in a restaurant and have a burger and fries exposed you to serious bodily harm. Walking past the stores on the Corner, especially at night, could be a terrifying experience. Exposure to the negative behavior of students and others who were hanging out there was unavoidable if you wanted to walk downtown to visit friends in the black community, as I did from time to time. Any effort to avoid the Corner's crowd added distance to the walk. Eventually, I learned to ignore the comments, keep walking, and not look at the people. That wasn't easy. There were some incidents.

One major episode occurred because of my unwillingness to do silly things such as stepping off the sidewalk to let others pass. Several times, this resulted in words being exchanged, and more than once, harsh words were uttered and blows were exchanged. Once it resulted in my damaging a young man's private parts with a well-placed field-goal attempt that cured his belligerent actions but not his attitude. Neither he nor his friends were aware that I ran track at Union, thus they were surprised when I won the race to safety, or vengeance from their perspective. I managed to get a ride back to Grounds later that night and avoided a rematch by doing so. Fortunately, our paths never crossed again. I believe that I was destined to lose any rematch. My pugilistic record, at and away from U.Va., does not distinguish me; suffice it to say, despite more than one fight, I graduated on time with mental scars but no physical ones.

ESTABLISHING A BROTHERHOOD, CREATING A LEGACY

In truth, upon reflection, even the mental scars are gone. As stated earlier, the black community in Charlottesville was the critical factor for my being able to endure my three years at law school. They were incredibly warm, friendly, and caring. They provided real southern hospitality at its finest—a meal, conversation, knowledge about Charlottesville and its people, and an important respite from stress. They provided a haven for me as well as for the three medical students and the handful of engineering students enrolled.

Interaction with those other black students was fundamentally nonexistent and, at best, infrequent. No surprise there since we were separated by different locations, classrooms, and courses of study. Engineering and medical-school blacks had the advantage of others with whom to relate, compare notes, and get sustenance. As you might imagine, the coursework demanded our full attention in that environment. My search for normal outlets, when not in class or studying, did allow us to meet and talk on occasion. Their experiences were similar to mine, but they had each other on a daily basis, something I didn't have but yearned for.

By way of background, all black students mentioned here attended U.Va. as a result of an abysmal, albeit deliberate, failure on Virginia's part to provide the equal part of "separate but equal" within its own borders. Virginia State College in Petersburg was the "separate but equal" higher education facility provided by the state for its "colored" population. It had no professional graduate schools, specifically no medical, engineering, or law schools. Instead, the state had a program wherein it would pay the cost for blacks to attend professional and graduate schools in other states if they could get admitted. Many, driven as much by economics as any other reason, wisely took advantage of this "perk" and became doctors, lawyers, engineers, and teachers, who served, and serve, America well. Master's and Ph.D. degrees were also obtained because of Virginia's largesse.

Although these "perks" were reluctantly available, they also represented clear evidence that the separate was not equal, nor did the state ever intend it to be. William and Mary has had a law school since 1866, Washington and Lee since 1779, and U.Va. since 1819. None entered into the diversity arena until after I established it at U.Va.

I will end with the surprise that made my U.Va. experience forever meaningful and involved what is one of the best days of my life.

In 1987, I took my daughter and niece to look at colleges. We visited Georgetown, the University of North Carolina, Duke, and U.Va. Somehow, U.Va. learned that we were coming and contacted me. A meeting was arranged with John A. Blackburn, the then-dean of admission at U.Va. Susan, my daughter, and Tabitha, my niece, were given a grand tour and seriously encouraged to apply. Tabitha chose to do so and went on to earn her undergraduate degree from U.Va. Susan, however, had her mind set on the University of Pennsylvania, where she earned a bachelor of arts degree in 1991.

After graduating from Penn, Susan wanted to attend law school, and her choice was U.Va. I first learned of her interest from Gerard Peterson, a longtime friend from Hartford, Connecticut, who had known Susan from birth and was one of the many friends with whom Susan discussed her interest in law school. My relationship with Susan did not include telling her what she should be. My only advice along those lines was that she should pursue her interests without any pressure from me and would, when she felt the time was right, speak with me about them. She was accepted at U.Va. and received her J.D. degree in 1994. At some point prior to graduation, a committee of her classmates invited me to deliver the commencement address at her graduation. The invitation was extended without Susan's knowledge and came as a complete surprise to both of us. She became the first child of a black graduate to receive a law degree from U.Va. Yes, she created the first black legacy at the law school, a legacy that took thirty-six years to create, but Susan made it happen.

That day, I was very proud of her, U.Va., and her classmates who invited me to speak. It validated my three years there, erased many negatives from my mind, and set a stage for more to come regarding diversity at U.Va. I worked long and hard preparing that speech. I did not want to embarrass Susan; I did want to make that day meaningful for her, her classmates, and others in attendance. I was never more nervous in my life than when it came time to speak. I have given many speeches during my life, but that one stands out for me. Susan tells me that some of her classmates still remember some of what I said that memorable day.

U.Va., especially under the leadership of President Emeritus John T. Casteen III—and the commitment to diversity endorsed by the late Dean Blackburn—has achieved a level of diversity in its student body and faculty that is admirable. The levels achieved rank it at or near the top of America's colleges and universities.

What really pleases me, in addition to my involvement in the 1950s, is that the effort is ongoing. It's good to know that I have been a part of something significant, worthwhile, and sorely needed, from inception.

BECOMING A DOCTOR IN A SEGREGATED WORLD

William M. Womack

LIFE BEFORE THE UNIVERSITY OF VIRGINIA

I was born in 1936 in Lynchburg, Virginia, where I lived out my childhood. I was an only child, born into a very educated family, especially for African Americans living in the South. I lived with my mother, a high school teacher, and my aunt, an elementary school teacher. I also had an uncle who was a veterinarian. My maternal grandfather, William Smith, was the first black merchant in the city of Lynchburg. He was known and respected in the community for having been a pioneer in black business. My father's side of the family was also well-educated. I did not live with my father, but he was a teacher and ultimately became a school principal. My paternal grandfather was a farmer, but five or six of his twelve children ended up becoming schoolteachers. Teaching was a good way to make a solid income during that time because schools were segregated, so there had to be teachers of color.

Clearly, education was of major importance in my family. I was encouraged to read and learn from a young age. At the age of five I made the rather unusual and clear determination that I would become a doctor. Although this was amusing to my mother and aunt because of my age, they never made me feel that this wasn't a real possibility.

Education was also a strong value in my Lynchburg community. Our teachers, themselves people of color, were tough on us about getting a good education. I remember a lot of emphasis on going to college. My friends and schoolmates were going to college so they could eventually get a job. I didn't really hear anything like, "What's the point of getting an education since all the good jobs are going to white people." I lived in a middle-class black community. There really was a class difference—we didn't run around with the people who weren't into getting an education.

By the time I entered high school in the 1950s, the climate in Lynchburg was one of segregation—in all ways. Black people rode in the back of the bus, were not allowed in restaurants, and could only sit in the balconies of theaters; of course, schools were also segregated. In addition, I remember white people not showing respect toward my mom—for example, calling her by her first name, Fannie, instead of "Mrs. Womack." That kind of disrespect affected me. However, I didn't engage emotionally with the reality of segregation—I couldn't deal with it. I remember feeling like maybe it was all some kind of bad dream and that someday I would wake up. Supreme Court rulings in the 1950s removed some of the barriers regarding travel and education for black people, but in the Deep South, things really weren't changing yet—that would come later in the 1960s with the civil rights movement.

Despite living in a segregated community, I was successful in school. After the third grade I became a straight-A student, and because I was able to skip a couple of grades, I was only sixteen when I graduated from high school as valedictorian of my class. I attended Lincoln University in Oxford, Pennsylvania. It was an all-male African American college with a sprinkling of international students. For example, several members of African royalty were students there. I pursued a double major in chemistry and math, and ended my senior year once again as valedictorian.

In 1954, while I was in college, the Supreme Court ruled in *Brown v. Board of Education* that state laws segregating public schools were unconstitutional. Universities could no longer deny education to a state resident because of his or her skin color. Virginia first tried to send potential students who were black to northern states, but finally the state's premier universities opened their doors to black students—albeit with a quota system.

I still wanted to be a doctor. I applied to Albert Einstein University in New York, but I didn't have a good interview experience and wasn't accepted. My parents suggested that I might want to go to the University of Virginia. It would be cheaper and closer to home. So I applied and was accepted. This was only a few years after the first African American students were accepted to U.Va.—and I had no idea what challenges lay before me.

MY TIME AT U.VA.

My biggest surprise when I got to the University was that I was no longer expected to be smart. At all my others schools I'd always been at the top of my class and was known as one of the smartest kids. But now, by virtue of my skin, I was no longer expected to be smart. In fact, I was expected to fail.

When I arrived, I was assigned to a dormitory where I had my own room. The friendships I formed were mostly around my anatomy course, since we had to work in partners to dissect cadavers and study together. I worked with, and then became friends with, another African American student named Robert Clinton Murchison. During the first six months, Clint and I sat together in the lecture auditorium. There were always vacant seats around us—people didn't want to sit near us. There was also a Jewish student from New York I worked with, and later we made friends with a white female student. Nobody else wanted to work with us. I think our first friendships were mostly with Jewish and northern out-of-state students. They were the ones who didn't care very much about the segregation stuff.

Aside from sharing instructional messages with others in the class, there was very little interaction between most of my classmates and me. Some of the medical students who were in fraternities were able to get old exams to help with studying, which, of course, were never shared with Clint or me. I think in the second half of that first year we somehow got access to old exams and did better. The dean of the medical school was responsible for looking out for the African American students. He never called me into the office to ask how I was doing, but he did have a couple of small gatherings for students of color. He would invite us for tea and cookies and he would ask us how we were doing. I didn't get the sense that things changed very much based on what we told him. I have no idea how much he did to address our concerns, but at least he listened. He was probably also checking to see how we were doing since there was the general feeling that we wouldn't do as well as the white students, although I didn't get the sense that he personally thought that.

Other professors were not so kind. One day during the first half of the year, I remember my biochemistry professor telling me something like this: "I just want you to know, Mr. Womack, that if this is hard for you, you shouldn't be too upset. I would suspect that for most people like you, this is going to be a very difficult course. And no matter what you've done before, I want you to know that I don't think it in any way guarantees that you will do well in this course. I wish I could tell you better news, but I thought I would just tell you this in the beginning so that you would know what to expect. My experience with people like you is that you have a hard time understanding this kind of course."

I had never been in a place before where no one believed in me. In every other institution I had been in, I had always been affirmed. Teachers would say, "You know you can do this Bill!" The only thing I got at U.Va. was, "No you can't. You're not smart enough to do this."

This "news" came during the first six months of the first year, when I was already feeling pretty depressed. Charlottesville and all of its public establishments (restaurants, movies, etc.) were still segregated. I thought about visiting Monticello but figured we weren't allowed up there either. I wasn't interested anyway, since I knew Jefferson had owned slaves. There were only two places close to the University I could eat—the University cafeteria and the sandwich shop next door.

I do have positive memories about the sandwich shop because the guy who owned it was northern and Jewish. He loved to talk to us, and we to him. He thought the whole segregation thing was bananas. We students of color really liked him.

But it was very discouraging to me to realize that segregation was such a reality. Up until that point I could act as if it was a dream. My parents were a wonderful buffer for me. No matter what would happen outside, I would come home and my mother would say, "Just forget about that, it doesn't matter." The first year of medical school was the end of my naivety.

My friend Clint was angry. He didn't like white people at all and didn't want to. But I was different. I was more like my mother—she didn't hate white people like my aunt did; she was more tolerant. I wanted the white students and teachers to like me. There was no reason for them not to like me—but they didn't. I didn't have to worry about anything like this before because all of my social activities were with blacks. This was new, and it was hard.

I went back home at Christmas and announced that I wasn't going back to U.Va. It was a shock to my mother because she had never before heard me say that I couldn't do something when it had to do with educa-tion or learning. She asked why it was so bad. I let her know about people being mean and my feeling so isolated. Mom responded, "You know Billy Martin, I think that it would be a good idea for you to try to finish this first year. I can't really make you go back, but I'd like you to try to finish the first year. It will be a little harder for you to drop out of U.Va. medical school and then find another school to accept you if you don't stay the whole year. But if you really want to do that I'll support you."

So I went back. It was soon after that that I found out I had made the dean's list. I had no idea I had done so well. It was an enormous lift to my spirits. It was a gift for me—to know that I could succeed in this hostile environment. After that, the feeling of isolation lessened. It didn't disap-pear, but it wasn't as important.

RESOURCES AND ALLIES DURING THE FIRST YEAR

I think one reason I did better in the second half of my first year was that I took classes that were more aligned with my undergraduate majors, that is, math and chemistry, whereas in the first half of the year I took anatomy, which was a bear. Also it was a team effort to learn anatomy. That, along with all the other social drama, was very difficult for me. But the second half of the year was more about books and microscopes—it was more my speed.

Although Clint was definitely one of my main resources that first year, we went through our own trials and tribulations. We had different person-alities. It wasn't that we didn't like each other; it's just that we might not have normally "clicked"—but because we were both there and wanted each other to finish, we threw our full support behind each other.

As I've already mentioned, most of our friends were New York Jews. There were two women in the class—one was standoffish but the other was very social, bright and bubbly, and very kind. She was one of the white students willing to sit next to us, and she did some partnering with us during the anatomy class.

During the second half of the first year there was a class party, but orga-nizers couldn't find a venue Clint and I would be allowed to enter. So as a group they sat down and discussed it with us. Some said, "Who cares, let's go where we want." And others said, "Well, that's not very cool." Finally, they found a place that would allow blacks, but in the end we didn't go. Clint didn't want to go because he couldn't really forgive them for involving us in the venue discussion and making it an issue to begin with. He thought they could have just found a place that allowed us to go without telling us. So he wasn't going, and I didn't want to go alone. Our Jewish friends didn't go either.

A big ally for me that first year was the Jackson family. My dentist in Lynchburg was Franklin Jackson, a close family friend with relatives in Charlottesville. I had looked forward to meeting Franklin's brother "Punjab," a tall and friendly man with a magnificent, rich laugh. He was married to a wonderful woman who also was a fabulous host and cooked great meals. We were always happily fed at their table.

Additionally, there was Teresa Walker. The Walkers were good friends of the Jacksons, and they too hosted many social events for African American graduate students. Teresa's brother Eddie had a nightclub outside the city limits that was specifically for black clientele. So on the weekends we would go there and dance.

The Jacksons and the Walkers had a reputation for being an anchor for African American students. Their door was always open if you needed a place to escape, if you were hungry or simply needed someone to talk to. They knew all the black graduate students at the University, not just the medical students.

As far as allies within the school faculty the first few years, there was only one I can remember—the dean, Dr. Thomas H. Hunter. It was clear he was struggling with how to adapt to the Supreme Court ruling, and, as I mentioned earlier, he held a few gatherings for us that first year. I felt he was a nice man, and I became quite fond of him and viewed him as an ally. There weren't any other faculty members I felt this way about at all—until Dr. Ian Stevenson in my last year. At best, many were simply neutral about my presence.

THE REMAINING YEARS

The next year included ongoing studies and more classroom instruction. At this point, the few friends that we had were more forthcoming in helping us get what we needed through the whole difficult situation. I decided to focus on my studies first and foremost and leave the drama to the side as much as I could. I also felt I had a social life with friends and contacts that supported my time away from medical school.

The third year was different—it was all clinical work. We focused on different areas, like pediatrics, surgery, and work in medical clinics. There were no restrictions about which patients African American students could see and treat, though we did not have much one-on-one time with patients. Mostly, we did all the "scut work"—the lab work, the blood draws, microscope work, urinalyses, and so on—at the request of the residents, who had more specific responsibilities for patient care.

By this point I had started a series of summer jobs at Raleigh General Hospital in Raleigh, North Carolina. This enabled me to get a lot of experience doing laboratory work. I got these jobs through a family friend who was a doctor. I worked at that hospital over the summers after the second and third years. I think that while working there, I became more settled in my career choice and more convinced I had the intelligence and skills to become a doctor.

By my fourth and final year, I had pretty much accepted the environment I was in. I was determined to simply do the best I could and then get out of there. Things overall went more smoothly, but we still had to deal with racism—some instances more overt than others. One example I remember from my last year was when I was working on an obstetrics/gynecology clerkship. The faculty decided they were not going to go against social norms regarding black men, white women, and sexuality. They weren't willing to take the risk of having black men exam white female patients. It was far too intimate. I think that during my third year I had been given a heads-up about this reality from the other African American students ahead of me. The wards in the U.Va. hospital were segregated, so I could only work with black female patients. That restricted the number of patients I had to work with. The white students had access to twice as many patients because white men could see black female patients without a problem. It felt very unfair.

CAREER DECISIONS

When I was maybe twelve or thirteen, I had picked up a book called *The 50-Minute Hour*. It was about unusual psychiatric patient cases. I felt as if I was reading a detective novel, it was so intriguing. The psychiatrist was, in fact, like a detective—asking questions and figuring out the root of each patient's problems. In high school, many of my older peers would often come to me and ask my advice. I liked that and found I had some talent for listening. When I did my psychiatry clerkship at U.Va., Dr. Ian Stevenson, the chair of the Department of Psychiatry, noticed that as well. He told me I had done a very good job on the clerkship and asked if I would consider going into psychiatry. I told him I would, but that I really had an interest in obstetrics.

Stevenson asked me where I had applied for internships. I had applied to all Midwestern schools. He thought they were all horrible choices, but I didn't want to stay on the East Coast and I couldn't afford to visit the West Coast. He encouraged me to look at the West Coast options nonetheless, in particular the State of Washington. He knew the chair of the psychiatry department at the University of Washington in Seattle, and he thought I would like it better than schools in the Midwest. It was a brand-new hospital and would provide good future opportunities.

Both financial concerns and potential military service factored into my decision. Everyone around my age was very aware of potentially being drafted for the Vietnam War. I thought about joining the Berry Plan (U.S. Naval Reserve), which would allow me to finish my specialty and then go into the reserves. Choosing psychiatry would mean that I would be able to finish my training, whereas they drafted young men with some other medical specialties before they were done with training. After reflecting on all of this, I decided to apply to the University of Washington and for active duty in the Navy (where I could also complete my training); I was accepted by both. I chose to go to Seattle under the Berry Plan and Naval Reserve because the active-duty Navy program required repayment after the training. Seattle was less money stipend-wise but there was no repayment program.

The mentoring I received from Dr. Stevenson with regard to internship applications made a significant difference in my life and set me on a successful career path. He was the only faculty member at U.Va. who specifically told me that I was a good clinician, that he was concerned about what I was going to do with my life and my career. Here was this white southerner who liked and respected me and truly was interested enough to give me advice. I didn't even know where Seattle was, I hadn't a clue about the University of Washington, and I couldn't afford to visit before moving there! It was a total leap of faith, but I chose to follow his advice. And, as it turns out, Dr. Stevenson was right—it was the best place for me.

AFTER GRADUATION FROM U.VA.

I moved to Seattle and began my internship at the University of Washington in 1961. I was a rotating intern, as I hadn't declared my specialty yet. During that first year I met the woman who I would later marry. She was a psychiatric nurse from Montreal, Canada, and she also happened to be white. The other nurses were very discouraging of her hanging out with me—it clearly wasn't considered appropriate for a white woman to date a black man. She didn't understand their efforts to "protect" her, because she didn't grow up in the United States with its racial divisions and tensions.

By the end of that first year I was still trying to decide if I should be an obstetrician or a psychiatrist, and I was feeling pretty unwelcome in Seattle. Several of the psychiatric nurses asked me why I wanted to come there: didn't I want to go somewhere else to be a psychiatrist? I was the first black intern in the department and, not surprisingly, there was a certain amount of hostility that came with that distinction. I chose to keep focusing on what I was there to do. And while I really liked delivering babies, and I thought obstetrics might be my first choice, I decided to do one year of psychiatry and quickly found that I liked understanding patients and listening to their life stories. I chose to stick with psychiatry.

My education and career development continued to include a series of firsts at the University of Washington Hospital: I became the first African American house staff officer; the first African American resident in the department of psychiatry; after a three-year residency in general psychiatry and two years of sub-specialty training in child psychiatry, the first African American child fellow; and, finally, the first African American chief resident in child psychiatry.

I got married in 1965 and joined the military during the Vietnam War. Since I was educated under the Berry Plan, I was required to serve in the Navy after completing my medical training. When I finished my residency and the Navy asked where I'd like to be stationed, I requested and was assigned to the Naval Hospital in San Diego. I was quickly reassigned, however, to Treasure Island in San Francisco when the chief of psychiatry in San Diego refused to have me as a faculty-attending after learning I was

African American. This was a horrible blow, and I felt very insulted. Once in San Francisco, however, we loved it so much that the whole situation ended up feeling like a blessing. I was stationed at Treasure Island in San Francisco for a year and then on the island of Guam for two years.

In 1969, my wife and I returned to the University of Washington, where I became the first African American faculty member in the psychiatry department. Overall, I had a very successful career there, but minority faculty rarely got promoted to senior levels, and despite a number of advocates who helped me over the years, I never made it to full professor. I believe it is easier for minority faculty now, as there are more mentors to guide them along their path.

I later was hired to work at the community psychiatric center at Seattle's Harborview Medical Center and became chief of psychiatry, running an inpatient unit for adults. I eventually became director of the center before leaving in 1982 to take the role as director of child psychiatry at Seattle Children's Hospital. That was probably another first, as I don't remember there having been any other African American directors at the hospital.

Living and working in Seattle while being an academic physician also gave me opportunities to continue to grow professionally. For example, for four years one of the local radio/television stations allowed me to develop two- to five-minute television segments called "Monday's Child" in which I talked about parenting issues and gave tips on how to be more understanding of child and teen behaviors. This kind of success made it easier to forget some of the racial traumas of the past.

REFLECTIONS ON U.VA.

The University of Virginia gave me the opportunity to have a profession and a wonderful and fulfilling career. It gave me an education. It gave me a piece of paper that told the world that I had passed many hurdles and become a physician. The state could not deny me an education, and I got it.

But for a long time I was not so willing to look back—to remember—or to visit U.Va. It had been such an unwelcoming place for me, so it seemed sort of ridiculous when people from Charlottesville would come to visit me, asking for contributions to the University and the medical school. I finally told one person, "Look, I'm not interested in helping you with money. You guys weren't nice to me—why would I want to give you money?" He made it his mission to find a way to change my mind.

In 2000, he asked if I would visit the University to speak about bio-feedback, one of my specialties. He also said that the University wanted to honor me as someone who had made a difference there.

I decided to go. I wanted to see for myself if things really were different for students now. While there, I participated in a roundtable discussion with a group of African American medical students, which was both rewarding and healing for me. I also finally went to Monticello for the first time and developed a more nuanced view of Thomas Jefferson.

During that visit I found something unexpected: forgiveness. What was done was done. None of my U.Va. difficulties were being repeated now; it was no longer necessary to remain bitter. Attending the 2009 reunion with other pioneering African American students at U.Va. represented a big turnaround in how I felt about the University. And it was gratifying to receive official recognition of the contributions we had made.

Finally, things had come full circle.

Henry Martin served as the University's first African American bell ringer from 1847 to 1909. In 2012, a plaque honoring Martin's tenure was placed near the Chapel. It reads, "Henry Martin rang the bell at dawn to awaken the students, and rang it during the day to mark the hours and the beginning and ending of class periods. He was beloved by generations of faculty, students, and alumni, and he remembered them all when they returned for visits." (Albert and Shirley Small Special Collections Library, University of Virginia)

In 1953, Walter Nathaniel Ridley earned a doctorate of education degree from the University of Virginia, becoming the first black graduate of the University—and the first black person to receive an academic doctoral degree from a traditional, predominantly white, southern college or university. He graduated with high honors, and his pioneering achievements in desegregating the University were noted in the national and international press at the time. A University article written some years later reported that he "opened new territory for future generations, and with courage and dignity set an example for others to follow." He was awarded the Distinguished Curry School Alumnus Award in 1988. (Albert and Shirley Small Special Collections Library, University of Virginia)

A graduate of the College of Arts and Sciences, George K. Martin was appointed to U.Va.'s Board of Visitors in 2011. In 2013, Martin's fellow board members elected him to a two-year term as rector of the University, making him the first African American to hold that position. (Dan Addison/U.Va. University Communications)

In 2009, almost two dozen of the first African American students to attend the University in the late 1950s and 1960s reunited at an alumni function held to celebrate the pioneering women and men who helped to desegregate the University.
(Dan Addison/U.Va. Public Affairs)

From left to right: Elmore Dundridge, Aubrey Jones, Robert "Bobby" Bland, James Trice, and Leroy Willis gathered at the 2009 reunion to remember—and celebrate—important changes they helped implement at the University. (Dan Addison/U.Va. Public Affairs)

David Temple, who earned his undergraduate degree in psychology and his master's in special education, was instrumental in establishing a chapter of the Pi Lambda Phi fraternity, the first fraternity in the country to accept male students without regard to race or religion. Coming back to the University was "an uplifting experience," he said. "Seeing all the students made it feel like we did something right!" (Dan Addison/U.Va. Public Affairs)

Female trailblazers, from left to right: Vivian Pinn, who in 1967 was the second African American woman to graduate from the School of Medicine; Susan Y. Dorsey, who has two degrees from the University and was the second African American woman to be appointed to the University's Board of Visitors; and Barbara Starks Favazza, who in 1966 was the first African American woman to graduate from the School of Medicine. (Dan Addison/U.Va. Public Affairs)

John Merchant, who in 1958 became the first black student to graduate from the law school, said it took him seventeen years to return to University Grounds after receiving his law degree. "I came, and I survived," he said. "I don't talk about my negative experiences, and I probably never will. I want to move forward." Merchant's daughter would later become the first black legacy student to graduate from the law school—and her father was invited to speak at her graduation. (Dan Addison/U.Va. Public Affairs)

During a special alumni weekend celebrating the pioneering work of the University's earliest African American students, family members and alumni watch a football game from the president's box. (Dan Addison/U.Va. Public Affairs)

"My biggest surprise while going to the University of Virginia was that I was no longer expected to be smart. . . . In fact, they expected me to fail," William Womack remembers about his first year in medical school. During the Christmas break, when he wanted to quit, his mother convinced him to stay on through the year, and it was soon after that learned he had made the Dean's List. "It was a gift . . . to know that I could succeed in this hostile environment." Attending the 2009 reunion with other early African American students represented a turnaround in how Womack felt. "It was gratifying to have official recognition of the African American pioneers at the school," he said. "Finally things had come full circle." (Dan Addison/U.Va. Public Affairs)

"It was as though we had the weight of the black community on our shoulders. If we failed, we felt that it would not only be a bad reflection on ourselves but it might keep other blacks from attending U.Va.," Aubrey Jones remembers. "There were times when many of us thought about quitting or giving up, but we couldn't do that because there was too much at stake. We couldn't let all those people down who were pulling for us to make it. But most importantly, we couldn't let ourselves down. So we stayed and helped each other. We relied on each other for strength and support. Harold Marsh said it best, 'Because Bobby Bland stayed, I stayed. Because I stayed, Elmore Dundridge and James Trice stayed. Because they stayed, Aubrey stayed.' Because we all stayed, others stayed, and we now have a rich black heritage that's still growing at U.Va." (Dan Addison/U.Va. Public Affairs)

The University's earliest black graduates gathered in 2009 for an alumni reunion during which they discussed their time at the University and their experiences, which paved the way for future generations. (Dan Addison/U.Va. Public Affairs)

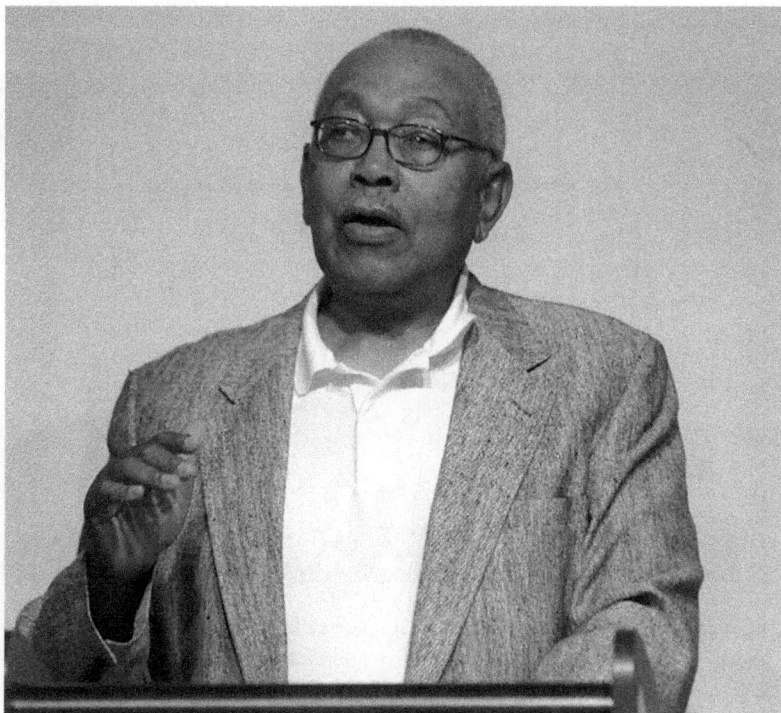

John Gaines is one of the earliest graduates and the only one who still lives in Charlottesville today. He is a frequent speaker in his community. (Dan Addison/U.Va. Public Affairs)

In August 2015, Gibbons House, a first-year residence hall, was named for William and Isabella Gibbons, who were enslaved by different professors at the University. Although husband and wife, they lived in different pavilions in the mid-nineteenth century. Once emancipated, Isabella became a teacher at the Freedman's School and William became a minister at Charlottesville's oldest black church, First Baptist.

"One of the recommendations of the President's Commission on Slavery and the University was to name one or more U.Va. buildings after enslaved persons who were connected to the life of the University," said U.Va. president Teresa A. Sullivan, regarding the commission she established in 2013. "This is part of a broad, ongoing effort to recognize the role of slavery in the University's history and to educate the members of our community about the role of enslaved persons at U.Va. as we approach our bicentennial." (Dan Addison/U.Va. University Communications)

During the "Donning of the Kente" ceremony, graduating black students receive stoles made of Kente cloth imported from West Africa, which symbolize their academic achievement. The event recognizes African American students the day before they graduate from the University of Virginia. (Chadia King/CkingDiamonds Photography)

LIFE ON MR. JEFFERSON'S PLANTATION

Aubrey Jones

THE MISSING APPLICATION

I became interested in attending the University of Virginia for several reasons. First, it was the best school I could afford to attend. As a Virginia resident, my tuition was relatively low, especially compared to students from out of the state. The second reason was that I knew someone who was already there, Rupert Picot, and he encouraged me to join him in Charlottesville.

I knew there were not many blacks attending U.Va., and I didn't know whether they would accept me, but I went ahead and submitted my application. I was stationed in the U.S. Air Force in Germany when I applied and wanted to enter midyear, but the admissions office told me that they only accepted first-year students in September. So I requested to be considered for the next class, which entered in September 1958.

After I was discharged, I learned that I had to take the entrance examination, now called the SAT. I studied very hard, but after I took it, I heard nothing from U.Va., and when I called to check on my status was told there was no record of my application. Naturally, I assumed that someone did not want me to attend and had conveniently lost my application.

I told Rupert what was happening, and he suggested that I come to Charlottesville and speak to the dean of the engineering school. I took his advice and headed up to meet with Dean Lawrence Quarles, who was very gracious. To my surprise, he told me I had already been accepted as an undergraduate to the School of Engineering; he could not explain why the admissions office said that it had no record of my application. While I was sitting in his office, he called someone and straightened out the situation.

He was very apologetic and assured me that he was looking forward to seeing me in September. I felt really good after that meeting.

I CAN DO IT TOO!

For a black, attending U.Va. in 1958 was a major event. I felt proud and excited about being accepted to Mr. Jefferson's University. My family and friends were proud, but I was also very apprehensive. I kept telling myself "I can do it," and if for some reason I couldn't, it would not be because I didn't try. There were other black students already there, but, sadly, many who had enrolled ahead of me, including Rupert, left because they were either unwilling or unable to put up with the pressure of being one of the first blacks to attend a southern white school. When some black people learned I was going to U.Va., their messages were mixed. Some said, "Why are you going to U.Va., you know you can't make it there!" Others said, "Don't go there and embarrass us!"

Many of us felt the pressure to succeed from family, friends, ministers, and teachers. It was as though we had the weight of the black community on our shoulders. If we failed, we felt that it would not only be a bad reflection on ourselves but it might keep other blacks from attending U.Va. We were in the spotlight—and under the microscope—of both the black and white communities. Of course, I put additional pressure on myself. Every quiz became a final exam.

I don't believe I could have made it at U.Va. right out of high school. The four years in the air force definitely helped give me the maturity and toughness needed to survive.

There were also a number of people who encouraged and supported me, and I thank them for that. But as a twenty-three-year-old veteran, I was much more mature than the average college student and I was better prepared mentally to handle the stress. I had a mission, I was focused, and nobody was going to stop me!

As a first-year student, I had to go to school a week earlier than the rest of the students. Freshmen week was uneventful, except for one thing that made me feel welcomed. When I went to the dining room, I sat at a table by myself. While many students stared at me, one, Gary Cuozzo, asked if he could join me. I didn't know at the time that he was a quarterback on the football team. His warm reception helped me feel a little more comfortable in the dining room, and later other students on my residence hall stopped by to introduce themselves. Basically, things went well for me during the first week.

Dean Quarles met with all of the first-year engineering students and he asked everyone who was either a valedictorian or salutatorian at his high school to raise his hand. More than half of the 250 students raised their hands. He made the point that we were all good students in high school otherwise we would not have been accepted to U.Va. But he admonished us that our high school record did not mean a thing from this point on. He told us that we had to prove ourselves all over again. That certainly put everything in perspective for us.

Another thing was made very clear to all of us. Mr. Jefferson's School was steeped in tradition. It was an all-male school, coats and ties were worn to class, and there was the Honor System. Being one of the few black students, I was not about to start breaking tradition.

I was in awe when I walked around the Grounds. Looking at the magnificent architecture, thinking about the history, made me feel proud. The Rotunda and the Lawn were ever-present reminders of the honor, responsibility, and gentlemanly conduct expected. And I must admit, I liked the prestige of being a student there.

I put a lot of pressure on myself, but after being out of high school for five years, I found myself challenged by the work. I did okay with math but chemistry and a class called "descriptive geometry," which was a course where you had to visualize things in three dimensions, proved difficult. I was able to get a tutor after midterm for chemistry but I failed the second half of descriptive geometry.

I had no social life during my first year because I spent most of my time studying. One of my problems, I discovered, was I really didn't know how to study in college. I put the time in, but I wasn't getting the return for my investment. Thanks to Arthur Walls, a black Ph.D. candidate who tutored me in chemistry, I learned how to understand the work rather than try to memorize a bunch of formulas. Because of his help, my grade went from failing at midterm to a final grade of B. I had known Walls back in high school; he had actually taught me science in the ninth grade and was now at U.Va. working on his doctorate—and dealing with his own problems of race on Grounds. I would never be able to thank him for his generosity and kindness in helping me.

Because my score on the entrance exam was not high enough in English, I was required to take remedial English. My first reaction was that I didn't need to take this non-credit course and believed I could pass English 101 without it. So I pleaded my case to the head of the department and, surprisingly, was given permission to jump ahead. Because of a scheduling conflict, however, I ended up in the remedial class after all, which turned out to be a blessing in disguise. At first, I was embarrassed because I was the only black in the class, but deep down I knew I needed it. It turns out it provided me the foundation for English 101 and helped me in subsequent courses.

During one of my English classes, we had a writing assignment and I said to my professor, "I know what I want to say but I don't know how to say it." He said, "That's a lot of bull. If you know what you want to say, just say it! Don't worry about using the right words, spelling, or grammar. Just write your thoughts as fast as you can." He told me to use "placeholders" for my thoughts until I was able to come up with the right words. I quickly got over my writer's block.

At that time, my vocabulary consisted of a lot of slang. In fact, I told my professor that I had a large vocabulary, but it was all slang. He smiled and said, "That's a start." Over the years, I made an effort to increase my vocabulary. Anytime I came across a word I didn't understand, I looked it up in the dictionary. Even after graduation, I kept a list of new words and tried to learn a new one every day.

One of the benefits of attending this class was that I met Professor Luther Gore. He was only three years older than I was, and very open-minded and supportive. I felt comfortable talking to him. In fact, several of the professors of the English department, including Graham Hereford and Alan Gianinny, were favorites because of their open-mindedness and support. One of the strengths of the engineering program was its English department. It stressed the importance of being able to communicate effectively, which proved to be one of the keys to my success in the corporate world.

Not only am I able to write specifications, business plans, and other documents, but I've gone on to write ten books on computers. I attribute a lot of this success to my English professors. One of the lessons I learned was that no matter how good your engineering or computer skills might be, you must be able to communicate. My engineering degree helped me get the job, but my communications skills got me promoted.

My roommate, Robert "Bobby" Bland, was a senior. They put all of the black students together, and I guess because I was the oldest of the undergraduates they made us roommates. But that was a blessing because Bobby was majoring in electrical engineering too and he was able to give me the scoop on all of the professors. Some professors were known to give the brothers a hard time, so we would try to avoid them if we could. That was pretty easy to do because the dean's office knew these professors. Thus, if you were a black student and there was another section available, all you had to do was to go see "Dean Jean" and she would make the necessary changes. "Dean Jean" was Jean Holiday, Dean Quarles's administrative assistant. As everyone knew, she ran the office! She was very helpful to all students but seemed to keep a special eye out for black students.

There was one math professor I was told to avoid because he had been identified as a racist. I needed to take differential equations, and his class was the only one available. Everyone told me I would flunk, so I jumped in expecting the worse. To my surprise, he was an excellent teacher who did an outstanding job of breaking down the lessons and making them clear. He was also quite entertaining—and never brought his politics into the classroom.

During the final exam, I was struggling to complete it on time and I was the last one left in the room. He told me to take my time and that he would wait until I was finished. At the end of the exam, I said, "Professor, I don't know whether or not this is ethical, but I just want to tell you that I thoroughly enjoyed your class." And he responded, "Thank you Mr. Jones. It must be unethical because no one ever told me that before." We both laughed and I left.

One lesson I learned was that in spite of his reputation, the professor treated me with respect and did not bring politics into the classroom. He did not have to like me, as long as he respected me. And yes, I passed his course.

BEHIND THE SCENES

We soon discovered that we had an extended family at U.Va.—a network of African American custodians, cooks, and maintenance people, all of them pulling for us to make it. Many had worked at the University for years, and they were clearly happy to see black students finally able to attend the University. They would give us extra helpings of food in the dining halls, unlock classroom doors so we might study late into the night, and point out the most racist professors based on their own experiences.

It was surprising how much information a maid or janitor could pick up, especially when some whites assumed that they were too ignorant to understand what they were saying. It reminded me of stories of how the slave masters on plantations used to treat the house servants. They talked openly about many things because they thought that their servants were too dumb to understand. One maid in particular at the engineering school was very helpful to us—and always concerned about our welfare and grades. She was among the first to check the bulletin boards when grades were posted.

Some evenings after dinner we would go back to the engineering school so that we could use a blackboard to work out problems. But classrooms were at a premium and you had to get there early to reserve one—unless you knew someone. All we had to do was to let her know and she would reserve a room for us and then lock the door until we got back. That allowed us time to take a brief nap after dinner in order to be ready to study the rest of the night.

We found incredible support among these ranks of black employees, who seemed to understand the importance of our being there to create a path for others, perhaps for their own children or grandchildren. Seeing us succeed gave them hope and filled them with a shared pride.

Charlottesville was a small college town with a very small black community. Many of the blacks in the town worked at the University in some capacity. And while some black students were young enough to date high school students, I was not. And there were few single young women who lived in town. When we had parties, oftentimes we would invite some of the young schoolteachers or student teachers, but most of the time I would have to go home to Richmond if I wanted to date someone.

Bobby Bland played another important role in my life. He introduced me to Alyce Brown, my future wife, although neither of us thought much about marriage when we met during my first year. In fact, she told me later she did not even like me initially and thought I was conceited.

A few years later, after Alyce returned from school in Ohio, that all changed. We became very good friends. She typed my term papers, invited me home for dinner, and was someone I could talk to when I was feeling down. Her mother, Alice Brown, became a second mother to me and we remained close even after Alyce's death in 1985.

THE BLACKS ARE COMING! THE BLACKS ARE COMING!

On weekends, when families and friends visited the University, many were still surprised to see black students. When we walked into the cafeteria, sometimes people would stop eating for a second and stare at us. It was a strange feeling because before we walked into the cafeteria, you could hear the buzzing of people talking. But, for one instant, the noise level would drop several decibels when they spotted us. You could almost read the lips—or minds—of some: "I didn't know that Negroes went here."

But we were there, although small in number. There was a widely held misconception that integration at U.Va. didn't begin until the early 1970s. But integration happened some twenty years earlier. In 1950, Gregory Swanson, a twenty-six-year-old lawyer from Danville, Virginia, challenged U.Va.'s right to continue the practice of segregation. In doing so, he challenged the law of the Commonwealth of Virginia, which forbade "race mixing" in tax-supported schools. Swanson took his case to court with the support of the NAACP and won his suit.

Although Swanson was admitted to U.Va., he did not live on University Grounds; he had to live in a black hotel in town. It is my understanding that he attended U.Va. for about a year to take additional coursework since he already had his law degree from Howard University. Even though Swanson did not graduate from U.Va., he helped pave the way for Walter N. Ridley, who became the first black to graduate from U.Va. in 1953, earning a doctorate in education. And in 1959, my friend Bobby Bland became the first black undergraduate to obtain a degree from U.Va.

The University's integration started before the modern civil rights era. Ridley received his degree before the U.S. Supreme Court ruled in 1954 that segregated schools were unlawful. This was before Martin Luther King, Jr., organized the bus boycott in Montgomery, Alabama, in 1956. It was before James Meredith integrated the University of Mississippi in 1961, and before Charlene Hunter broke down the barriers at the University of Georgia.

Here is a bit of history. All of the first black undergraduates were engineering students since none of the black colleges in Virginia offered engineering curriculums. Prior to 1954, any black resident who wanted to pursue a curriculum that was not offered at a black college in Virginia could attend any out-of-state school of his or her choice—on the state's dime. Many blacks took full advantage of this free education and enrolled in northern schools to obtain their degrees. After the 1954 *Brown v. Board of Education* decision by the U.S. Supreme Court, Virginia had to admit blacks into white colleges. Initially, U.Va. admitted blacks for only those courses not being offered at black schools in the state, such as engineering, law, and medicine. In the early 1950s, there were some students who entered at the graduate level in law (Swanson), education (Ridley), and medicine (Edward Wood and Edward Nash), but the undergraduate schools were still segregated.

In 1955, the first undergraduates were admitted to the School of Engineering: Robert Bland of Petersburg, George Harris of Lynchburg, and Ted Thomas of Chesapeake. In the following year, Harold Marsh and Rupert Picot, Jr., both of Richmond, entered the school. Four first-year black students were admitted to the engineering school in 1957: Walter Payne, Jr., of Charlottesville; Nathaniel Gatlin of Petersburg; and Elmer Dandridge and James Trice, both from Richmond. In 1958, I entered, followed in 1959 by Leroy Willis. A year later, Bland became the first black undergraduate to finish with his bachelor of electrical engineering degree.

In 1960, after a year in the engineering school, Willis decided to challenge the system. Until then, undergraduate blacks at U.Va. were only allowed to attend the engineering school. Being able to attend the College of Arts and Sciences had been denied to black students in spite of the 1954 Supreme Court ruling that said all schools were to desegregate "with all deliberate speed." U.Va. had decided to remain with the old law of "separate but equal" until Willis challenged the University's stance.

In 1960, Willis was quietly allowed to transfer into the College, switching his major from chemical engineering to chemistry. He later had the privilege of opening yet another door. He became the first black student to live on the Lawn in 1961.

To live in one of the fifty-four Lawn rooms was—and remains today—a great honor at the University. Located in Jefferson's original buildings, these rooms are truly in the center of University life. In fact, the Lawn, anchored at the north end by the Rotunda, still looks and functions much as it did in Jefferson's era—as a vital community organized around learning.

Leroy was one of the real pioneers, making it easier for those who came after him. I did not suffer as many racial slurs or find insulting signs hanging on the dorms because by the time I was admitted, blacks had been on campus for several years. Sure, there were times when many of us thought about quitting or giving up, but we couldn't do that because there was too much at stake. We couldn't let down all those people who were pulling for us to make it. But most importantly, we couldn't let ourselves down. So we stayed and helped each other. We relied on each other for strength and support.

Harold Marsh said it best: "Because Bobby Bland stayed, I stayed. Because I stayed, Elmer Dandridge and James Trice stayed. Because they stayed, Aubrey stayed." Because we all stayed, others stayed, and we now have a rich black heritage that's still growing at U.Va.

THE NO-NAME FRATERNITY

The social life of the University was centered primarily on fraternity life. If you were not in or allowed to be in a fraternity, opportunities for socializing were few. As expected, the doors to fraternity life and other social clubs were closed to blacks. People would often ask me if I belonged to a fraternity, and I usually answered that there were no black fraternities at U.Va. Later, I thought about my answer and realized that I actually did belong to a fraternity. It was not formally organized, it was not incorporated, it had no secret rites, no secret handshakes, and no name. But it was a group of brothers who were bound together with a common purpose, a common interest, and a common cause. Initially, we came together for survival— not for fun. But as it turned out, we did everything together. We studied together, shared each other's pain together, went to church together, and partied together. Sounds like a fraternity to me!

Sometimes after a rough exam, we would take a break. We would all gather in one of our rooms and put on some music and just talk, tell some jokes, and tell some lies too. We had fun.

Occasionally, we would go to town if we knew of a party. Some of the young black men in town did not like the U.Va. students because we had a "semi-celebrity" status, which appealed to the young ladies in town and to their parents. The local young brothers were not so welcoming. There were occasional fights, but nothing really serious.

The truth is that we honestly did not have a lot of time to party. We were focused on our academic work—and our need to prove ourselves and to succeed.

One of the things our no-name fraternity did was to save old exams, reports, and homework assignments so that we could pass them down to those who followed us. The white fraternity brothers had been doing this for years and had access to much more information, but it was a start for us. The University had a very strict Honor Code, and if you cheated, lied, or stole you could be kicked out of school. Each student had to write the following pledge on all exams and other work as designated by the professor and then sign it: "On my honor I have neither given nor received aid on this exam." The professors usually handed out the exams and then left the room because they did not have to worry about anyone cheating.

Black students had to be very careful that no one accused them of cheating. It only took two students to accuse you. Then you would have to go before the Honor Committee to defend yourself. We were all paranoid about this system because if two racist white students wanted to swear that you were cheating on a test, they could do so. Fortunately, it never happened. But one of the things the no-name fraternity warned new students about was to never put yourself in a position where there could be the slightest reason for someone to accuse you. For example, I would always sit up front and make certain that there was nothing around me that looked the least bit suspicious. So in addition to trying to study and pass an exam, you had to worry about making certain that you were above reproach.

U.Va. had a reputation of being a hard-drinking school. So Harold Marsh gave us some survival tips on attending sporting events, including to be aware of the impromptu playing of "Dixie." When the band played "Dixie," most of the spectators would stand and sing along. He told us that we should not stand. In 1958, U.Va. did not have a very good football team, but the band still played "Dixie" and the drunken spectators sang along: "I think we need another drink for the glory of U.Va." Mix "Dixie" and drunks and you have a formula for problems.

Fortunately for me, I can recall only one isolated incident at a football game. Jim Trice and I were sitting in the stands and the band played "Dixie." Most of the spectators stood; we did not. One drunk spotted us and yelled, "There they go, two N———." Interestingly, nobody laughed at what he said and just looked at him as if to say, "Shut up and sit down!" He did not get the response he was hoping for, so he shut up and sat down. What a relief, and perhaps a sign that a change in attitudes by the majority of the people was beginning to take place.

THE STRUGGLE MAKES YOU STRONGER

More good things happened to me than bad while at U.Va. It was a little easier for me because Bobby, Harold, and Elmer had preceded me. But I will always remember how some people reacted when they saw us on campus, and how they treated us.

There was one lesson I would not soon forget. I failed descriptive geometry during my first year and took the course again the next year. The final exam was 50 percent of my total grade. I had a passing grade going into the final, but ended up with a 73 total; 75 was passing. The reason I failed was because of a problem I felt was graded unfairly.

Typically, if you only needed a couple of points to pass, a professor would usually give the student the benefit of the doubt. This was especially true if you were taking a course that was not a prerequisite for any other course. My professor would not budge. I said to him, "You mean to tell me you're going to fail me a second time with a 73?" He said, "If it will make you feel any better, I will lower your grade and flunk you with a lower score!"

I was really upset with this guy, and I had to restrain myself to keep from punching him, but I did not want to get kicked out of school. At that point in my life, I did not cry easily, but I went to the field behind the physics building and just ran around the field with tears streaming down my face. I had to let off some steam because I was about to explode.

The next day, I went to see the head of the department to plead my case. Interestingly, he agreed with my interpretation of the problem but said he could not change my grade. He did, however, make a good suggestion. He told me to forget about that course for now because it was not a prerequisite; he advised that I concentrate on my other courses and retake this course later. He also offered encouragement by telling me that I had done well to have only failed one course because more than 50 percent of engineering students either flunk out or transfer to another major during the first two years. That made me feel a little better, but this story does not end there.

Two and a half years later, during my last semester, the course I failed was one of the three I needed for graduation. When I signed up to retake it, I made certain I didn't get the same professor whom I had had twice before. In fact, my professor was now the same head of the department who had given me the good advice. As luck would have it, my professor became ill and guess who I got as my professor again? You got it! But I made up my mind that this course was not going to keep me from graduating. I went into the final exam with an A average and my final grade was a C. It didn't matter because I was graduating with praise—"Thank You, Lordy!"

U.Va. was a microcosm of the real world that I would have to face after graduation. The lesson I learned from this incident is that life is full of obstacles and challenges, and if you give up every time you are faced with a challenge, you'll never accomplish anything. I learned the struggle makes you stronger.

THE "RAT PACK"

During my third and fourth years, I joined a study group composed of four other guys and myself. Four of us were veterans and everyone except me was married—and white. Because we were older than the typical students, we had one thing in common: we were there to study, not to party. We were very focused. We hit it off well and even jokingly called ourselves the "Rat Pack," based on that popular Hollywood group of actors in the 1960s made famous by Sammy Davis, Jr., Frank Sinatra, and Dean Martin.

Bill was my lab partner for most of the electronics labs. Since both of us had been electronic technicians in the U.S. Air Force, the labs were easy for us. I believe Bill and I started to study together first and then Bob, Jim, and Larry joined the group later.

Bill was a nice guy; he was very open and honest with me. Although we did not discuss it a lot, Bill knew the challenges I had at U.Va. He lived off campus and on several occasions invited me to his home for dinner. Bill graduated in 1962, and I graduated six months later in February 1963. We both moved to the Philadelphia area after graduation and stayed in touch for a while.

The lesson learned from this study group was similar to the lesson that

I learned in the air force. You cannot say all whites or all blacks do this or that. You have to judge people on their merits. Christians are taught, however, "to hate the sin but love the sinner." I don't want to imply that I am totally there yet, but I'm working on it. Another lesson I learned was that some whites will accept you and talk to you, but they will not accept other blacks. Sometimes they might even say to you, "You're different."

I do remember times when a student might speak to me in class, but if he saw me on the Corner he would not bother to say hello. I learned not to let it bother me if someone didn't want to speak to me. It was his problem, not mine.

PUTTING A LITTLE LIGHT ON THE SUBJECT

There were some other benefits to attending U.Va.—in addition to the great education. It prepared me for the corporate environment where I would have to deal with biased opinions and myths about blacks. At U.Va., I had the opportunity to talk to a number of white students to get a better understanding of how they felt about certain issues. I remember sitting in one of the study rooms in my dormitory when I overheard some white students discussing what was wrong with "colored people." They had no idea that I was in the building, much less that I was within earshot. I tried to ignore the conversation until they started making statements like "all colored people are inferior, they steal and have no moral values," and so on. I could not resist the temptation to see who was doing all this talking and quoting statistics like he was an expert on colored people.

The door to the room where they were having this discussion was open, so I went and knocked on the door and said, "Excuse me, but I could not help overhearing your discussion; perhaps I can put a little light on the subject?"

There was silence and an embarrassed look from the guy who was doing all the talking. So I continued by saying that he was certainly entitled to his opinions but asked, "Where are you getting all the statistics from that you are using?" And by the way, "Where do you live?" To my surprise, the man said Richmond. "Richmond?" I said. "I live in Richmond and I know what you are saying is not true." Further, I said, even if all of the black people you know did all of those things you claimed, that would be a very small sample. He admitted after more discussion that he was no expert on the matter but was basing everything on what his parents had told him. We continued our discussion and when I left, I believe I had earned his respect. He could at least say that he had met a black person who could not be stereotyped.

Like it or not, reluctant or not, I was a trailblazer and role model. That did not change for me in the corporate world. I have had to shine a light on a lot of topics over the years. But more importantly, I learned: "I must let my light so shine before men, that others might see my good works and glorify my Father which is in heaven." Amen.

<h2 style="text-align:center">I'M OUT OF HERE</h2>

After graduation in 1963, I thought I would never return to the University. I must admit that I was proud to be a graduate and enjoyed the prestige and recognition of being one of the first blacks to graduate from such a prestigious institution. I had enjoyed the excitement of breaking the barriers of segregation, but I knew I would not miss the stress and pressures I had endured. While I liked being part of a great tradition, I never really felt a part of the University. I was an unwanted guest in someone else's home. So I was happy to be leaving, my goal achieved.

Twenty-four years later, in 1987, I decided to attend the very first weekend held by the University to honor its earliest black graduates from the 1950s and 1960s. There were more than 220 black alumni in attendance, and surprisingly, I had a great time.

The keynote speaker was John Merchant, the first black to graduate from the law school. He challenged us to raise a half-million dollars for minority scholarships in honor of Walter N. Ridley, the University's first black graduate. The Ridley Fund has given us a reason to feel a part of U.Va. Just as someone paved the way for us, we can continue to help the brothers and sisters who follow us. Today there are 25,000–30,000 black alumni.

In 1990, I was invited back to U.Va. to speak to the Council of Black Student Leaders. They were rightly concerned about a recent rash of racial incidents on the campus. Racial slurs had been written on the sidewalks, and some whites were displaying hostile attitudes toward some of the black students. During my speech, I told them that I did not know how it was at U.Va. for them today, but I believed that it had to be better than it had been thirty years before when I was there. I pointed out that they had a lot more support both within the student body and the administration. I envied them their black student associations, fraternities and sororities, their Office of African-American Affairs, and their black professors and growing number of black alumni. At the same time, I empathized, not wanting to minimize their very real concerns.

My point was simply this: "If we made it with much less support, then you can do it too." But it was never easy, and I understood all too well their frustrations and why they were unwilling to put up with the things that should have been eradicated by then. I reminded them that "life is full of obstacles and challenges and if they give up every time they are faced with challenges, they will never accomplish anything." I challenged them to keep the faith and believe in themselves and each other, and that together they could handle any challenge, including dealing with racism at their university, in their communities, or later in their workplaces.

LOOKING BACK

Barbara S. Favazza

Growing up in the 1940s and 1950s in Kentucky and later Virginia, I thought that I might become a teacher one day. My grandfather was a teacher. My mother was a teacher. One of my favorite aunts was a teacher, and my father taught for a few years. Most of my parents' friends were also teachers. Teaching was an honorable profession for Negro men and women in those days, and playing school with friends was one of my favorite activities as a child. I always chose to be the teacher.[1] One of my mother's friends, however, was a nurse, and she later played a significant role in my life.

I have always felt fortunate that my parents and grandparents valued education. My father and mother both graduated from Hampton Institute (now Hampton University) in Hampton, Virginia. My mother may have been the only member of her family to attend college. Her older siblings, recognizing that she was very smart, provided financial assistance as best they could so that she could earn a college degree. It was my parents' expectation that if they had children, those children would go to college as well.

Long before high school I became interested in science and medicine. I enjoyed reading about doctors and scientists who determined the causes of diseases and developed effective treatments for them. The contributions of women in this area made a great impression on me. Everything about the medical field seemed so interesting, and I began to think about a career in nursing so I could help the sick and, hopefully, save lives. Although I had read about famous female physicians, the only women I knew in the medical field were nurses. The thought of being a physician never entered my mind.

By the time I was in high school, my mother's friend had become director of nursing at the local hospital. Like everything else in Virginia, the hospitals were segregated. The Negro hospital was a good one with excellent nurses and physicians on the staff. My mother's friend was an outstanding administrator and the hospital was well run, administering quality care to its patients. The Negro physicians on staff were men, of course. Except for one physician, the Negro physicians could not obtain staff privileges at the white hospital. An exception was made for a Negro surgeon who was said to be the best in the city. He was given staff privileges and allowed to perform surgery on white patients as well. All of our Negro physicians were quite busy, serving the entire Negro community. They saw patients in their offices, treated them at the hospital, provided emergency coverage, and even made house calls.

Throughout high school my interest in medicine and science only increased. I again was fortunate to attend a high school notable for the achievement of its students in academics, music, and athletics. Our teachers were extremely dedicated and expected us to work hard. I am grateful for the preparation they gave me for further education. My biology, chemistry, English, and math teachers were my favorites, always making the most difficult material understandable—and fun.

I still remember having to stay after school (and I was not alone) to repeat a lab assignment in chemistry. Our teacher entertained us with jokes so we didn't feel bad about messing up earlier. He'd say, "Since we all have to stay after school today we might as well have some fun while we work." One never forgets a teacher like that.

I soon decided that nursing would be my career after high school, and my family was pleased about my interest in medicine. My mother suggested I talk to her friend, and soon after I was offered a summer job at the hospital as a nurse's aide. I jumped at the opportunity, although I could have earned more much-needed money at another job.

I loved being at the hospital, and I was eager to go to work each day. The work was far from glamorous, and there was rarely time to eat or take a break. Changing soiled bed linens, emptying bedpans, stocking supplies, and other tasks made me feel useful. The nurses were eager to teach me about their work, allowing me into the delivery room to observe babies being born and the operating room to watch surgical procedures.

I was taught to prepare the formula for the newborns using strict sterilization procedures. Whenever I had a break, I went straight to the newborn nursery to feed or hold the babies. What could be more fun than that for a teenage girl?

The nurses were amazing—so smart and knowledgeable about medicine—and I wanted to be like them. They handled crises calmly and efficiently until a physician arrived, and even delivered babies who could not wait with skill equal to the doctors. Every minute was an opportunity to learn, and the nurses never tired of my endless questions. The physicians, on the other hand, were rather intimidating. They always seemed in a hurry and wanted their orders followed right away. It was clear, however, that they respected the nursing staff and appreciated their good care of the patients.

I was reluctant to bother the physicians with my questions, but I finally gathered the courage to approach the pediatrician with my list of questions. He laughed but answered every one.

Unbeknownst to me, the pediatrician and the surgeon at the hospital, independently of each other, were taking note of my interest in medicine, my curiosity, and my enthusiasm about my work at the hospital. They were aware that I was a good student, and they knew my parents. While I was helping in the newborn nursery one day, the pediatrician asked me if I had ever thought about becoming a doctor. I said no, that I wanted to be a nurse. He replied that nursing is a good career but believed that I could do more. He thought I could be a doctor and encouraged me to think about it. On another occasion the surgeon passed me in the hallway and told me the same thing, urging me to eventually consider medical school.

Throughout the summers I worked at the hospital, these physicians gave me the confidence to apply to medical school. Had they not seen my potential, served as mentors, and encouraged me, I would not be a physician today. My mother's friend and those physicians changed my life, and I will be forever grateful to them. So when I entered college in 1958, my goal was to complete the requirements for admission to medical school.

Segregation was a way of life where I grew up. There were separate water fountains, separate areas of city parks and beaches, separate doors and seating at the movie theater. We rode in the back of the bus. At the same time, I lived in a thriving Negro community in which we had Negro teachers, doctors, dentists, bankers, hairdressers, lawyers, store owners, and nurses. A newspaper published by a Negro businessman kept us in touch with issues in the community. Segregation was the status quo, and most people just lived with it, or so it seemed.

The pastor of our church received information about a college for women in Pennsylvania, and he passed it on to me. I applied and was accepted at Beaver College (now co-educational Arcadia University). I was given a scholarship and off I went. I was eager to see what living in the North would be like as well. The college offered small classes with a lot of faculty interaction. I majored in chemistry and had excellent teachers in both the sciences and liberal arts. The number of students majoring in science was small, and we formed lasting friendships. Although I didn't relish the demands of my biochemistry course at the time, I appreciated them later when I got to med school.

In college I was the only Negro student in my class, and while I didn't venture far from campus very often, I saw no signs of segregation. I visited the homes of several students and attended events in Philadelphia with classmates. My race never seemed to be an issue, or if it was, I was too busy to notice. Several classmates were very interested in learning about my experiences growing up in the South. During my last two years of college, I roomed with two other students: one was from Japan and the other from New Jersey. Looking back, I suppose we were an interesting trio.

One of my classmates was active in social causes and student affairs. She was supportive of the civil rights movement and endeavored to get other students involved. Several of us joined her and students from nearby colleges for trips to Washington, D.C. Our task was to stage "sit-down strikes" at lunch counters and restaurants where Negroes were not allowed to eat. Students, both white and Negro, crammed into buses for these trips. The strikes were well-organized, and we were given precise training. White students would enter a dining establishment and occupy seats. Negro students would then enter quickly and occupy the seats they vacated. We remained seated until given the signal to leave. We then moved on to the next location. The camaraderie among the participants was heartwarming and inspiring. We tried not to think about the risk of being killed or hurt or of being arrested. We felt compelled to do something to bring about equal rights for all Americans. The strikes were something we could do to make a difference. Fortunately, no one from our group was ever harmed or arrested.

I knew my parents would not approve of my actions and would have forbidden me to participate. As a result, I never told them what I had done.

When it was time to apply to medical school, I chose to apply to only two schools, one in New York and one in Virginia, hoping that I would at least have a chance at my state medical school. I thought that my applicant's interview at the University of Virginia went okay, but during the tour of the school and the hospital, I didn't see any Negro faces. I began to worry, but then the good news came that I had been accepted. I was both excited and scared to death. The support of family and friends boosted my confidence and kept me focused.

At the end of the summer in 1962, I went to Charlottesville to begin medical school. The first-year class gathered in the large auditorium. I arrived early and took a seat in the front. Several male students were already sitting in the back of the room and were joined by more and more men. Finally, two other female students arrived, and they sat next to me. We were the only female students, and I was the only Negro student in the class.

The only women on the campus at that time were nursing or graduate students, and there was one dormitory for all of us. As female medical students we realized that we were in the same boat, and we supported one another every day. Although we didn't speak about it, each of us was determined to show our classmates and teachers that we were capable—and that we deserved to be there. Many male physicians did not believe that women had the ability to become physicians and they appeared to resent women students for taking slots away from men. As a Negro woman I was not sure what I would face, but I knew that it might be very difficult.

Segregation was in full force in Charlottesville, so my race would again be an issue. But I entered medical school with resolve that my race and gender would not be issues for me. If they were issues for anyone else, I would just have to deal with it.

Throughout the four years of medical school, I was treated like any other student for the most part. While there certainly were hurtful situations and interactions, I tried hard not to dwell on them. Some classmates, those from northern states in particular, were especially kind. There were a few female physicians on the faculty, and that helped ease things somewhat. Interestingly, at some point, our male classmates noticed that we three women took detailed notes in class; at test time we received several requests to borrow our notes. Suddenly, we had become an asset to the class. In addition, my strong background in chemistry gained me a number of supporters. Noticing that I usually finished my lab assignments in biochemistry early, several classmates asked for help, which I gave readily. Any doubts about my ability to master the tough medical school curriculum were erased.

Medical school was hard work—and demanding. There were classes all day, seeing patients in the clinics and hospital, nights on call, and, of course, homework. There was so much to learn about the human body and about disease and treatment. Every day was simply amazing, however, and I couldn't imagine doing anything more rewarding than being a medical student.

My second year another Negro woman—Vivian Pinn—moved into the room next to mine. She was a first-year medical student, the only woman and the only Negro student in her class. We were concerned about her and offered our support and guidance, but we need not have worried too much. Vivian was strong and independent, handling her situation extremely well. It didn't take long for her to earn the respect of her classmates and teachers.

I am forever grateful to Vivian for her friendship but also for her boldness in rescuing both of us from the dormitory. We had had enough of dorm life, but apartments were expensive and none near the medical school were available to Negro students. Through hometown connections—and her great powers of persuasion—Vivian convinced a landlord to rent an apartment to two Negro women. That we were medical students was in our favor. Frankly, I don't know if the other tenants even knew that we were even there; we left early in the morning and returned late at night. I would not have had the guts to do this on my own. Thank you again, Vivian.

I am so very proud of Vivian and of all that she has accomplished in her amazing career. It was such a pleasure and an honor to share those years in medical school with her. While we were in medical school, Vivian and I had no idea that we would be the first Negro women to receive medical degrees from the University of Virginia School of Medicine—but we were, and we did it together. I received my degree in 1966, and Vivian received her degree in 1967.

During summer breaks I worked either at the University Hospital or my hometown hospital. My experience with a teenage patient on the psychiatric ward was one factor that led me to pursue a career in child and adolescent psychiatry. From medical school I went to an internship in Boston, where I was the only Negro physician. A year later, I was off to do a residency in general psychiatry and a fellowship in child and adolescent psychiatry at the University of Michigan where I was one of two Negro residents. The other was a man.

By then I was accustomed to being the only Negro professional in many situations, and often the only female physician. When I first left my home and the security and comfort of my Negro community, someone told me that I would be representing my race wherever I went. He said that I would meet people whose negative attitudes about Negroes as a race could be positively influenced by my behavior. I remember discussing this with Vivian and talking about what a responsibility it was to represent a whole group of people. I certainly felt in medical school that I needed to succeed as a woman and that I needed to succeed as a Negro. I believed that my success would show that women and Negroes should be admitted to medical school and be allowed to become physicians. There were so many reasons why I simply *could not* fail.

I later settled in Missouri, which is where I have spent most of my career. My primary focus has been clinical work, treating children and adolescents with severe emotional and behavioral problems. I have been a clinician at a state mental health clinic and at the University of Missouri Hospital and Clinics. I also have been a faculty member at the University of Missouri Medical School and served on its admission committee. But more importantly, I have had the privilege to teach and provide clinical supervision to medical students, residents, and fellows. I have been able to pass on to many physicians all that I have learned throughout my career caring for patients. And I have upheld the family tradition; I became a teacher.

Most of all, I have endeavored to improve the lives of children and their families, a highly important task and a challenge that we as a society continue to face.

NOTE

1.   I have used the word "Negro" throughout because that was the terminology at the time. We were members of the Negro race.

AN INTERVIEW WITH TERESA WALKER PRICE AND EVELYN YANCEY JONES

Maurice Apprey and Shelli M. Poe

Teresa Price and Evelyn Jones were, in many ways, substitute mothers to the young African American men, and later women, who attended the University in the 1950s and 1960s. They and their Charlottesville families provided a respite from the stresses of University life—and from the fears that often permeated their days on Grounds. In this interview, conducted on May 1, 2013, with Price and Jones, their memories take us between the past and the present, speaking both to the community's presence—and support for the University's African American students—and their own questions as to why there is so little connection between black students and the community today.

MAURICE APPREY: What did the students look like in the early years?

EVELYN JONES: They looked like lost boys in a sea of white. They looked like teachers' children, custodians' children, often the first person from their families to go to college, children who had been at the top of their classes.

TERESA PRICE: Yes, they had a certain confidence—and at the same time, some uncertainty.

EJ: You know a lot of local kids didn't want to go. My brother [Charles Yancey] went kicking and screaming. Our parents were attempting to provide a debt-free education for the two of us and choices had to be made. It was necessary for us to go where it was affordable, and living at home and going to U.Va. was affordable, plus it provided a quality education.

MA: That's a great link between the community and the University.

EJ: It was necessary for the students at that time to have a link between the University and something that resembled normal, something homelike for them, because everything else was foreign.

EJ: Well Teresa's house was always open. There were many people at the table.

TP: Yes, we'd say, "Come on, come on."

EJ: The first time they came, they were guests. After that, they were family, so they'd do the dishes, wash clothes, and so on. Yeah, two of the guys lived with us for a couple summers. Leroy Willis stayed for at least one summer, Wesley Harris stayed two summers. It's interesting to follow their careers now. They were close friends with my brother and became lifelong family friends.

And it was interesting to watch what was happening at the local schools at the same time as integration was happening at U.Va. In the elementary and high schools they were breaking barriers as well. Everyone had to band together. It was a tense time for everyone.

You know, Valerie Gregory, the outreach director for undergraduate admissions at U.Va., would ask black students to go to the University of Virginia, and they would reply, "We don't want to go to the plantation." Valerie used to be a local school principal, and she knows the community well, so she was concerned because that mentality continued to exist for a very long time.

I'm concerned today about something else. It looks like black U.Va. students exclude themselves from our local community. That makes a void in their lives. They can't live balanced lives without back and forth between the community and the University. Do you think they lose their identity?

MA: The Office of African-American Affairs tries to address this. We ask students to think about how they can make a difference as a black doctor or lawyer or teacher. We ask them how they can bring added value to the classroom and world as black people.

EJ: Well, that's what kept the early students going. Many were the first to go to college. Their parents wanted more for them. And the students wanted to know, "How can I make a difference?" Students now are more self-centered and concerned about their future careers and have little to no interest in the community. They appear to have the attitude that they are beyond the community and there is nothing to be gained. Students now test the social limits; during the late 1950s and early '60s this simply was not an option.

TP: They were fighting two battles at once: surviving on the plantation and succeeding in school.

EJ: Failure just was not an option for them. When you look at them now, you can see it exemplified in their lives. What they learned in school they're doing for others now. For me, with the current students not being integrated into the community, that's what they miss. They don't see things around them. They only see the prestigious academic community. But next to them there are people who have been living in public housing for fifty-plus years, who haven't gone more than ten square miles from where they live, single-parent homes where children don't have the encouragement to end up at a university. If you don't put the effort in, it escapes you.

TP: It surprises me that there are people in the community who haven't been on campus. And students and black faculty are losing the opportunity to come into the city.

EJ: We miss opportunities to interface with them. We don't know about opportunities we could be involved in.

TP: It's a communication thing. But it's difficult to break old habits.

MA: What are some of your most affectionately remembered stories?

EJ: I remember Leroy Willis's graduation. His father was a Baptist minister and his mother was a homemaker. When I saw them on the Lawn—the awe in their expressions. They looked like, "We can't believe we're here, that this is our child." That's my hope for parents—to see their dream realized, that their children wouldn't have to live in the same poverty they did. Then Leroy got married at the University Chapel and had two kids who graduated from the University.

TP: The gentlemen [students] were so special in their comings and goings. I was their biggest fan club. They helped me raise my children. They'd come to play with my children; it was a release for them. In fact, Harold Marsh taught Frank [her son, Franklin Walker] how to tie his shoes. His brother Henry was an attorney and helped with litigation in desegregation suits, but Harold is gone now. In Richmond about seven years ago, he had a case where the persons involved were not satisfied with the outcome. They shot him at a red light.

I met these children because of the Jackson family. They were in with the fraternal organizations. So when parents sent their children to school here, they'd get in touch with the Jackson family downtown. Most who went to that house would also come to mine.

EJ: Those were the connected students. But then there were also the "commoners," the ones who had to make their own connections.

TP: My brother ran a dance and restaurant conglomerate. It was a great gathering place—called Bren Wanna on South 29. He provided a safe place for black students to go and to have the occasional good time.

Bobby Bland also had an aunt here—Rosemary Byers. She also became a support for Bobby and many of his friends.

Early on, eating establishments were closed on Sundays. So they'd come spend time with us.

EJ: In those years many restaurants were not integrated. My senior year in high school was when the marches and sit-ins started.

TP: I remember Marsh coming to the house one Sunday night and telling us: "I'm so full. I've been in and out of all the restaurants seeing who would serve me." He had gone from Madison House on Rugby Avenue all the way to Tenth Street. It was another milestone accomplished.

EJ: That was another huge divide, and a place where we broke ground. Prior to '63, no one could go into any local restaurants and get served a meal.

TP: That's why John [Merchant] got mono, I think. He didn't have money to find good food. He wasn't eating properly. It was a very hostile environment.

EJ: Participating in the academic environment was hard enough. It's amazing they did as well as they did.

TP: They had self-determination. They used to sing the song: "Bobby stayed, I'm staying. Bobby stayed, I'm staying" [referring to Bobby Bland].

EJ: It was a testament to their academic preparedness. They came from segregated schools where people were saying, you know, they couldn't be educated properly. But they *were* well educated.

EJ: No marriages happened immediately after college. They were focused. And it's a testament to the wonderful teachers they had in school. That's something that is overlooked. Their teachers in high school were well-educated. They had to do more than teach, too. They had to take care of the students, give them clothes and food. That's what steered me toward social ministry.

TP: The distinguishing thing about those gentlemen was, they had their priorities in focus. School first. They didn't let girls deter them. They didn't spend hours at my house either. They'd eat, ask if they could do something for me, and then they'd go. It was relaxing to them. I would play the piano and John [Merchant] would play the guitar. We'd do that a little while. Then they'd say, "See you later." I thought that was admirable. Then they'd walk back to school—no one had cars at the time—to study.

And these gentlemen sought out the church. First Baptist, Zion Union, Ebenezer, Mount Zion. I don't know why. Well, to feast their eyes on the pretty girls! And to establish contacts. Rev. Benjamin and Mrs. Emma Bunn did a lot with those boys.

[William] Womack went to D.C. after graduation and never looked back. The University had a hard time getting him back, and now he has been back more than any medical student, I think. [James] Trice's son came back as a resident. But now black students don't seek out community; they think they don't need to.

A SON OF THE SOUTH

An African American
Public Servant

David Temple, Jr.

THE CONTEXT: HISTORICAL AND GEOGRAPHICAL

I am Virginia born and raised, a son of the South. An African American son of the South.

Historically, the Commonwealth of Virginia was at the very center of our founding and its evolving American experience. Dubbed "the Mother of Presidents," central Virginia was home to Thomas Jefferson, James Madison, and James Monroe, who powerfully penned and contributed to the nation's democratic tenets. George Washington, the nation's "Father," sat at the helm in the northern part of the state. From the outset, Virginia's accessible geography and its leadership defined its prominence and its capacity to frame public opinion. Likewise, the institution of slavery became the inexorable economic, political, and social vehicle for southern wealth and power. Jefferson and the others were slave owners. And Jefferson's University, founded in 1819, quickly became a must-attend school for southern, well-rounded, male leadership. Slave labor helped to build Jefferson's University.

Usher in the Civil War in 1861. Richmond is named the capital of the Confederacy and Virginia becomes defined by a searing rebellion and separation from the very nation it earlier founded and led from its inception. U.Va.'s sons are among those who enlist and fight. After the war, it is black labor that helps to rebuild Richmond and other cities across the state.

Midway through the new twentieth century, the U.S. Supreme Court would rule against separate and unequal educational opportunities, ushering in new and unprecedented chapters in race relations between the large white majorities and the suddenly empowered black grandchildren of the region's past slave institution. Reactions across the South were immediate, recalcitrant, and often violent. Virginia and its Richmond capital led the South in a "massive resistance" to desegregation that closed white public schools rather than adhere to the court's ruling.

Large percentages of these state lawmakers were white sons of Virginia and alumni of the University of Virginia. As federal leadership enforced new laws, national black religious and civic leaders issued demands. Dr. Martin Luther King, Jr., pointed the way forward through the use of disarming and highly effective passive resistance, and the stage became set for descendants of slaves to enter and attend the formerly all-white, southern, post-secondary bastions, including "Mr. Jefferson's University."

THE PRE-U.VA. EXPERIENCE: FAMILY, CHURCH, AND SCHOOL

My father, David Temple, Sr., was born in King William County, Virginia, in 1911. My mother, Helen Burnette Jones, was born in the deeply rural Charles City County, Virginia, in 1919, the eighth of nine children born to Thomas and Magnolia Jones. She excelled academically in that economically and racially suppressed area. However, family needs ended her formal education before grade nine, which was not atypical in those years.

My parents met in Richmond and later married in October 1946, not long after my father returned from his naval service in World War II. I was born in July 1947 at Richmond's St. Phillips Hospital. Two years later, my brother Riley was born.

For more than forty years, Dad was a Richmond-based insurance agent with the historically black-owned North Carolina Mutual Life Insurance Company, moving up the ranks until eventually becoming the top sales agent, a position he held for many years. A time would come when hundreds of black families in East Richmond's Church Hill neighborhood would be insured through my dad, and generations recalled him in their kitchens or their churches or their civic-social clubs.

My parents bought a home in Church Hill, within blocks of numerous family members. Everyone attended the same church, where my father soon became a deacon and later the deacon board's chairman.

After my brother and I started school, Mom went to work on Richmond's Broad Street, long considered the retail district's main street. Reportedly, she was the first nonwhite "sales girl" on Broad Street at Harper's children's store. Despite her restricted academic experience, she developed superior computational, grammatical, and composition skills. When she retired from Richmond's Miller and Rhoades Department store, she had served as a retail buyer and retail accountant. Throughout Riley's and my K–12 experience, she never missed a school performance or parents' night. I later became a church-affiliated cub scout, then boy scout, a junior usher, and a singer in the Mount Olivet Baptist Angelic Choir. By this time, Dad was also publisher and editor of the church bulletin and president of the Astoria Beneficial Club, a black men's civic association. He and other community black leaders served as directors of the Richmond Community Hospital.

Dad had been befriended and mentored by another Church Hill African American insurance man, Robert Wilder, who with his wife, Beulah, became lifelong friends. Their son L. Douglas Wilder was, of course, the history-making Virginia politician who became a state senator, lieutenant governor, and finally governor.

I attended segregated George Mason Elementary School and was blessed to have been taught by highly skilled and caring black teachers. During those years I learned to play the violin and began cello instruction, but I also recall reading the state-required Virginia history textbook that taught us about "happy, contented Negroes" who "lollygagged, danced, and were well cared for" by plantation owners. At the same time, our black teachers taught us poetry by such greats as Langston Hughes. I had French and the earth sciences in sixth grade, and by seventh grade had been identified for accelerated courses in mathematics, science, and English in a program that would define my secondary school years and that laid the groundwork for my acceptance into college.

In fact, college attendance was as expected as getting dressed every day. I would become the first college student and college graduate on either side of my immediate family.

Meanwhile, and inexplicably, by age nine, I had become compelled by politics. In particular, I watched the Democratic and Republican Conventions, gavel to gavel. This fascination pleased, though bewildered, my folks, who had always voted, even when the poll tax was required. My political engagement and activism would later become a hallmark of my life and profession.

During the 1950s my parents made certain that my brother and I attended all of the Armstrong High School commencement exercises. At one memorable and life-changing ceremony, I saw Wesley Harris of Church Hill receive his diploma, and along with it seemingly endless cascades of honors and scholarship offers, including one from U.Va. It was not the greatest of the awards he received, but it seemed to represent a massive breakthrough in the 1950s for those of us not accustomed to blacks attending white schools, especially U.Va. His success raised the standard for me, and I wanted to follow him there when the time came.

THE PRE-U.VA. EXPERIENCE: POLITICS AND COMMUNITY

In 1960, during my middle school stint at East End Junior High, John F. Kennedy was seeking the Democratic nomination for president. He seemed to speak directly to me, insisting that our generation must move the country innovatively forward and create a new frontier of opportunity and excellence: a new frontier for "all races of Americans," he said. Kennedy had a galvanizing presence, and I never once doubted him. Meanwhile, Dr. Martin Luther King's call to blacks, whites, Christians, Jews, and others to march for freedom and justice captured me and gave affirmation and fundamental substance to Kennedy's soaring rhetoric for change.

Kennedy's victory and inaugural speech pronounced that "the torch has been passed to a new generation of Americans," and that we must "ask not what our country can do for you, rather what you can do for your country." I fully breathed and absorbed every word. From that moment to this day, public service would define and drive me.

Then came the summer of 1963. A small cohort of African American teens and I had become active with the Student Nonviolent Coordinating Committee and the NAACP. For months, my friends and I fine-tuned restaurant sit-in procedures. We were fully absorbed in nonviolence, turning the other cheek, locking arms, and falling limp. The worst we got were streams of spit, beer, and hate-filled, flush-faced "nigger-bombs." Since I was only sixteen, I was too young to be sent to jail, but I wanted desperately to bring attention to the courageous work of Dr. King and those who were working in far more perilous circumstances. So, when the police arrived at Tony's Kitchen, I lied about my age, suddenly becoming eighteen.

That fall, the climate in Mrs. Williams's trigonometry class was always tension-filled, not the least because she customarily walked the room with a menacing yardstick. For me the tension was even thicker because mistakes in trig came easily to me. One day, without notice, a radio feed came over the intercom, an unprecedented action. Lots of jumbled noise and confusion but through it all we heard the words, "... and President Kennedy was seen to slump over into Mrs. Kennedy's arms.... We are told that the injured president is being rushed to Parkland Hospital in Dallas." A short time later came the announcement that the president had died.

Kennedy was seen as a friend to us, had called for civil rights and voting rights legislation. He had "passed the torch" to me and others like me. I had come to see a way for the nation's and my future, and to view the organizational political vehicle as an asset. I had come to be proud of our country.

After a morose, dark, tearful and increasingly worrying weekend (after all, Vice President Lyndon B. Johnson, as a Texas senator, had voted against all civil rights legislation), I returned to school on that following Monday and, gratefully, to France Brinkley's history class. He insisted that we lift our chins and imagine a new president who would pick up the fallen banner and make it his own. Imagine too, he said, that he pushes through civil rights, voting rights, public accommodations, housing, and more. Imagine these things because the nation wants these things of the new president, to honor Kennedy's life.

President Johnson did just that.

THE U.VA. EXPERIENCE (1965–1969): THE DECISION-MAKING PROCESS

I planned early on to select U.Va. as my first choice and, gratefully, was accepted.

It seemed that many of my high school contemporaries were headed to Howard and Hampton. My father's friends and associates were pressing me to become a "Morehouse man." But King was asking that we reach out as blacks and whites, and the University of Virginia seemed the right place to do that. While Charlottesville was only seventy-five miles away,

I decided I would not be returning to Richmond on weekends. I would invest myself fully into the U.Va. experience, whatever that might be.

The housing application asked if "I would accept an 'other-race' roommate." I indicated in the affirmative, of course. My full experience agenda would suggest nothing else. John Lipscomb, from Richmond's all-white Douglas Freeman High School, had done the same. We were assigned Dunglison House, a then new dorm considered an experiment in group living. Each suite included five rooms, housing two students per room, plus a living room and large bathroom. Approximately 1,300 men comprised the entering class. Of those, five were black. I was the only black in Dunglison.

John had not told his mother that he had agreed to have a nonwhite roommate, and she paled visibly when he introduced us. He flushed. I smiled and shook her wobbly hand. Later, she demanded he change rooms, but he refused. I came to understand that I was the first African American with whom he had engaged in social or academic conversation. And while his world had been light years away from mine, he eagerly welcomed the new perspectives coming his way. John and I became close and trusted friends.

In short order we were oriented to the Honor System, the jacket-and-tie tradition expected of "Virginia gentlemen," and the institution of student-led governance. The fraternity system produced the leaders. Non-frat men were followers. This system was promoted, in particular, by the dean of students, B. F. D. Runk, who took immense pride in this way of life on Grounds: fraternity men first and fraternity men in leadership positions, a strong tradition worth keeping—in his mind.

I wanted the full collegiate experience at U.Va., which, clearly, included fraternity life, but I suffered no delusion that I would be recruited. The handful of black upperclassmen had generally confirmed my assessment. In fact, on bid night, I dressed in a "V" sweatshirt and jeans. John wore the customary U.Va. uniform: blue blazer, red bowtie, white shirt, khaki pants, penny loafers, no socks. Sure enough, the knocks on our door began— fourteen in all—every one for John. Many men arrived to ask him about his career interests, his likes and dislikes, "would he be able to get a date for the coming rush event?" Sitting at my desk, I was pretty much a potted plant, even though John never failed to introduce me. Beyond perfunctory greetings, none accepted his subtle prompts to engage me in conversation.

Then came what can only be called a "slip up." Three men came to the door asking for David Temple. I will always remember the contorted and gape-mouthed expressions on the ashen-faced young men. Although clearly stunned, they began to rapidly mumble their "script" while simultaneously extending uncertain hands. I indicated that I might be able to attend, knowing well that I was simply trying to get through this moment. John was thoroughly embarrassed and suddenly schooled in the repugnant, crude, and sad face of racism.

It was not until a year later that a group of us became interested in recolonizing Pi Lambda Phi. The dormant Virginia Omega Alpha chapter had been a member of the University fraternity community prior to World War II. We discovered that it was an international, nonsectarian, nondiscriminatory fraternity. It was this central mission that we found compelling and worthy of trying to rebuild as a part of their social and political activism, and their University legacy. This would become *our* mission, one that might shatter stodgy and unyielding race- and religion-based University traditions. We would desegregate U.Va.'s fraternity system and bring together Jews, Catholics, Protestants, and others. Runk and the Inter-Fraternity Council (IFC) insisted we apply for "colony" status and await future decision making after a suitable period, initially set at three years. When their three-year plan failed, the IFC disapproved our application, citing among other reasons that "we were not diverse *enough*." This further emboldened us since we were the only fraternity with any identifiably diverse elements whatsoever. The ongoing administrative blocks were useless. By 1969, Pi Lambda Phi had been rechartered and was invested as a member of the IFC.

We purchased a chapter house on fraternity row at 504 Rugby Road. We had conducted two successful class recruitments, and chapter photo composites were now hanging on our walls. This was a substantial and historic advance at Jefferson's academical village, where sadly, legal restrictions on race and gender were also a hallmark.

We attended college during a powerful, innovative, tumultuous, deeply inspiring and wholly tragic period for an impressionable young person of any race in American life. I had auditioned for, and was selected into the U.Va. Glee Club from my earliest days on Grounds. By 1967, I had become baritone section leader. Throughout, I was the club's only student of color. It was at the annual Glee Club Spring Concert performance in

April 1968 when they interrupted the program to report that King had been assassinated. A deafening silence fell across the Old Cabell Hall auditorium where I, the sole black person, now stood absorbing the horror, pain, shock, and isolation caused by that event. It seemed that every head on stage and those in the four-hundred-person audience had turned to me.

SURROUNDED AND EMBRACED; ISOLATED AND ALONE

I and my fraternity brothers were all working together on our cause. Nonetheless, I did not feel comfortable sharing my personal challenges as a black man at U.Va. It was not really possible for me at the time, but in retrospect, I wish I had had the confidence to seek out or create African American mentors, people who might have helped me feel better about what I believed was a lack of preparation for unanticipated differences in communication and instruction. I felt uncomfortable sharing *any* perceived weakness, fearing that it might get unfairly generalized by some and used against all blacks, present and future. My response was to suck it up, to feed myself with false pride and chin up, and to keep moving.

It took a while but I came to realize that I was learning, gaining valuable insights, and giving back to others within the community. I found that I was spending more time staying up late talking, debating, sharing views, socializing, and, yes, learning with a broad diversity of students. I rationalized that to be my responsibility. It was, of course, fundamentally irresponsible, since study time occasionally—or too often—got preempted by personal outreach between a black man and other-race individuals.

SCOTT STADIUM AND "DIXIE"

The jacket-and-tie uniform was also worn to Scott Stadium football games, or what passed for football in those days. Losing was a tradition as well, but it was handled better when washed down by deep swallows of Rebel Yell or Virginia Gentlemen. Predictably, by the second quarter we would be treated to endless choruses of "Dixie." Drunken male students, wishing to "take a stand to live and die in Dixie," did not react well to slights. As such, some of my fellow students thought it better to stand (though not sing), and urged me to do the same, fearing an outbreak of violence. I admit to standing once during the first two home games, just to head off any possible problems, but by the third game standing was not an option. Eventually several white students joined me in sitting.

FINALLY, A UNIVERSITY ALUMNUS

In 1971, two years after graduation, I returned to the University to work on a master's degree in special education at the Curry School of Education. I also met the woman whom I would later marry, a doctoral student in philosophy.

For many years I served on a number of alumni committees in the Washington area, including for the Jefferson Scholars program and as a director of the U.Va. Club of Washington. I worked with other black alums and the alumni association to create the Walter Ridley Scholarship Fund and served on its board for many years. It took several years for us to create a biannual Black Reunion Weekend, and we worked hard to help recruit and engage potential black first-year students.

Importantly and perhaps ironically, in 1986 Virginia Governor Gerald L. Baliles appointed me deputy secretary of education. The irony was that state education officials overseeing K–12 schools, community colleges, and four-year institutions reported to the secretary—and me—on the governor's behalf. Whenever I would return to Grounds with oversight responsibility, I could not completely jettison a sweet personal sense of irony, recalling the early years with the racially recalcitrant Dean Runk and the Dixie lovers.

STARTING A CAREER AND BACK TO U.VA.

What to do with a liberal arts degree in psychology? As it happened, the Commonwealth of Virginia's Correctional Department was experiencing meaningful growth, largely as a result of increased arrests of drugs-involved juveniles/youths. They sought counselors for these kids, who were incarcerated at Beaumont School for Boys about twenty miles west of Richmond. Once offered the position I grabbed it without hesitation. My career had finally begun.

The overwhelming majority of students were young black boys, mostly from Richmond, Petersburg, Newport News, and Norfolk. They lived and slept in cottages organized along a spectrum of age, size, and degree of criminal behavior. Each cottage was assigned a counselor and a house mother and father. My assignment was L Cottage, home to the youngest, nonviolent students. My job was to intervene in their patterns of dysfunction, engage their teachers, and prepare them to return to their homes, communities, and schools, hopefully within six months.

One day, a Curry School professor arrived with a group of graduate students, and we fell into conversation. He asked if I would consider returning to the University for a master's degree in special education training for emotionally disturbed school-aged populations. I had not but eagerly welcomed the possibility. One month later, I had returned to Charlottesville.

Shortly after earning my master's degree, I was recruited to teach in the Fairfax County Public Schools at Edison High School. I was also elected to the Fairfax County Democratic Committee; later the Fairfax County Board of Supervisors appointed me to the newly formed countywide Human Rights Commission.

By 1984 I had served two years as the Mount Vernon District Democratic Party chair. I had also reconnected with my Wilder family friend, State Senator Doug Wilder (D-Richmond). He let me know that he was planning a run for lieutenant governor in 1985. At a Virginia Education Association convention I had escorted and walked him through delegations, introducing him to rows of colleagues representing the counties of Fairfax, Fairfax City, Arlington, Prince William, and Loudoun, and the cities of Alexandria and Manassas, all residing and politically active in Virginia's 8th and 10th congressional districts. These jurisdictions comprised the northern Virginia region. I agreed to manage and direct this regional all-volunteer campaign.

I asked my good friend and Fairfax County Democratic Party Chair Patricia C. "Pat" Watt to assist me in this exciting effort. Pat had earlier run and lost her campaign to become chair of the Fairfax County Board of Supervisors. She would become an irreplaceable asset to the outcome. A victory would make Richmond-born Wilder, the grandson of slaves, the first black to win statewide election in Virginia and the first black to win a statewide executive office in the South since Reconstruction. Doug was intent and adamant on local fundraising to support this unprecedented effort. That is, any expenses would be paid for from funds raised by volunteers—none from corporate coffers.

Our northern Virginia effort, and the campaign overall, is well chronicled by author Dwayne Yancey (staff reporter for the *Roanoke Times and World News*) in *When Hell Froze Over* (1988, updated 1990).[1] Yancey selected the title from comments made by U.Va. professor Larry Sabato, who predicted that "hell would freeze over" before such an election could succeed statewide.

On that chilled November evening, I was able to report to Richmond and to those assembled, nervously waiting, that over fifteen thousand votes had been won in the 8th and 10th congressional districts, providing Wilder the majority needed statewide to become lieutenant governor, completing a victorious Democratic sweep for the offices of governor and attorney general. It made Doug the nation's highest ranking black elected official. And it set the stage for his second, and more impactful, 1989 history-making electoral effort, his election as governor of Virginia, the first African American so elected in the United States.

Days later, in a letter dated November 13, 1985, Doug wrote to me the following:

Dear Dave:

From the outset you were there and during the trials and tribulations, your support never wavered. You not only were instrumental in galvanizing perhaps the best organizational effort ever seen in the Northern Virginia area, according to many, many people who are far more knowledgeable, historically, of the area than I, but your enthusiasm was cancerous and had a contagion about it which infused the spirit of others to climb and move to greater heights. I will never say the things appropriately, and have not done so in terms of my appreciation, but I know of no single person more deserving of the credit for our victory than you, and I want you to know how much it means to me personally.

Best regards to all and we will see each other soon.

Sincerely,
Doug

That result brought me profound pride in our state, the capital seat of the defeated Confederate States of America. For me, it was a deep sense of civic and racial exhilaration. Our centuries-delayed, hard-won votes had joined those of white voters to elect the grandson of Virginia slaves. Recalling my much earlier, sixteen-year-old Richmond arrest and jailing (restaurant "trespassing"), and my unwelcoming arrival and "student career" at U.Va., it seemed that the arc of progress was a solid one, and one that blacks nationally could not fail to notice.

A PUBLIC SERVANT IN PUBLIC SERVICE

My professional education, workforce development career, and civic endeavors have been fully dedicated to public service and, more specifically, to executive and managerial leadership. I was fortunate to have served on numerous state and federal commissions and boards throughout my career, mostly focused on improving and expanding access to education. I have worked hard to be an advocate for young people and to improving their opportunities for success in all areas, including science, mathematics, and technology. I wanted to make a difference—and to fulfill the dreams of both King and Kennedy.

In 2005, I accepted Governor Mark Warner's appointment to Virginia's P–16 Education Council, an umbrella commission that sought to coordinate policies among pre-kindergarten, elementary and secondary, community college, and higher education institutional programs and policies. I also directed the statewide "Partnership for Excellence—Workforce Virginia 2000," a state government–led, public-private enterprise that resulted in a blueprint for the development of new inter-education partnerships. From 2003 to 2008, I served as a program director with the Education and Human Resources Directorate at the National Science Foundation.

I accepted two cabinet posts from then Washington, D.C., mayor Sharon Pratt Kelly, which included leading the mayor's Youth Initiatives Office, where within a period of six months we opened four full-time after-school social, health, educational, and family services programs in middle schools in economically distressed areas across the city.

I have been remarkably blessed to be able to serve the people of Virginia and the United States, and to have the sufficient skills and God-given will to put ideas to good effect. Without the collaboration and humor of willing others, my life as supported and molded by my U.Va., civic, professional, and political experiences, none of this would ever have occurred.

It is and has been an extraordinary ride—and I have learned and enjoyed much from every compelling moment.

NOTE

1. Dwayne Yancey, *When Hell Froze Over: The Untold Story of Doug Wilder: A Black Politician's Rise to Power in the South* (Dallas: Taylor, 1988).

U.VA.—AN ESSENTIAL EXPERIENCE

Willis B. McLeod

When I was a very young man, it never occurred to me to dream of going to the University of Virginia. It would have seemed too expensive, far beyond my grasp, or too elite, too white. But I did end up going there. And it changed my life.

I am a trailblazer. It's not a boast. I grew up in the segregated South, the child of a poor but proud mother who wore a permanent groove into her shoulder from the sack she dragged so constantly through the cotton fields where she worked. I came of age during the battle for civil rights and did my time on the streets of Fayetteville—and have the arrest record to prove it. I was among the first African Americans to earn master's and doctoral degrees from the University of Virginia, which was founded by a slave owner who wrote stirring words about all men being created equal. I was an educator and went from teacher to principal to assistant superintendent to superintendent. Then I became a university chancellor. I owe my professional heights, in large part, to my time in Charlottesville. This is my story.

I was literally born at the end of a cotton row in 1942. My parents were sharecroppers in rural Sampson County, North Carolina. They had married perhaps a year before but weren't starry-eyed and excited at life or their future. My mother, Hattie Lee, was forty-two when I was born. My father, Bud, was ten years older. They married late in life but loved each other and lived and worked on a farm owned by a Quaker family who judged people by their character, not their skin color. That was a blessing.

My father wasn't involved in my life. But as for my mother, nothing was too good for her baby, her only child. I saw her sacrifice. She could have forced me into the fields to work, the way so many families did with their children. Many families didn't have a commitment to their children's education. They wanted their children to graduate from high school and immediately become financial contributors to the family. That's not what my mother wanted. I worked in the fields in the summer but not during the school year. She wanted me to graduate from high school and go to college. She'd tell me she wanted me to have a better life than she had. I'm happy that I learned early to appreciate her sacrifice. I excelled at school and loved pleasing her. I would drag her out to PTA meetings so she could hear the teachers say good things about me.

Although both of my parents worked in the fields, my mother was more consistent. Even so, my dad cleverly made his own kneepads out of leather, rather than buying them at the store, to assist him when he had to spend a lot of time crawling to pick cotton. I have them on display in my home today, along with his burlap sack, to remind me. There's also a Pepsi bottle in the display. That's what he used for his libations. He liked alcohol, and that's what he worked to buy. He'd get enough money for a supply and then he'd be off the circuit for two to three weeks. He'd get drunk and lie around the house but he didn't bother anyone. Because he wasn't mean, I didn't dislike him. He just wasn't involved with me much. He'd give me a few dollars now and then. When I was about to graduate from high school, he took me to a department store and bought me a suit. That's the most fatherly thing I remember him doing. That was fatherly. He did that. But when I became a breadwinner, a father, I modeled my behavior on what he wasn't most of the time. I decided that never in my life would my refrigerator lack the basic things that I would need.

My mother always worked. She was a strong woman and built her reputation as a worker, specifically in cotton. She would get two of the burlap sacks used to collect cotton, take them apart, and sew them together again as one big sack. If she didn't pick three hundred pounds of cotton in a day, she didn't think she had accomplished anything. She was at least seventy and still working out in the fields when I was just getting going on my own. My dad had died years before. Then she got sick. We didn't discover until it was too late that she had cancer. By then, it had spread practically all over her body. Not long afterward, we lost her. I'll never forget: When she was in the hospital, she pulled her gown off her shoulder to show me the deep groove in her shoulder from pulling those sacks in the fields all those years.

All that work had left a trench. It touched me very deeply because it told the story of her toils and her life of work. That groove is what she had to show for it. That, and me.

She could read at maybe a fifth-grade level—well enough to read the Bible. She didn't read much else. She couldn't write, though. When I was perhaps nine or ten, she took me to the bank with her one day and introduced me to the president of the bank, and I guess she told him that she couldn't write. He told her to mark her Social Security checks with an X and I could bring her checks to the bank and get them cashed. I was very embarrassed by that. All of my close friends' parents were much more literate. I know she knew I was embarrassed, even though I didn't say that to her. I probably said to her one night that I was tired of working on my homework and why didn't I teach her how to write her name. And I did. It didn't take long. She was a fast learner. She had problems signing exactly on the line but she learned to sign her name in cursive. She wouldn't have ever asked anyone to teach her, and wouldn't have let anyone do it but me.

Even though she couldn't write, she watched me closely when I did homework. Somehow she could tell if I was really doing it. There was an expectation that I would do it, and I did. I made good grades, and she was proud. In high school, I also played trumpet and made the first team in football all four years. Back then, what I really wanted to do after school was play professional football. I wasn't good enough coming out of high school to attract scholarships from schools that would put me in the limelight where I'd be seen. But later, at Fayetteville State Teachers College (now Fayetteville State University), I played on the football team all four years and was invited to tryouts by both the Minnesota Vikings and the Miami Dolphins. By then, much to my mother's relief, I had decided that I was going to pursue teaching. She reminded me of that television commercial where the pro quarterback is speaking to school kids. He tells the kids what he does for a living and looks proud. Then this little girl says, "*That's not a job.*" That's the way my mother was. She thought being a teacher was the height, not playing football. And it was. When I was coming along, being a teacher was *the* job to have. It's too bad that teachers aren't respected and revered today like they were in my day.

In 1960, I entered Fayetteville State Teachers College, where I made the dean's list every semester, played football, and was elected student body president. I also started organizing student civil rights protests in Fayetteville. What pushed me forward? It was the feeling that "I deserve this as much as you." But it was also the fact that I was looked upon as the one to do it. I don't know why, but I was always the leader of the pack, whether I wanted to be or not. I guess it's the way I carried myself, and my character, and how I portrayed my values. I was the president of the student body when the movement in Fayetteville started. I felt it was my responsibility to lead the movement since I was in that position. At the eleven other historically black colleges and universities, the student government presidents were basically taking leadership roles, expressing feelings and taking action in organizing student protests. The person I looked toward and whom I decided to try to emulate was Jesse Jackson, who was president of the student government at North Carolina A&T in Greensboro at the time. He was organizing student protests and demonstrations there. But that wasn't why I'd gotten into student government at Fayetteville State. I'd felt the need to lead—and I was drafted into the job by my fellow students. I didn't mind. I'd been involved in student government in high school, and it was kind of an ego boost to be drafted. But at the same time, I always felt like, "Mac, you've got to do it." It was something that had to be done, a need that had to be filled. That's how I saw it, so I didn't shy away when they asked me to serve. I always said yes and then tried to do whatever the job demanded. At this point, I felt it demanded action on the part of students.

It concerned my mother. She was worried about my safety. There used to be a program on one of the radio stations here called "Around the Market House," and the Rush Limbaugh of the program was a man named Johnny Joyce. That name I will never forget. Boy, did he beat us students down with his tongue. When we started the downtown protests and folks started gathering, one of my fellow students got hurt one Saturday evening. They were throwing tear gas at us and other things in bottles and cans—that scared my mother to death. She was concerned about my safety and very survival. But had it not been for me, and this isn't egotistical at all, there would have been nothing to live through in Fayetteville because nobody else would have stepped up to the plate. I was aided by the fact that I was president of the student government and also an honor student, I was well-respected on campus, and none of the professors could really hold anything against me or vilify me because I was the kind of student they liked to brag about, whether they appreciated what I was doing or not. Plus, even on black college campuses there was what I call an *Uncle Tom's Cabin* mentality among blacks: You don't go but so far. Don't push it because you don't want to make the white folks mad. My mother suffered from this a great deal because she was a sharecropper's daughter. She'd had a very hard life and had her own method of coping and surviving. I remember her telling me that periodically the Klan would show up at their house at night and scare them to death. They'd come just to scare them, just to be mean. She had her reasons. But I had mine, and I felt I had to act and lead.

We wanted to be allowed into segregated businesses, like the cinema, and we wanted stores that served blacks to hire blacks, not just whites. We were protesting peacefully—but our opponents didn't appreciate our opinions and weren't quiet about it. I was arrested five times during that period. Once, a police officer said he arrested me to get me out of the sight of a sniper on a nearby hotel roof. Eventually, things in Fayetteville did change.

In 1964, I graduated from Fayetteville State and accepted a position teaching algebra and general mathematics at a new junior high school in Richmond, Virginia. There I met my first wife, who bore my only child, a wonderful son named Jeffrey.

I had been encouraged early in my teaching career to consider going into administration. To achieve that goal, I needed a master's degree. That motivated me a great deal. Plus, while I was teaching in Richmond, I was selected for a special leadership program at U.Va. that had been set up by a generous donor. The superintendent of schools in Richmond nominated me for the program, which was an inroad to the university's School of Education. That started my relationship with U.Va. I had never really thought about going there. I never would have thought I could get in.

There were fifteen of us, all black, all involved in education, and we were exposed to the most talented professors in the education school at U.Va. We also had the opportunity to visit and interact with state and federal officials who held positions of responsibility in education. The program, funded by a grant from U.Va., lasted four or five years, concurrent with my master's program at U.Va. It was at that time that I developed my passion for educational leadership. It was an exciting time. I became charged by the experience because it said to me that earning a master's in this program would set me apart in terms of my educational preparation. Because I had the U.Va. brand, I would get a closer look than I would have otherwise.

Frank E. Flora was the administrator in the School of Education and William H. Seawell was the dean of the school. While Dr. Seawell accepted the leadership program, other professors in the department were much more receptive to it than he was. He was tough. He had a military-style demeanor and it seemed the members of the leadership program really had to pass muster with him. The first time I met him, he said, "McLeod, we're just like the Marine Corps, we only want a few good men." That scared me silly at first. Being black and feeling somewhat tentative, I didn't quite know how to take his comment. When I told Dr. Flora about it, he quickly put me at ease. Apparently, Dr. Seawell said that to every new student.

Although I respected Dr. Seawell, I never felt close to him. He gave me a particularly hard time with my dissertation, which was on the role of school personnel officers in collective bargaining. I don't know that I ever completely satisfied him with its overall quality. In part, I think it was because I did not seek him out when choosing my topic. He was friendlier with the white students. I knew he enjoyed a good shot of bourbon, and he would have a drink with them at times. I never got an invitation. But I didn't necessarily want one. I just wanted to do my work and get out of there.

I did develop friendships, though. I'd already been acquainted with Russell M. Busch, another black educator from Richmond who was enrolled in the doctoral program at U.Va. We became close friends over the course of our time at U.Va. We rode together between Richmond and Charlottesville and got together at other times. It was nice to have someone else to bounce ideas off of. Our families became close and we remained friends after we graduated. Much later, when I went to Columbia, South Carolina, as a superintendent, I took him with me to run our federal programs. He's in Richmond now, and we still talk about once a week. We have a lot of fun laughing about things that we endured back then—including things that probably wouldn't have seemed very funny to us back then!

I also became very close with Doug Magan, a white student in the School of Education. We had a couple of classes together and somehow migrated toward each other. He was a brilliant man, made a perfect score on the SATs. We spent time together at Dr. Flora's house and at Doug's house. Doug and I just hit it off. We shared common values. Our lives growing up mirrored each other. He had this tremendous intelligence and got a lot of encouragement, I think, like myself. I know he was the first in his family to go to college. We worked together for four years and then went in separate directions. We have fallen out of touch but I think about him and wonder how he's doing. I think we had the kind of friendship that could be reignited in a second.

Finally, I developed a particular friendship with Dr. Flora. He used to call just to call, especially during my dissertation phase when I was dealing with Dr. Seawell. I'd get down and Frank would be there to pick me up again; he had my back. Over my years at U.Va., I came to feel that I was a part of his family. If I was in Charlottesville and not on campus, I was typically at his house. I helped to do things but mostly he just liked my being around his kids. Both children are now school superintendents. Frank became one of the best friends of my life, period. Even today I miss him a great deal because he was such a giving guy. He was, in my opinion, an unusual man during that period because he was white but didn't appear to be molded in the same way as some of his white colleagues. I don't know if the leadership program was Frank's idea to facilitate integration or if someone else had the idea and passed it on, but it was a miracle that he ended up heading the program. That was a great decision by the dean. Nobody else could have done what he did. None of the others could have developed the same kind of relationship with black students. He was so humane and down to earth and personable and caring. When he died, his family called and said he had wanted me to be on the funeral program to give remarks. There were so many people whom he could have chosen. Two people gave remarks that day and I was one of them. I was very honored by that.

I didn't have the same kind of close relationship with my colleagues in the leadership program. We enjoyed each other but we weren't problem-sharing friends. We didn't get down to the gut level in our relationships. What we did develop was respect for each other through our association and through the program. We observed and listened to others in their discourses as they shared things about their lives. I got to know them more that way than I did apart from the program.

I didn't feel prejudice from white students at U.Va. I felt it more from professors, which might not be too surprising because professors are vain anyway. It caused me some concern but it never really got me down. The only time I remember getting down was when I received a grade that I felt should have been much better, while others got higher grades for work I felt was no better. It was that kind of thing that got me down. That seemed racially motivated. There was just no way that I could do as well as white students in those situations.

The closest experience I had with talking about race-specific subjects when I was a student at U.Va. was one night when a group of us were in a colleague's room and we were all having a good time. We were celebrating something. I was the only black in the room. After a couple of drinks, the comfort level got to a point where one of the guys finally came out with some of the things that were on his mind. I'll always remember that he asked me why black men wear mustaches. I wore a mustache. Still do. I explained that it had always been a part of our dress. We didn't really feel dressed up without a mustache. And generally the opposite is true with white men. In any case, I thought the fact that we felt comfortable speaking to each other on such a personal level was pretty profound, and I felt an even deeper sense of closeness with them than I had before. The fellow who asked me the mustache question had come out of a redneck situation, but he was a nice guy. I think I helped him with his comfort level by talking about the mustache. Just by interacting and being in each other's presence, we both learned about the other. There were a number of eye-opening moments for me too. I thought, "Hey, this person isn't the way I thought he would be. That stereotype isn't as valid as I thought it was." It was an opportunity to interact and learn, which helps a lot in changing ideas, perceptions, and impressions.

During my years at U.Va. and after them, I held a number of administrative jobs in education. I was principal of two schools in Richmond; a Head Start administrator in Wilmington, Delaware; and personnel director in the Richmond schools. Then I worked in several school systems in the South as superintendent or assistant or associate superintendent. While I was superintendent of schools in Northampton County, North Carolina, the school system became accredited for the first time, voters approved the first bond referendum, and, with the proceeds, two new schools were built and others renovated. After eight years there, I became superintendent of the school system in Petersburg, Virginia. Four years after that, I became associate superintendent in charge of instruction in Richmond.

My career might have ended in Richmond, where it had begun, but in 1994, I took a superintendent job in Columbia, South Carolina. There, my staff and I were able to make key personnel changes and get the curriculum aligned.

One day, while on my way back to the office after a school visit, I received a phone call that was absolutely life changing. C. D. Spangler, president of the University of North Carolina, wanted to know if I'd come to Chapel Hill to discuss the leadership position at my alma mater, now called Fayetteville State University (FSU). I was thrilled. In 1995, I became the chancellor at the school where I'd received my undergraduate degree.

During the ensuing eight years, FSU's enrollment grew from 3,943 to 5,329. The school also began offering a bachelor's degree in nursing, established undergraduate degree programs in banking and finance, and a master's degree in social work. Furthermore, it received over $34 million in sponsored research and foundation grant support, and a residence hall was opened for students who maintain academic excellence. My term at FSU also saw development of the school's first master campus plan, renovation and expansion of the student center, and an increase in retention and graduation rates. We had ten different athletic championships during my eight-year tenure. My pride and joy was passage of a $46 million fund referendum. I left FSU in 2003. Because of my time at FSU as an undergraduate and as its chancellor, and because I now live in Fayetteville with my second wife, Jackie, Fayetteville State is probably the educational institution closest to my heart.

Even so, U.Va. was likely the most significant milestone in my life because it opened up the world. It opened up so many avenues for me: the people I got to know; the places I got to go; experiences that I had, personally and professionally, that I never would have had otherwise. The members of the leadership program visited our congressmen in Washington, D.C. We visited the Virginia state legislature and met the state superintendent. That was a big deal for us—a *big* deal. And these people were proud to see us, happy to see us. They were happy to show themselves off to us, and at the same time they were glad to see the state was beginning to make some progress. *Some* progress.

Had it not been for my U.Va. experience, I probably would have ended up retiring as an elementary school principal in Richmond at the most. Not that there would have been anything wrong with that. But had it not been for U.Va., I never would have fathomed the idea of becoming a central office administrator or an assistant superintendent, much less a superintendent or, eventually, a university chancellor. It was through that experience that I learned the possibilities were there. We were coming upon a time when school systems, by virtue of federal program requirements, were required to hire blacks in the administration. So my timing was good.

I haven't been back to U.Va. often. I went back once for a gathering of black alumni. Of course, I went back for Frank's funeral and to a couple of football games. Otherwise, I haven't seen the campus. I'm not one to go back to old landmarks. That's sad for me to do, to look back instead of looking forward. I can say, "Here's where I lived" and so forth. Well, so what? What else? I'd much rather say, "Here's where I live now, and where I live now is a consequence of life's opportunities and experiences. And here's what I'm doing now, and I'm doing it because of those opportunities and experiences." It served its purpose and served it very well. U.Va. was an essential experience in my life.

As for my accomplishments, I've helped thousands of young people through my work in school systems, through my work at the higher-education level, and I've helped adults as well. For the most part, I've had a positive influence on principals and teachers. That's what I feel good about. Not the buildings that I built or the programs that I developed. What means something to me is to go to a special activity on the Fayetteville State campus and see a youngster who was there when I was there, and how they greet me and so often express appreciation. I was always someone who felt a real desire to touch those with whom I worked and served. So I spent a lot of time talking and interacting and taking advantage of every opportunity I had to try to influence how a kid or group of kids thought. I never turned down an invitation, even as a chancellor, to come and speak to a first-grade class. I was an example for them. They could see, live and in living color, what is possible.

My professional career is now over and I am eternally grateful to U.Va., God, and good friends for the quality of life that I have had. U.Va. did indeed serve as a catalyst for much of what happened in my professional life and, to a degree, my personal life. I am pleased that my tenure as a U.Va. student helped to pave the way for so many wonderful opportunities that are now equally available to all, without regard to race, creed, color, sex, or national origin.

AN INTERVIEW WITH
VIVIAN W. PINN

Maurice Apprey

It was July 7, 2014, exactly thirty years since the creation of the University's Medical Academic Achievement Program (MAAP), an enrichment program to facilitate admission and retention of underserved and underrepresented students who wish to pursue careers in medicine or dentistry. Dr. Vivian Pinn, the second African American female student to matriculate at the University of Virginia School of Medicine, was on hand as keynote speaker to welcome the young women and men in the thirtieth class. What follows is an interview with Pinn about her experiences as the only woman and only black in her class some fifty years earlier.

MAURICE APPREY: As you may remember, when we started the Medical Academic Advancement Program [MAAP] in 1984, which is the forerunner of the SMDEP [Summer Medical and Dental Education Program], I wanted you to be among our first speakers but it was, at first, difficult for you to accept an invitation to return to the School of Medicine. What changed that allowed you to eventually return, and to return now, as often as you have?

VIVIAN PINN: Well, I think several things happened over the years, including my realization that my medical career was built on my education at U.Va. In spite of some of the unpleasant challenges that I faced during my school years, there were and have been some very positive changes, and to ignore my responsibility to assist in those changes at this institution would be selfish of me. I remember my very first day. The class was to meet in the auditorium in the old medical school. I knew no one there, so I went in and up the stairs and sat in the back of the room and looked around. I saw no other women and no one else of color, but I figured they were just late. Then the dean came in and called the roll. Everyone was there, which is when I thought, "Oh my goodness, what have I gotten myself into?" No other women, no one else of color. I could see the guys talking to each other. They had friends from their fraternities and people they knew from college, and I sat there alone wondering, "How am I going to get through this?"

When we got ready for the morning coffee break, the dean said, "I want you to get yourselves into groups of four. Those are going to be your anatomy partners for the year, so organize yourselves in groups during the break." I stayed put in the back of the room, still thinking about what next. I knew anatomy was very important, and getting good lab partners could make a big difference in getting through the first year. So I'm trying to decide, thinking to myself, "This isn't going to work; maybe I should just leave."

As I started down the steps to the bottom of the auditorium, really feeling dejected, two classmates came up to me, one of whom would eventually became a department chair at the medical school, and said, "We'd like for you to be our lab partner." Just like that.

I said, "Okay." They went and found a fourth guy to complete our lab group, and then said, "Let's go have coffee." That made such a difference on the first day.

I often tell that story because to me it points out how a very small gesture can make such a difference in someone's life and career. I thought I was going to be stuck with whoever didn't get other lab partners. There was no one like me, and it was going to be tough enough, and maybe I should go home. Then all of sudden I had lab partners who invited me to be part of their group. And when it was time for lunch, they said, "Come on, let's go." So I went with them but didn't find out until later that some of the places we went that year had not been integrated before. So I integrated some of those places on the Corner because I didn't know any better.

It turned out I had some very smart lab partners, who were very good people, who really looked out for me. That first day made such a difference in my orientation. It was not easy being here, but the fact that there were a few episodes like that, where there was goodwill from some of my classmates, where I felt they were really looking out for me, encouraged me to stick with it—because being a doctor was what I wanted to do.

When it got difficult and I just couldn't take it anymore I went home to Lynchburg and my father, who was not a physician but who understood what I was dealing with, gave me the support to stay the course. He gave me some fruit and a good meal and said, "Now get back up there and do what you're supposed to do." He gave me the tough love I needed, and so I got the through my years at U.Va.

I remember another episode from that first year that might interest you. Barbara Starks [Favazza], a second-year med student, arrived with her class a couple of weeks after the first-year students. I was so happy to see her because there she was, another person of color. We were both in the same residence, Mary Munford Hall, the first women's dormitory at the University, which was secluded from the predominately male campus at the northwest corner of grounds, in rooms next to each other. That made a big difference because now there was Barbara, plus the guys in anatomy looking out for me. She became a true friend and provided incredible support. I don't know what she did the year before when she had no one to provide support to her as she did for me. We are still good friends, going all the way back to the fall of 1963 when I started.

We decided we should move out of the dorm at the end of the year and get an apartment together. Some classmates had suggested I look at the apartments where a lot of the married couples lived, and they gave me the name of the people who owned it. They happened to be owned by someone on the University's Board of Visitors whose son also worked in the Athletic Department. I called and said I was looking for an apartment but that we would need twin beds. He said that would be no problem. We were in the midst of our final exams but wanted to see the place before the end of the academic year. So between exams, Barbara and I went over. I had been up all night, and then took my exam, came back to take a nap to get ready for the next exam when I got a phone call. And you know, back then there were no cell phones, just a phone booth in the hallway, and I still remember that cork paneling in the phone booth.

I went to the phone and it was the guy who owned the apartment, saying he was sorry but he couldn't let us have the apartment because he couldn't get the twin beds. My temper went off. I said, "It's not because you can't get the beds, it's because you saw us and saw we were black. You should be ashamed of yourself because I'm a part of this university and you're on the board here and your son works here. It's just because you saw us, and I am right in the middle of my exams and trying to study." I was so angry and so upset; it got to me. There were a lot of other incidents throughout the first year, but that one kind of capped things off at the end of the year.

I went to a number of the deans at the medical school saying this shouldn't happen, that he shouldn't get away with this. But no one seemed to take any interest in trying to do anything. I was just told there really wasn't anything to be done because he owned the property personally. As it turned out, someone else told us about an apartment on Brandon Avenue and that worked out well because it was right across the street from the school and the hospital. Barbara and I lived there together until she graduated.

I really felt someone could have attempted to do something about that first apartment. I found out later that one of my classmates was so upset over what happened, he went to his father, who evidently was a federal officer, and asked him to look into it. It turned out, because of the number of units or something, they couldn't bring in a federal agency to do anything. But the fact that one of my classmates tried to do something without ever saying anything about it, but quietly tried to do something, was encouraging. There were a lot of incidents like that where something negative was balanced with something positive.

I didn't like how they handled my internship, but that's another story. In any case, I did get into Harvard for my internship. I was trying to adjust to what I went through, but I did believe that I was well-prepared for the rigors of Harvard. U.Va. had provided the education I needed, and at least I had my medical degree. I had that feeling I could stand on my own, and I owe the school that.

A few years after graduation, I was invited to attend a meeting of the Alumni Association, but after learning that one of the featured speakers was someone who was reputed to have started an institution at that time to allow families to avoid having to send their children to integrated schools, I did not wish to come as my small way of protesting. And I decided to withhold any contributions to U.Va. But, in time, and after meeting or hearing of other students of color at the medical school, I realized that if I was going to have a role in bringing about change so that students coming after me would not have the same degree of challenges that I had faced earlier, then I needed to be a contributor to the school in donations of money and of effort. And that really marked the true beginning of my years of involvement with the medical school since that time, as well as being able to witness the very promising changes that have taken place since that time.

My cousin came here to U.Va. Medical School a few years after I graduated

MA: Are you speaking of Melvin [T. Pinn, Jr.]?

VP: Yes. He had a rough time even though he's brilliant. He finished a few years after me and did not have an easy time of it. I remember him saying, "Why didn't you tell me?" And I said, "If I told you not to go, you would've thought it was because I had gone. But maybe it would've been different for you." So it is something he had to go through himself, even if the same thing happened to me. I found out much later that another African American male from my hometown who graduated from the medical school before I came had experienced some very unpleasant incidents while at U.Va., but he never told me. When I asked him about this, he said, "You never know how people are going to react in a situation and it is something you have to experience for yourself to see how it will go."

But seeing progress and the faces of the diversity of students and faculty has been very encouraging to me and has inspired me to continue to lend my support to the change in atmosphere and attitudes at the medical school—and university. Some folks looked out for me—extended courtesy and kindness—and without them I probably would've left the first day. Maybe in spite of the bad things there were enough good things to keep me going. I got my degree and the education had been good. So that's when I decided that if I wanted to have a voice, I couldn't just be on the outside criticizing. I needed to play a role and get involved in contributing to change. I had stopped going to class reunions, but after that I started going to reunions and got to know people. I got involved. Then you invited me to speak, and I think those old mixed feelings returned—and I was reminded of those things I had lived through.

MA: Can I put it in your own words? "It is hard to come back, because when I come back I have to look at the faces of the same people that gave me a tough time when I was there."

VP: You are right; that is it. In one episode I remember so clearly, during the spring of my senior year, a dean, I won't say his name, who had never spoken to me, was heading toward me in the hall, but he quickly turned and walked up the stairs. Maybe that's where he was originally going, I don't know, but I took it as an intentional slight. You couldn't miss me; I didn't look like anybody else. So I marched in his office and fumed to his secretary because there were all these things about being a Virginia gentleman, but he wasn't courteous enough to speak to one of the students. He didn't speak to me my entire four years, and while others tried to reassure me that it was just him and it was nothing personal against me, I still wanted to talk to him. I had had it. He never came to the office while I was there.

So after the University commencement exercises that year but before we went back to the medical school to get our diplomas, my father and I got into a receiving line. He was really the one with the big temper (whatever temper I had, I got it from him). When we got to the dean, I said, "Doctor, I'm Vivian Pinn." And he said, "I know who you are Vivian." I said, "I thought you didn't, because you have not talked to me my entire four years here."

My father pulled on my robe and whispered, "Just wait thirty minutes and you'll have your diploma!" Then he turned to the dean and said very calmly, "How do you do, doctor? I am Vivian's father." Then he pushed me on my way. I never forgot that.

When I got the position at the NIH [National Institutes of Health], I received a handwritten note from that same dean, who was then retired. He said he had followed my career and was proud of me and of what I had accomplished. I kind of forgave him because he probably had no idea the impact he had on my life and the impact he had on my four years at U.Va. A small thing like not speaking to me really hurt me, but he took the time to send me that handwritten note, not a dictated one, to tell me he was proud of me. I didn't forget the feelings of slight I had experienced back then, but his note to me did make me think that he probably had no idea how his actions had affected me, but that was 1991, some twenty-four years later.

I looked back on some of the things that happened and I realized many of them had to do with the times. They were acting how they were used to acting without realizing the impact they had on others. Now I feel like maybe if I can share some of my stories with some of the students today, maybe they will understand that what they are dealing with these days isn't as bad as it might have been, and that if I made it through they can do even better. So that's been my philosophy.

When you got me to come back and talk to the students—I have always loved to teach—that was such a great experience. I still run into people who say, "I remember when you spoke to me at U.Va." So it has been such a special thing.

Incredibly, there are some faculty members here who were good to me back then, some of those others who have gone on, and some whom I just don't remember.

But I must admit there were some things that happened that were definitely worse than what I described, but they were not things that I liked to talk about. When I got the job at NIH, there were many interviews and media stories; everyone knew I had been the only woman and only minority in my class at U.Va. They wanted some sensational sound bites, the bad stuff I'd had to deal with. But I would not give it. I told them about my classmates who invited me to be their lab partner and how that made a difference. Certainly the bad things may have made me look good, on the one hand, but on the other hand, I was a U.Va. alumna and it wasn't going to make me look good to make the school look bad. So I did not share, not even some of the things I just told you, because I did not think it was either the time or the place to bring up the old wounds.

MA: What were some of the internal strengths that allowed you to soldier on? Also, what were some of your external support system: people like Teresa Price, the people in the community, and church?

VP: I think three things gave me the support I needed. First, there was my close family. I lost my mother when she was just forty-six and I was nineteen and away at college. I'm an only child, so I wanted to come back home and be closer to my father. It had been a rough death for both of us because our family was very close. My family sustained me.

Second, there was my father, who was very proud that I was in medical school. He was a physical education teacher who worked two extra jobs to provide for me. What did teachers make? Not that much in a segregated school system in Lynchburg. In fact, even after I finished medical school, here I was, a doctor at Harvard getting fifteen dollars from my father to get a good meal because it meant so much to him.

He was so proud of what I was doing that I couldn't let those other things keep me from focusing on my work. He could appreciate what I was going through and knew how to support me. He would say to folks, "You can't bother her, she needs the quiet. She needs to focus, to study." He understood that I needed the peace and quiet to get myself together, and he knew when to say, "Alright, get yourself together. You need to get back up there. You can do it." He was really my major support throughout.

Third were friends of my parents who lived in the Charlottesville area, who were there for us and who reached out and provided support. You knew you could call them because of your parents' network. So yes, it was the community support. There were a few faculty members that were very special to me, and some were not so nice. There was one woman professor who simply wasn't very nice to other women. So there were no women or minorities to go to for help on the faculty. There were a few people who tried to understand what we were going through and could be there for us, but no one who could really share the same experiences. You were always very careful about whom you talked to. You didn't want it taken as a weakness, so you just didn't share that much.

I think that because of the lessons accrued from my experiences as a student, I became a different kind of faculty member at another university. I wanted to help students and found I worked well with them, and finally I was named assistant dean of student affairs at Tufts University School of Medicine. The dean told me I was already doing the job so I might as well have the title. My experiences as a student helped me to support students dealing with all sorts of issues. There were some other supportive faculty members, but it was not the same as having someone who understood the issues related to being a woman or a minority in a town that was not integrated or at an institution with few if any other minorities on the faculty.

At the end of my senior year here at Virginia, some of my classmates wanted to have the senior party at the Boar's Head Inn but were informed that I could not attend as it had not yet been integrated. Funny—I remember that clearly although classmates that I have mentioned this to do not. That was before U.Va. took it over. So when I came back to give the commencement address at the University, I remember mentioning that I was trying to make the point that U.Va. is steeped in tradition. Some traditions needed to be kept and respected, and some needed to change. One example was that the very hotel I stayed in the night before I gave the address would not allow me in there my senior year at U.Va. There was a tradition that changed, that needed to change.

MA: I have been here for decades and I have been to just about every commencement. Yours was the only one that I remember ever received a standing ovation. Did you know that?

VP: No, I did not know that. That really touches me. [Tears come to her eyes.]

MA: What does that mean to you?

VP: I guess I never knew that. I was really frightened because when I was called by someone in the president's office, I said I would do it for the medical school but they told me, "No, this is not for the medical school; this is for the University." I said, "I can't do it. There is no way I can do the commencement address for the whole University."

I was just thinking I would really be on the spot. There would be criticisms. I was told by whoever called me, after I turned it down, "You have to do it; the president wants you to do it." So I did.

I had met President [John T.] Casteen earlier when I received the Alumni Achievement Award and he was very gracious. I felt honored to be asked, and I worked on my speech. I wanted to get across the message that U.Va. provides a great education—and a bit about tradition. There is so much tradition related to Thomas Jefferson that is good, but there were other traditions that were a part of this University history that no longer should exist. To do that without it coming across like I was preaching, without coming across like I was bitter, and still get the message across, was important to me. I did not want folks to say, "She is black, she is a woman, and she caused a couple of problems when she was here." I took the invitation very seriously, thinking we have people from philosophy, computer science, English, and so on, and my grammar had to be just right because I was afraid of the criticism I might get.

MA: Your address was very personal to the students. They were touched. They were moved. I know I was, and I would like to say, again, thank you for your countless contributions to the field of medicine and to health-care policy at the national level, among others.

VP: You are very welcome.

OPENING THE DOOR

Reflection and a Call to Action for an Inclusive Academic Community

Shelli M. Poe, Patrice Preston-Grimes,
Marcus L. Martin, and Meghan S. Faulkner

Official histories create and maintain the unity and continuity of a
political body by imposing an interpretation on a shared past and, at
the same time, by silencing alternative interpretations of historical
experiences. Counter-histories try to undo these silences and to
undermine the unity and continuity that official histories produce.
—JOSÉ MEDINA, "Toward a Foucaultian
Epistemology of *Resistence*" (2011)

As anyone on the underside of history knows, the privileges, powers, and perspectives of official historians are not irrelevant. Official history tends to suppress "the stories of resistance and dissent against the status quo and presents the past either as the triumph of the deserving or as inevitable."[1] Counter-histories, on the other hand, highlight the narratives of those who have challenged the existing state of affairs, representing progress as a result not of the inevitable march of time but of the courage of human subjects to struggle against injustice.

This book reflects critical history about the University of Virginia during its transition from an academic institution designed for the sons of the white, southern elite to a public university whose aim is to educate students from across the Commonwealth of Virginia and the nation. By contributing their own counter-histories, the school's early African American graduates witness to their struggle for justice and their achievements of excellence in spite of the obstacles they faced.

Each author in this volume speaks to the importance of women in their lives as they struggled to attain their goals. In this concluding chapter, we draw together the stories of the women who are peppered here and there within the early graduates' counter-histories. By doing so, we acknowledge the countless African American women who have been tragically forgotten—women who may have their own counter-histories to tell. It also serves as an introduction to our survey of the progress that has been made at U.Va. in recent years and its present challenges, many of which relate to sex and gender as well as race.

AFRICAN AMERICAN WOMEN AND THE EARLY GRADUATES

The "invisible faces" and "forgotten stories" with which Ervin Jordan opens his chapter in this volume include enslaved people, faculty and administrative slave owners, and freed African Americans employed at U.Va. after the Civil War. Among them were women who labored at Thomas Jefferson's plantation and who experienced interlocking systems of oppression on account of their race, class, and sex. We retain the names Lily and Fanny Hern, Catherine "Kitty" Foster, Maria (unknown last name), Isabella Gibbons, and Sally Cottrell Cole. For every name remembered, however, countless have been forgotten, recorded only as "cook," "seamstress," and "laundress." And then there were those by whose reproductive labor were produced children who were subsequently sold away to protect white male students. Most of these invisible faces and forgotten stories cannot be reconstructed.

The efforts of Alice Jackson to enroll as an undergraduate student in 1935 serve as a benchmark in the push to transform a white, male student body into a community that was more representative of the population of the Commonwealth of Virginia. Even after black women began matriculating as students at the University, however, its undergraduate population was almost exclusively male until 1970. Subsequently, a disproportionate number of male names are well known and reflect the progress in desegregating U.Va. over the years. For example, Dr. Luther Porter Jackson was the first black lecturer, Gregory Hayes Swanson was the first admitted black student, Walter Nathaniel Ridley was the first graduate of any kind, with a degree from the School of Education, Edward Wood was the first graduate in medicine, John F. Merchant was the first to earn a law degree, Robert Bland was the first to earn an undergraduate degree, and Amos Leroy Willis was the first black Lawn resident. The list continues into the present. For instance, five African American men have served as dean of the Office of African-American Affairs. Only in 2008 was Deborah McDowell chosen to direct the Carter G. Woodson Institute, itself named for "the Father of Black History."

More recently, significant progress has been made in the University's health system. In 2014, Pamela Sutton-Wallace was appointed CEO of the Medical Center, the first woman and the first African American to hold that position. A year later, the University named Dr. David S. Wilkes dean of the School of Medicine. Wilkes, the first African American to lead the school, is a specialist in pulmonary disease and critical-care medicine.

In light of these facts, we pause to notice the relative invisibility of black women at U.Va., who, as Jordan notes in his opening chapter, "had an especially hard road to travel." In an attempt to better understand that road and those who traveled it, here we highlight the histories of those women to whom the early African American graduates are indebted as integral players in their success.

Foremost among such women are the early graduates' mothers. In many of the autobiographical narratives contained in the previous pages of this volume, the early graduates' mothers are portrayed as reliable people who expected much from their children and who worked tirelessly to equip them for the tasks they would undertake. We begin with John Merchant's mother, a domestic worker in Greenwich, Connecticut, who raised him from the time she and his father separated when he was two years old. She was the one who took him to the hospital after he had fallen out of a tree and dislocated his wrist at age nine, who waited with him for the only black doctor in the area to arrive and treat him. She was the one who begged Dr. Samuel D. Proctor to "take her son off the streets" because "she was terrified he was going to wind up in jail." She persuaded Proctor, who then convinced Merchant, to enroll in U.Va.'s law school. She was the one whose "firm, but unsubstantiated belief that it would be okay" served as a source of strength for her son.

Likewise, William Womack's mother, Fannie, acted as a buffer from the segregated, racist world around them. When William would come home discouraged, his mother would say, "Just forget about that, it doesn't matter." Fannie Womack was a teacher who encouraged her young son to follow his dream of becoming a doctor. And when he was on the verge of dropping out midway through his first year at medical school, she convinced him to stay the course—and at least complete his first year before making a final decision.

Willis McLeod's mother, Hattie Lee, inspired her son with her own strength and pride. A sharecropper's daughter, she would pick three hundred pounds of cotton daily, worked well into her seventies, and, as a result, "wore a permanent groove into her shoulder from the sack she dragged so constantly through the cotton fields where she worked." Hattie Lee sacrificed for her son, not allowing him to work in the fields but expecting him instead to finish high school and go to college. While not literate herself, she made sure McLeod did his homework and was proud when he decided to become a teacher. She became concerned for his safety when he began to lead student demonstrations in the civil rights movement, remembering her own childhood when the Klan would appear at her house to scare her family.

David Temple's mother, Helen Burnette Jones, was born in 1919 and excelled academically until her education was cut short due to family needs before the ninth grade. She stayed home with David and his brother in his early years. And then, breaking boundaries herself, she worked as the first saleswoman of color in Richmond's retail district, at Harper's children's store. Finally, Barbara Favazza's mother, a college graduate herself, expected her children to go to college. These mothers of the early graduates inspired much, expected much, and deserved much.

They are joined by the early graduates' aunts, sisters, wives, nieces, and daughters in the community of women who enabled their sons, nephews, brothers, spouses, and fathers to succeed. Aubrey Jones, for instance, met his future wife, Alyce, in Charlottesville. As he explains, she "typed my term papers, invited me down for dinner, and was someone I could talk to when I was feeling down." David Temple's Aunt Bea took care of him after school. John Merchant's two sisters, Barbara ("Bobbie") and Elizabeth ("Liz"), were wonderful people he loved and leaned on, having grown up with them in a "rat-infested attic on Charles Street" and having sung with them in the junior choir at First Baptist Church. It was with them that his "chauvinistic approach" to the allowance they shared was "abolished by a failure to gather the votes." And it was with his niece's and daughter's work at U.Va.—Tabitha's achievement of an undergraduate degree and Susan's attainment of a law degree—that Merchant's three years at the University were validated. In particular, his daughter Susan's graduation as the first child of a black University law student "erased many negatives from [his] mind, and set a stage for more to come regarding diversity at UVa."

Other women in the Charlottesville community served as sources of strength for the early African American graduates as well. For Merchant and others, these community members included Punjab and Mae Jackson, Edward and Eunice Jackson, and Teresa Walker Price and her sons Bo and Frankie. It is notable that faculty member Charles O. Gregory invited Merchant to his summer home in New Hampshire for dinner. "His wife, a wonderful woman," prepared lamb chops. William Womack also acknowledges Mae Jackson as "a wonderful woman who also was a fabulous host and cooked great meals. We were always happily fed at their table."

Add to this list those workers, administrators, and professional mentors who helped the early graduates along the way. Aubrey Jones mentions Jean Holiday, Dean Lawrence Quarles's administrative assistant. Everyone knew, he says, that "Dean Jean" ran the office, and she was especially helpful to the black students. He also mentions an unnamed housekeeper at the engineering school who would ask the black students how they were doing and offer "words of encouragement." Upon request, she would reserve a much-need classroom for the students to study in after hours and lock the door until they arrived. Nameless other cooks and servers in the dining halls gave the early African American students extra helpings of food. Barbara Favazza emphasizes the role in her life's trajectory of many women nurses, but especially her mother's good friend, who was nursing director at a local hospital. The nurses "were amazing—so smart and knowledgeable," writes Favazza, and she wanted to be like them. Her mother's friend landed her a summer job as a nurse's aide. It was through this connection and her own enthusiasm for nursing that Favazza was encouraged to become a physician. Of course, Favazza and Vivian Pinn have their own stories to tell about being women at the University. They and countless other female students supported one another as they struggled to achieve their goals.

These are only bits and pieces of recollections about women's contributions to those early African American graduates of U.Va., reconstructed from larger autobiographical narratives. They represent merely the tip of the iceberg in terms of women's efforts to desegregate the University. The memory of these women accompany us as we detail the recent progress and current challenges at U.Va. and elsewhere. Here we affirm the need for institutions of higher education to focus on those who continue to be burdened by American society's approaches to race, class, sex, gender, and sexual orientation.

RECENT PROGRESS AND CURRENT CHALLENGES

The voices of the early African American students, buoyed with resilience, emotion, and community support, would foreshadow institutional responses over the next three decades. Three separate U.Va. presidential calls-to-action—in 1986, 2003, and 2013—remind us that the pace of structural change often moves slowly. University presidents Robert M. O'Neil, John T. Casteen III, and Teresa A. Sullivan each appointed internal commissions to study University policies and programs that could enhance the educational climate and recommend ways to create and sustain opportunities for all students and faculty at the University. Two of these commissions emerged from student protests calling for administrative action due to incidents of racial injustice and insensitivity on the Grounds. The third commission arose from efforts to acknowledge formally the contributions of African Americans to the University's history and to build relationships with a local community that has not always viewed the University as inclusive and welcoming.

In 1986, O'Neil appointed the Task Force on Afro-American Affairs "to define an institutional policy designed to promote integration and enhance the educational opportunities for Afro-American students at the University of Virginia."[2] The sixteen-member interracial task force included faculty, administrators, and student representatives. Its ten-month fact-finding study consisted of holding open student and faculty forums; surveying students, alumni, faculty, administrators, and the local community; and contacting other institutions to determine their activities related to minority affairs. The 295-page report, *An Audacious Faith,* was delivered to O'Neil in the spring of 1987. The task force chose the following words from Dr. Martin Luther King, Jr., to embody its hope for the future of race relations at U.Va.: "I accept this award with an abiding faith in America and an audacious faith in the future of mankind. I refuse to accept the idea that the 'isness' of man's present nature makes him morally incapable of reaching up for the 'oughtness' that forever confronts him."

King's admonition here, uttered while accepting his 1964 Nobel Peace Prize, came at the same time that the University's early African American students were enduring the isolation and bigotry that accompanied their collegiate experience. The students, like King, were determined to triumph not only for themselves but for all who would follow. In this spirit, the commission's overarching policy recommendation was to "welcome blacks on an equal basis to full participation at all levels in the mainstream of all University endeavors." The report includes twenty-seven supporting policy and programmatic recommendations with five areas for improvement, including the recruitment and retention of faculty, the recruitment and retention of students, student academic services, community relations, and administrative structure and employment policies. The task force concluded that "the self-transformation of the University of Virginia into a genuinely integrated institution equally receptive to people of all races is far from complete." They admonished, "The strategic goal of genuine integration can and must be achieved at the University of Virginia if the University is to maintain its place as an ethical leader, the flagship of the Commonwealth's system of higher learning, and an institution of increasing national and international prominence. The goal is a difficult and elusive one, however, that can be accomplished only through major and unequivocal commitment at two levels: (1) the level of institutional leadership and (2) the level of community ownership."[3] The degree to which the University administration addressed the task force recommendations across Grounds varied over the next several years. To a significant degree, the University left individual academic departments and administrative units to set their own policies for the recruitment, retention, and development of support services for African American students and faculty.

By the spring of 2003, however, a series of overt racial incidents toward African American students across the University's Grounds created widespread cause for concern, which led to the creation of a second commission. In September 2003, Casteen appointed the President's Commission on Diversity and Equity (PCODE) and tasked the commission with determining "the quality of the student experience within the University in all of its aspects, with special attention to experiences unique or generally germane to women and minority students."[4] Unlike *An Audacious Faith,* this report examines University populations other than African Americans and includes feedback from parents, alumni, and community representatives. It is similar to the earlier report in its scope, rigor, and identification of key issues (i.e., student life, climate, recruitment and retention; curriculum; faculty and staff recruitment and retention; and business/community relations). During the year-long study, commission members gathered and analyzed data and held dozens of meetings, focused discussions, and consultations within the broad spectrum of the University and city of Charlottesville constituents.

The PCODE report, *Embracing Diversity in Pursuit of Excellence,* was presented to the Board of Visitors, the University's governing body, in June 2004 and submitted to Casteen three months later. The overarching recommendation was to "appoint as soon as possible, after a national search, a chief officer for Diversity and Equity, structured as recommended in the full report."[5] In September 2005, Casteen named William B. Harvey as the University's first vice president and chief officer for diversity and equity, with direct reporting responsibilities to the University president. Many programs, efforts, and offices recommended by PCODE have since been initiated (e.g., the Office of Graduate Student Diversity Programs and its Mentoring Institute, University membership in the Sustained Dialogue Campus Network with program implementation across Grounds, and a University Sexual Misconduct Board). Others were enhanced (e.g., the Outreach Office of the Office of Undergraduate Admissions and the Office of African-American Affairs).

Still, the recruitment, retention, and advancement of African American faculty remains a challenge, even with the development of a recruitment and hiring training program for all faculty search committees and hiring officials, effective in 2005. The PCODE subcommittee addressed this dilemma, stating, "The issue then, is not that we as an institution have failed to find the ways that we can achieve greater diversity among our faculty and staff. The issue is that we have not effectively implemented the policies that have been recommended to us by our own investigations. The problem is not one of collective know-how, but of collective will."[6]

From the onset, PCODE members expressed their intention to "do more than write another well-crafted report."[7] Thus, the remaining challenge for current faculty, administrators, staff, and students is to respond to the dedicated work of the Task Force on Afro-American Affairs and PCODE to diversify and provide equity among the student bodies, faculty, administration, and staff. Both commissions challenged critics and cynics to persevere toward the principles embodied in the Jeffersonian traditions of excellence and enlightenment through national (and global) leadership.

Such leadership also includes attention to sex and gender. A number of successful initiatives to improve the climate of the University have been implemented as a result of PCODE recommendations. One of these is Sustained Dialogue, a contracted independent organization of the University. U.Va. is one of the nine original members of the Sustained Dialogue Campus Network national organization. Each week during the academic year, students of diverse backgrounds come together throughout the University in small groups to discuss a variety of social issues. At the end of the academic year, groups complete social action projects that they have collectively chosen during the course of the group meetings. Since the program's beginning in 2001, hundreds of undergraduate students have participated in regular group discussions as part of Sustained Dialogue. A similar program, called Dialogue across U.Va., has extended this principle to the larger University community. The program uses the Sustained Dialogue model to bring together faculty, staff, and students in small discussion groups to explore topics such as race, gender, class, religion, and U.Va.'s relationship to the larger Charlottesville community.

PCODE also recommended that the University promote mentoring efforts for youth in the local community. Among programs created are the Young Women Leaders Program, which connects U.Va. undergraduate women and seventh grade girls with a focus on enhancing the qualities of competence, connection, and autonomy in young women. Similarly, the Men's Leadership Project pairs undergraduate men and boys in the community and strives to develop leadership skills and healthy conceptions of masculinity in program participants.

Another PCODE recommendation highlights sex and gender by noting that the University should improve benefits in areas such as sick leave funding for professional research staff, tuition remission for worker's families, and health benefits for domestic partners/same-sex spouses, which has since been implemented. One direct benefit of this discussion was the creation of the LGBT (Lesbian, Gay, Bisexual, Transgender) Committee, a subcommittee of the University's Diversity Council. The LGBT Committee was formed in 2011 and is charged with discussing and addressing items of interest to the LGBT community, reviewing best practices of other institutions, and making regular reports and recommendations for the Diversity Council. One of the early successes of the committee was to provide feedback to the Faculty Senate on its faculty survey, which now provides an option for participants to identify as lesbian, gay, bisexual, and/or transgender. It is anticipated that this will be extended to the next version of the staff survey as well.

The third president's commission grew from the efforts of students and community residents over the years to acknowledge and remember the contributions of African Americans who built and labored at the University from its inception. In fall 2013, President Teresa Sullivan appointed a President's Commission on Slavery and the University (PCSU) with the directive that the commission "provide advice and recommendations . . . on the commemoration of the University of Virginia's historical relationship with slavery and enslaved people. From the early 19th Century until the Civil War, slavery was an integral component of the University. Enslaved people terraced the lawn, cleaned up after cadaver dissections, served the students and faculty, and built much of the University."[8] Once again, the commission's structure mirrored the previous two task forces, with an array of faculty, administration, staff, student, and community representatives selected to participate. Since then, several working groups have been formed, and the PCSU hosted a symposium—"Universities Confronting the Legacy of Slavery"—in October 2014, which included national and local participants.

Other events and activities give hope for ongoing change at the University. The election in 2013 of the first African American rector of the University, Board of Visitors member George K. Martin, and the University's deep commitment to supporting an annual community-based celebration recognizing the life and legacy of Martin Luther King, Jr., are oft-cited examples. In addition, the July 2014 issue of the *Peabody Journal of Education* features articles delineating best practices in the University's Office of African-American Affairs (OAAA), which have received national attention for two decades. For instance, a strategic OAAA goal has been to increase African American achievement, measured by those who, after earning an undergraduate degree, continue successfully in graduate schools, the workplace, or public service.

The question remains as to whether these and other efforts will unlock the door to a culturally diverse and inclusive academic community, or whether these actions will become merely symbolic benchmarks of a University that maintains the status quo. The voices of the early African Americans and others who have heretofore been on the margins of the history of the University highlight the need to continue to press for change in order to uphold the equality and dignity of all.

NOTES

1. Beverly Wildung Harrison, *Making the Connections: Essays in Feminist Social Ethics,* ed. Carol S. Robb (Boston: Beacon Press, 1985), 250.

2. See Task Force on Afro-American Affairs, *An Audacious Faith* (1987), https:// blackfireuva.files.wordpress.com/2012/02/an-audacious-faith.pdf.

3. Task Force on Afro-American Affairs, *An Audacious Faith,* 29.

4. PCODE, *Embracing Diversity in Pursuit of Excellence: Report of the President's Commission on Diversity and Equity* (2004), 2, https://pages.shanti.virginia.edu/ucare /files/2011/06/EmbracingDiversityReport_04.pdf.

5. PCODE, *Embracing Diversity,* 4.

6. PCODE, *Embracing Diversity,* 45.

7. PCODE, *Embracing Diversity,* 3.

8. Board of Visitors, Special Committee Meeting on Diversity (agenda item summary minutes), p. 1, February 21, 2014, Rotunda, U.Va., http://www.virginia.edu/bov /meetings/14feb/'14%20%20FEB%20%20DIVERSITY%20COMMITTEE%20 %20BOOKLET.pdf.

ADDENDUM

Strategies for Creating a Sense of
Place and High Achievement

Maurice Apprey

When I undertook the project of capturing the experience of the early African American graduates at the University of Virginia, Teresa Walker Price, one of the African Americans who had created a home away from home for many of those individuals, wondered if they would be able to write their stories. In her words, perhaps "it would be too painful for them." She was right. It was painful for them at the beginning to even contemplate the remembering. But then they began to write and to talk—and to remember. Shelli Poe and I owe an immense gratitude to them for allowing us to document their experiences and to preserve them for posterity. We all stand to learn from their stories of courage, perseverance, and leadership.

This book is structured with the stories of the early graduates at the core. The opening and closing chapters bracket their stories, providing additional historical and experiential contexts. The introduction by Deborah McDowell speaks to the imperative for open doors within higher education so that all may flourish. The lead chapter by Ervin Jordan provides a comprehensive historical trajectory of the presence of African Americans at the University.

Here in this addendum, I would like to pay tribute to the extraordinary work by many of my former and current colleagues in the University community and in the Office of African-American Affairs (OAAA) who have worked tirelessly to ensure the success—academically, socially, and professionally—of our African American students.

Their collective achievements and ongoing initiatives are the best way

I know to thank our early graduates for their pioneering efforts to create a path for future generations—and to let them know that their efforts to desegregate the University of Virginia, to graduate, and to achieve their own successes were worth their all-too-often painful and lonely labors. Their hard-won successes were accomplished so that others might stand on their shoulders to create an even greater and more diverse community of living and learning, a true "academical village" as envisioned by Thomas Jefferson, the University's founder.

Today, and in relative terms, African American students can prosper without the fear and impact of legal segregation. In addition, for the past twenty-five years, the University of Virginia consistently has received top honors among its peer flagship public universities in the rankings of retention and graduation rates of African American students. The 2015 graduation rate of the University's African American students was 86 percent, while the national average lagged at 42 percent.

So just how far has the University come? And how did it get to where it is today? It was not by happenstance. Rather, institutional commitment and strategic decision making fostered this competitive advantage—and an evolving understanding that graduation rankings could not be the only measure of success.

Increasing grade-point averages—literally doubling the number of African American students in the 3.4–4.0 range in the last ten years— became pivotal so that graduates would be positioned to go on to graduate or professional schools, as well as to compete for the best jobs after graduation.

This approach involved not only academic goals but also included noncognitive goals that would address skills and competencies for the workplace: emotional intelligence, team building, project management, and leadership development. It also embraced fostering an interest in African American culture as a major force in our pluralistic society.

Much of this work landed with the OAAA, which was established in 1976 and charged with assisting academic and nonacademic units in meeting the challenges of delivering an array of services to African American students. The office became one of the keys to making progress and to creating a supportive environment that promoted students' full participation in the life of the University.

Under the OAAA there are a number of programs that support our aspirations and have been the foundation of our success. They include the Peer Advisor Program, charged with facilitating students' entry into the University and helping them adjust to it; the GradStar Program, responsible for student retention and preparing them to enter graduate and professional programs and competitive workplaces; the Luther P. Jackson Black Cultural Center, charged with assisting students to develop skills and competencies in a culturally supportive environment; the STEM Enhancement Program, whose goal is to enhance students' quantitative skills in science, technology, engineering, and mathematics—including tutoring and mentoring services; and, finally, the Faculty-Staff Mentoring Program, in which University faculty and staff are paired one to one with undergraduates for individual mentoring and support and cross-cultural understanding.

All of these initiatives, as well as several others, focus on raising the bar for our students, helping them to develop into leaders who are well-rounded in both cognitive and non-cognitive spheres, and who have the informational influence to make decisive and substantive impacts on knowledge generation and knowledge transfer. In addition, our hope is that they will develop an informed and sustained commitment to society as the index of their leadership.

Throughout these students' time at the University, we impart four consistent messages that we believe contribute to their success:

- Motivation: Stay focused; clarify your goals; be persistent; and, most importantly, sustain your drive to become a teacher, lawyer, doctor, and so on.
- Exposure: Test your motivation by engaging in an internship or any set of activities that would allow you to know what you are about to get into and what ethical challenges there are in the anticipated profession.
- Academic preparation: Protect your grades; study broadly and deeply; be as well-rounded as possible.
- Leadership: Learn to lead from the front, the back, and the middle; treat leadership as a function of commitment to a purpose or a cause, not necessarily where one is in a hierarchy.

In all these efforts, we are building on the pioneering efforts of our first African American students.

I want to end by providing my lasting impressions from the stories in this book. In these pages, we find sometimes a wound here, a vicarious sense of triumph there, but never a regression to cynicism or recalcitrant resignation. The affective presence of each narrative leads me, above all, to feel a sense of hope and a collective sense of remembering in order to refashion our world.

To paraphrase the sociologist of knowledge Maurice Halbwachs in his *On Collective Memory*, I am reminded that we need others to remember, and reminiscing with them allows us to affirm that we are never alone. My greatest wish is that our readers will be enlightened as I was—and will remember always *with* our narrators.

CONTRIBUTORS

Maurice Apprey, a professor of psychiatric medicine at the University of Virginia's School of Medicine, has devoted his life to the practice of psychiatry as well as addressing diversity issues. For the past nine years, he has served as the University's dean of the Office of African-American Affairs. As the former associate dean for diversity at the medical school, Apprey was involved in the successful recruitment and retention of minority students to the school, and taught undergraduate and medical students, residents in psychiatry and psychology, and hospital chaplains. While at the medical school, he set up federally funded programs to provide student academic support and professional counseling to medical and premedical students, resulting in a thirteen-year run of 100 percent retention of minority and disadvantaged students and significant increases in the number of minority students in entering classes. He is one of a handful of students trained in London by Anna Freud at the Hampstead Clinic where he graduated in 1979. He has published extensively in three interrelated areas: conflict resolution and social change management; modern French and German phenomenology; and child, adolescent, and adult psychoanalysis.

Meghan S. Faulkner is assistant to the vice president and chief officer for diversity and equity for programs and projects at the University of Virginia. She joined the Office for Diversity and Equity in 2010. A native of Charlottesville, Virginia, she earned a B.A. in English from Tufts University and a M.Ed. in social foundations of education from the University of Virginia.

Barbara S. Favazza was the first African American woman to graduate from the University of Virginia's School of Medicine in 1966. Between 1985 and 1987, Favazza became the director of the Child and Adolescent Psychiatry Residency Training Program and director of the Child Psychiatry Outpatient Clinic at the University of Missouri Health Science Center. In 1987, she was appointed a clinical associate professor of child psychiatry at Missouri. As a member of the

Missouri State Mental Health Commission, appointed by the governor in the mid-1970s, she made many contributions to Missouri's mental health organizations and facilities. Favazza retired from clinical practice in 2004.

Aubrey Jones entered the University of Virginia School of Engineering in 1958. A resident of Richmond, Virginia, he matriculated as a twenty-three-year old veteran after serving four years in the U.S. Air Force. Jones was part of the cohort admitted to the School of Engineering during the first three years it opened its doors to black students.

Evelyn Yancey Jones grew up in Charlottesville and attended Jackson P. Burley High School. She is the sister of Charles Yancey, who studied at U.Va. in the early years. Students congregated in the Yancey home when there were very few places they could go, especially on Sundays.

Ervin L. Jordan, Jr., is an associate professor and research archivist at the University of Virginia's Albert and Shirley Small Special Collections Library. He specializes in Civil War and African American history and is the author of three books including *Black Confederates and Afro-Yankees in Civil War Virginia,* named one of 1995's best nonfiction books by *Publisher's Weekly.* He has contributed to a variety of academic and general publications including *The African American Odyssey, The Encyclopedia of the United States in the Nineteenth Century, The Western Journal of Black Studies,* and *Voices from Within the Veil: African Americans and the Experience of Democracy,* a collection of essays exploring the four-hundred-year journey of African Americans in America. Since 2015 he has been an affiliated faculty at the John L. Nau III Center for Civil War History, University of Virginia College and Graduate School of Arts and Sciences.

Marcus L. Martin is vice president and chief officer for diversity and equity and professor in the Department of Emergency Medicine at the University of Virginia. He served as chair of the Emergency Medicine Department as well as assistant dean in the School of Medicine at U.Va. He is the principal investigator for the Virginia–North Carolina Alliance, the goal of which is to increase the number of underrepresented minority college students who receive undergraduate degrees in STEM fields. He is also a member of the Kenan Institute of Engineering Technology and Science Board of Directors. He co-chairs the President's Commission on Slavery and the University.

Deborah E. McDowell is the Alice Griffin Professor of Literary Studies and director of the Carter G. Woodson Institute for African-American and African Studies at the University of Virginia. A member of U.Va.'s English department since 1987, McDowell is a well-known writer, scholar, and editor of African American literature for both academic and general audiences. She is the author of *Leaving Pipe Shop: Memories of Kin* and *The Changing Same: Studies in Fiction by African-American Women,* along with numerous articles and book chapters. Raised in a small town outside Birmingham, Alabama, McDowell received her B.A. from Tuskegee University and both her M.A. and Ph.D. from Purdue University.

Willis B. McLeod was a 1964 graduate of Fayetteville State University, and thirty-one years later was appointed chancellor of his alma mater. He became the ninth chief executive officer of the 135-year-old institution and its first alumnus to serve as chancellor since FSU became a constituent of the University of North Carolina. McLeod retired as chancellor in 2003 with emeritus status. He received both his master's and doctorate degrees in education from the University of Virginia.

John F. Merchant was born and raised in Greenwich, Connecticut, the son of Virginia natives. In 1958, he became the first black student to receive a law degree from the University of Virginia School of Law. His daughter later would become the first child of an African American alumnus to receive her law degree, and Merchant spoke at her graduation. He is retired from the law firm of Merchant and Rosenblum. At the insistence of friends, in 2012 he self-published his autobiography, *A Journey Worth Taking: An Unpredictable Adventure.* His chapter in this book is excerpted from that work. Merchant earned a B.A. from Virginia Union University in 1955.

Vivian W. Pinn is a physician, scientist, and pathologist known for her advocacy of women's health issues, as well as for encouraging women to follow medical and scientific careers. She was born in 1941 in Halifax, Virginia, and raised in Lynchburg, where she attended segregated schools. In 1967, she received her medical degree from the University of Virginia's School of Medicine where she was the only African American and the only woman in her class. She went on to do her residency in pathology at Massachusetts General Hospital while also serving as a teaching fellow at Harvard Medical School. In 1970, Pinn joined the faculty of Tufts University School of Medicine and served as assistant dean for student affairs. In 1982, she moved to Washington, D.C., to become professor and chair of the Department of Pathology at Howard University College of Medicine, becoming the first African American woman to chair an academic pathology department in the United States. In 1991, Pinn was appointed the first full-time director of the Office of Research on Women's Health at the National Institutes of Health. She graduated from Wellesley College in 1963. In 2005, Pinn delivered the keynote address at U.Va.'s graduation, the first African American woman to do so.

Shelli M. Poe is a visiting assistant professor of religious studies and director of Vocation, Ethics, and Society at Millsaps College in Jackson, Mississippi. She currently serves as co-chair of the Schleiermacher Group at the American Academy of Religion. She has published in religious studies, the study of teaching and learning, and higher education. She earned a Ph.D. from the University of Virginia, a M.Div. from Princeton Theological Seminary, and a B.A. from Bethel University in St. Paul, Minnesota.

Patrice Preston-Grimes is an associate professor in the Curry School of Education and associate dean of African-American Affairs at the University of Virginia. Her research focuses on southern public education before the civil rights era, with a special interest in local history and culture. She earned an MAT and Ph.D. from Emory University and a B.S. from Northwestern University.

Teresa Walker Price is a member of the Charlottesville community who often reached out to African American students, offering them support and some sense of home. In 2004, she was awarded the first annual Reflector Award, recognizing her service to the Jefferson School City Center and to the community at large. The award, given to a community member whose service embodies the core values that drive the work of the center, including activism, entrepreneurship, and social and cultural equity, is intended to "reflect the progress of our community and race."

David Temple, Jr. was born in 1947 in Richmond, Virginia, the first of two sons to David, Sr., and Helen Jones Temple. His only sibling, Riley K. Temple, was born in Richmond in 1949. In June 1965, David graduated from Richmond's Armstrong High School, one of two city high schools lawfully designated for black students. He and his brother graduated from Armstrong with honors. In 1969, David graduated from the University of Virginia with a bachelor of arts degree in psychology. He also earned a master of education degree in special education from U.Va.'s Curry School in 1972. Among other public and volunteer posts, David has served locally as a Fairfax County teacher and principal, on the state level as Virginia deputy secretary of education, and as program director at the National Science Foundation's Directorate for Education and Human Resources, where he helped to recruit thousands of Hispanic, black, and Native American post-secondary college students into STEM (science, technology, engineering, math) professions. During his career, David received the U.S. Department of Commerce Silver Medal for Workforce Development. He was awarded Vice President Al Gore's Hammer Award for Excellence in Government Reinvention. At its 2012 national convention, the Pi Lambda Phi International Fraternity presented David its Big Pi recognition, "awarded to alumni Brothers who are held 'in high esteem' for bringing honor to the Brother and Pi Lambda Phi Fraternity." On hand were several of Virginia Omega Alpha Chapter brothers, those who desegregated the IFC at U.Va.

William M. Womack graduated from the University of Virginia School of Medicine in 1961. In 1962, he completed his internship at the University of Washington Hospital in psychiatry, staying at Washington to do both his residency and a hospital fellowship. He has practiced psychiatry in Seattle for more than fifty-three years.

INDEX

ACC (Atlantic Coast Conference) titles, 26
AccessUVa, 47n48
Aerospace Engineering and Engineering
　Physics, School of, 20
affirmative action, 22, 31, 36
African Americans at U.Va.
—administrators: first affirmative action
　and equal opportunity officer (Lincoln
　Lewis), 22; first black administrators,
　21–24; first black dean of academic
　department (Bonnie Guiton Hill), 22;
　organizations, 25; women among, 163
—alumni: difficulty of returning, 4, 108,
　149, 153–54, *gallery;* Distinguished
　Alumna Award, 27; first Black Alumni
　Weekend (1987), 19, 108, 133; number
　of, 38; Pinn returning as speaker and
　taking active role, 152–53, 155; reunion
　of black students from 1950s and 1960s
　(2009), *gallery;* Temple serving on alumni
　committees, 133
—faculty: Afro-American Faculty-Staff
　Forum (1980s), 23, 25; first black faculty,
　21–24; first black female faculty member
　(Joan C. Franks), 22; first black tenured
　faculty couple (Nathan & Joan Franks),
　22; number of, 22–23, 38, 109; organiza-
　tions, 25; recruitment and retention of, 166
—firsts: admissions of black students (1950s),
　19, 84; African American and woman as
　Medical Center CEO (Pamela Sutton-
　Wallace), 161; black administrators and
　faculty, 21–24; black athletic director

(Craig K. Littlepage), 27; black College of
Arts and Sciences graduate (Amos Leroy
Willis), 20, 121; black dean of academic
department (Bonnie Guiton Hill), 22;
black dean of School of Medicine (David S. Wilkes), 161; black female faculty
member (Joan C. Franks), 22; black
female graduate (Louise Stokes Hunter),
19; black female law school graduate
(Elaine R. Jones), 18; black female medical
school graduate (Barbara S. Favazza),
114–17, *gallery;* black graduate (Walter
Nathaniel Ridley), 19, 160, *gallery;* black
Lawn resident (Leroy Willis), 102–3, 121,
161; black law school admission (Gregory
Hayes Swanson), 18, 160; black law school
graduate (John F. Merchant), 18, 49–82,
161; black law school professor (Larry
Wilson), 22; black medical school graduate (Edward Wood), 19, 161; black rector
(George K. Martin), 168, *gallery;* black
scholar to lecture (Luther Porter Jackson),
18, 160; black student-athletes, 26–27;
black undergraduate to receive B.S. (Robert A. Bland), 20, 101, 161; desegregated
fraternity (Pi Lambda Phi), 130–31, 132
—students: black faculty linked to recruitment of, 23–24; change in attitudes of
present black students, 120–21; characteristics of first black students, 119–21;
fostering success of, 172; organizations
and publications, 24–25; percent of
students (2016), 36

African Americans at U.Va. (*continued*)
—workers: displaced by whites in Great
Depression, 15; in early 1800s, 9–10; first
black department supervisor (Randolph L. White), 19; in late 1800s, 14;
supporting early black students, 99–100,
163
African American college graduates, number
in Virginia (1930), 16
African American entertainers, U.Va.
appearances of, 21
Afro-American studies program, 27–28, 30,
33–34
Allen, George, 20
Allen, Howard "Hank" Webster, 21
Alpha Kappa Alpha sorority, 24
alumni. *See* African Americans at U.Va.:
alumni
American Athletic Union softball tournament, 78–79
Anglo Saxon Clubs of America, 15
Apprey, Maurice: interview with Jones
and Price, 119–23; interview with Pinn,
149–57; as OAAA dean, 29, 32–33; on
race-based admissions, 5; "State of Race"
address, 33; strategies for creating sense of
place and high achievement, 171–74
"Around the Market House" radio program,
142
Asian American students, 36
Astoria Beneficial Club, 127
athletics. *See* sports and athletics
Atlantic Coast Conference (ACC) titles, 26

Baldwin, James, 20
Baliles, Gerald L., 133
Barringer, Paul, 15
Barristers (law-school softball team), 78
Battle, John S., 58
Beaver College (now Arcadia University),
114
bell-ringers, 11–12, *gallery*
Berry Plan (U.S. Naval Reserve), 90–91

Beta Bridge racist graffiti incident (May 1,
2013), 35, 47n49
Blackburn, John A., 81, 82
Black Culture Week, 24
blackface, 32, 37, 47n49
Black Student Alliance (BSA), 24–25; Black
Students for Freedom (original name),
24, 28; calling for Afro-American studies
department, 33; criticism of Puryear as
OAAA dean, 30; on Honor System, 35;
"Proposal for the Establishment of an Office of Minority Affairs at the University
of Virginia" (1975), 28
Black Voices (student choir), 24
Bland, Robert A. ("Bobby"), 20, 99–103,
105, 122, 161, *gallery*
Board of Visitors: black members, 20, 24; of
Central College (later U.Va.), 9; demands
for resignations of members, 27; Farming-
ton incident (1976) and, 28–29; Jackson,
rejection of application for admission,
16; member refusing to rent to black
female medical students, 151–52; protest
over lack of black member, 20; role of,
24; slavery prohibition on Grounds, 11;
statement of regret issued for slavery that
helped build U.Va., 37
Boar's Head Inn (Charlottesville), 156
Bob (slave), 13
Bowen, William, 6
Boyle, Sarah Patton, 20
Bren Wanna (social establishment), 122
Bressant, Ronnie, 64
Brinkley, France, 129
Brown, Alyce (wife of Aubrey Jones),
100–101, 162
Brown, Henry Box, 3
Brown, Joseph A., 29, 31, 32
Brown v. Board of Education (1954), 2,
49–51, 55, 76, 84; effect on Virginia, 5,
58, 102
BSA. *See* Black Student Alliance
Bunn, Benjamin and Emma, 123

Busch, Russell M., 144

Byers, Rosemary (aunt of Robert Bland), 122

Byrd, Harry F., 58, 59, 72, 78

Carter G. Woodson Institute for African-American and African Studies (formerly Institute for Afro-American and African Studies), 33–34, 161

Casteen, John T., III, 82, 157, 164, 165–66

Cavalier Daily (U.Va. student newspaper), 18

CBS (Concerned Black Students), 24–25

Central College (later U.Va.), 9–10

Chapel, University, 12

Charlottesville African American community: church role in, 123; free blacks, housing for, 10; hospital services for (late 1800s), 14; importance of link with University, 119–20, 164; mentoring for youth in, 167; present black students' detachment from, 120–21, 123; public school desegregation, 20, 120; welcoming students into, 4, 53, 72, 80, 103–4, 119–23, 156, 171; women's role in, 163

Charlottesville Tribune, 19

cheating. *See* Honor System

civil rights movement, 58–59, 84, 114, 141–42; sit-ins, 114, 122, 128, 136

Civil War, 13–14, 125

Cole, Reuben (free black), 12

Cole, Sally Cottrell (slave), 12, 160

College of Arts and Sciences: black faculty, 23; continued segregation in 1950s, 102; first black graduate (Amos Leroy Willis), 20, 102; increase in number of black graduates (1978 to 1981), 30

College of William and Mary, 19, 81

Columbia University, 17

Commodore, Lewis ("Lewis the Bell-Ringer," slave), 11

Concerned Black Students (CBS), 24–25

Confederate flag, 3, 57

Consultative Resource Center for School Desegregation, 21–22

Conway, Ishmail, 23

Coppeto, Barbara, 74

Corner, the (retail shops and restaurants adjacent to U.Va.), 79, 107, 150

corpses stolen from black cemeteries, 11, 13

Correctional Department, Virginia, 133

cottonpickers, 139–41

Council of Black Student Leaders, 35, 108

Council of Graduate Schools/Peterson's Award for Innovation in Promoting an Inclusive Graduate Community, 37

counter-histories, 159–60

Crispus Attucks Community Center (Greenwich, CT), 63

Cuozzo, Gary, 96–97

Curry School of Education: black professional and administrative staff, 21–22, 23; first black graduate (Walter Nathaniel Ridley), 19, 160–61, *gallery;* special leadership program of, 143–45; Temple earning master's degree in special education at, 133–34

Dabney, Richard Heath, 15

Dandridge, Elmer, 102, 103, *gallery*

Dawson, Martin, 29

Delta Sigma Theta sorority, 24

desegregation (1960s and 1970s), 19–20, 49–50, 125–26; Charlottesville public schools, 20, 120; the Corner, 150; Fayetteville businesses, 143; Richmond businesses, 162; Southern opposition to, 15, 59, 126

Dialogue across U.Va. program, 167

Dillard, Hardy C., 65–66

diversity: achievements of U.Va. in student body and faculty composition, 82; *Embracing Diversity in Pursuit of Excellence* (report, 2004), 166; first vice president and chief officer for diversity and equity (2005), 35, 166; minority groups represented in student population (2016), 36; need to foster, 38; Office of

diversity (*continued*)
 Graduate Student Diversity Programs,
 166; President's Commission on Diversity
 and Equity (PCODE), 165–67; Sustained
 Dialogue Campus Network, 166, 167
"Dixie" song, 3, 104–5, 132–33
"Donning of the Kente" ceremony, 33,
 gallery
Dorsey, Susan Y., 24, *gallery*
Dovell Act (1936), 17
Du Bois, W. E. B., 6
Dunglison House (dormitory), 130

Easley, Ken, 34–35
education: ban on teaching of blacks
 (pre–Civil War), 10; black school teachers
 seeking graduate and summer school
 admission, 19; blacks in administrative
 positions, initiatives for, 148; high
 school and higher education of blacks,
 opposition to, 15; pre-college education
 of black students, 122; teaching as career
 choice of blacks, 83, 111, 141; Temple as
 advocate for improved access to, 136. *See
 also* desegregation
Elizabeth City State Teachers College
 (North Carolina), 19
Ellison, John M., 50
Ellison, Ralph, "The World and the Jug," 4
Elwood, William, 20
employment discrimination, 54, 61, 63, 65
equal opportunity, education as key to, 6;
 hope for improved conditions, 38, 76, 114,
 148, 165, 169, 174
Equal Protection Clause, 18, 36

faculty: civil rights movement and, 20;
 interactions with black medical students,
 85–86, 156; Law School faculty during
 Merchant's time, 65–66, 163; Medical
 School faculty during Pinn's time, 156;
 Medical School faculty during Womack's
 time, 88–89; obstructing scholarly

research on African American studies,
 30; prohibiting blacks from residing on
 school property, 10; racism of, 15, 24–25,
 35, 98–99; as slaveholders, 10, 11, 13–14,
 160. *See also* African Americans at U.Va.:
 faculty; mentoring
Faculty-Staff Mentoring Program, 173
failure not an option, 52, 60, 66, 121
Farmington incident (1976), 28–29
Faulkner, Meghan S., 159
Fauntroy, Walter, 64
Favazza, Barbara S., 111–17, *gallery;* family
 and early years, 111–13; medical school as
 option for, 113; mother of, 162; Pinn and,
 116, 117, 151–52, 163; post-medical school
 training, 117; renting apartment near campus, 116, 151–52; on segregation, 113–14;
 undergraduate school in Pennsylvania,
 114; U.Va. medical school experience of,
 115–17; on women nurses, 112–13, 163
Fayetteville, VA, 139
Fayetteville State University/Fayetteville
 State Teachers College, 141–42, 147
First Amendment rights, 37
Flora, Frank E., 144–45, 148
Foster, Catherine "Kitty" (domestic worker),
 12, 160
Foster family cemetery, 12
Founder's Day protests, 23
Franks, Joan C., 22
fraternities, 103–4, 130–31; Pi Lambda Phi
 as first desegregated fraternity, 130–31,
 132, *gallery*
free blacks, 10–12, 160
fugitive slave narratives, 3

Gaines, John, *gallery*
Gaston, Paul, 20
Gatlin, Nathaniel, 102
G.I. Bill of Rights, 18
Gianinny, Alan, 98
Gibbons, William and Isabella (slaves), 12,
 160, *gallery*

Gilmore, Jim, 20
Glee Club, 131–32
Gordon, Vivian Verdell, 22, 28
Gore, Luther, 98
grading: improved grade-point averages of black students, 172; unfair, 24, 60–61, 69–70, 105–6, 146
Gratz v. Bollinger (2003), 36
Great Depression, 15
Greenwich, CT, 53, 54, 57, 61–63, 161
Gregory, Charles O., 66, 163
Gregory, Valerie, 120
Grounds: blacks prohibited from living on (late 1800s), 14; slavery prohibition on, 11; use of term, 39n2
Grutter v. Bollinger (2003), 36

Hackney, Caesar, 21
Halbwachs, Maurice, *On Collective Memory*, 174
Hampton Institute/Hampton Normal and Agricultural Institute, 16, 19, 111, 129
Harborview Medical Center (Seattle), 92
Harris, George, 102
Harris, Wesley L., Sr., 20, 120, 128
Harris, William L., Sr., 20, 29–30, 32
Harris, William M., Sr., 29
Harvard University, 1–2, 4–5, 6, 26, 152
Harvey, William B., 166
Hassell, Leroy R., Sr., 28
HBCUs (historically black colleges and universities), 2, 6, 50, 64
Hereford, Graham, 98
Hern, Fanny and Lily (slaves), 10, 160
Hern, Thrimston (slave), 10
Hill, Bonnie Guiton, 22
Hill, Oliver, 58
Hispanics, 36
historically black colleges and universities (HBCUs), 2, 6, 50, 64
Holcombe, James, 14
Holden, Matthew, Jr., 22
Holiday, Jean ("Dean Jean"), 99, 163

Holland, Elsie Goodwyn, 20, 24
Honor Committee, 34, 104
Honor System, 34–35, 97, 104, 130
Houpis, John, 70
Howard, Henry, 12
Howard University, 129
Hughes, Langston, 127
Hunter, Charlene, 101
Hunter, Louise Stokes, 19
Hunter, Thomas H., 88

"I, Too, Am Harvard" (multimedia project), 1
inclusive academic community, call for, 164–69
Institute for Afro-American and African Studies. *See* Carter G. Woodson Institute for African-American and African Studies
Institute of Government (now Weldon Cooper Center for Public Service), 30
integration. *See* desegregation; African Americans at U.Va.: firsts
Inter-Fraternity Council, 131

Jackson, Alice, 15–17, 160
Jackson, Edward and Eunice, 53, 163
Jackson, Jesse, 142
Jackson, Luther Porter ("Mr. Civil Rights of Virginia"), 18, 29, 160
Jackson, Punjab and Mae, 53, 88, 163
Jackson family (Charlottesville), 53, 88, 121, 163. *See also individual family members*
Jacobs, Linwood, 21
James, Arthur Curtiss, 15
Jefferson, Thomas: "Academical Village," 6, 7n8, 131, 172; and house of prostitution near U.Va., 12; slave ownership of, affecting attitudes of black students, 86; slaves owned by family of, 12; tradition associated with, 157, 167; U.Va. campus design by, 9–10, 11, 39n3, 102; Virginian as U.S. president, 125; Womack on, 93; women slaves owned by, 160

Jefferson's University. *See* University of
Virginia
Jews, 15, 85–88, 131
Jim Crow laws and practices, 2, 58–59
Johnson, Alex M., Jr., 22
Johnson, Elizabeth, 21
Johnson, Lyndon B., 129
Johnson, Nathan Edward, Sr., 21–22
Johnson, Sheila C., 24
Jones, Aubrey, 95–109, *gallery;* application
for U.Va. admission, 95–96; on benefits of
attending U.Va., 107–8; class choices and
avoiding racist professors, 98–99; as Coun-
cil of Black Student Leaders speaker (1990),
108–9; on exam taking and grading, 104,
105–6; at first Black Alumni Weekend
(1987), 108; mother of, 126–27, 162; on mo-
tivation and life lesson, 106, *gallery;* on "Rat
Pack" study group, 106–7; on social life,
103–5; on support from other blacks on
campus, 97, 99, 103; U.Va. staff employees
and, 99–100; wife of, 100–101, 162
Jones, Donald W., 21
Jones, Elaine R., 18
Jones, Evelyn Yancey, interview with, 119–23
Jones, Helen Burnette (mother of David
Temple), 126–27, 162
Jones, Howie, 64
Jordan, Ervin L., Jr., 2, 9, 160, 161, 171
Joyce, Johnny, 142

Kappa Delta Pi honor society, 19
Kelly, Sharon Pratt, 136
Kennedy, John F., 128–29
Key, Glynn D., 24
Key, Thomas Hewitt, 12
King, Martin Luther, Jr.: assassination of,
132; celebration to recognize life and
legacy of, 168; civil rights movement,
galvanizing role of, 126, 128; on desegregation, 19–20; Montgomery bus boycott
and, 101; Nobel Peace Prize (1964), 165;
public accommodations focus of, 75–76;

Task Force on Afro-American Affairs
quoting from, 164–65; Walker and, 64
Ku Klux Klan, 2, 15, 20, 50, 58, 75, 143, 162
Kurzweil, Martin, 6

Lawn: first black to live on (Leroy Willis),
102–3, 121, 161; historical import of, 97;
Jefferson's design for, 39n3
Law School (U.Va.): Barristers softball team,
78; dormitory life, 57–58; faculty during
Merchant's time at, 65–66, 163; first black
admissions and graduates, 18, 54; first
black law school graduate (John F. Mer-
chant), 18, 49–82; first black professor
(Larry Wilson), 22; student body of, 62.
See also Merchant, John F.
Leitao, Dave, 27
Lewis, Lincoln, 22
LGBT (Lesbian, Gay, Bisexual, Transgen-
der) Committee, 167–68
Lincoln University, 84
Lipscomb, John, 130–31
"Little Canada" neighborhood, 10
Littlepage, Craig K., 27
London, Mike, 27
Loury, Glenn, 1
Luther P. Jackson Black Cultural Center,
29, 173
Luther P. Jackson House, 29, 30
Lynchburg, VA, 83

Madison, James, 9, 125
Magan, Doug, 144–45
Maria (slave), 12, 160
Marsh, Harold, 102, 103, 105, 121, 122, *gallery*
Marsh, Henry, 65, 121
Marshall, Thurgood, 16, 18
Martin, George K., 168, *gallery*
Martin, Henry (enslaved bell-ringer), 11–12,
gallery
Martin, Marcus L., 159
Martin Luther King, Jr., Community Award
(Charlottesville), 20

Mary Munford Hall (dormitory), 151
McDowell, Deborah E., 1, 34, 161, 171
McLeod, Bud (father of Willis), 139–40
McLeod, Hattie Lee (mother of Willis), 139–41, 162
McLeod, Willis B., 3, 139–48; civil rights protests, participation in, 142–43, 162; college education at Fayetteville State Teachers College, 141–43; family and early years, 139–41; grading at U.Va., race as factor in, 146; in master's program for special leadership program at U.Va., 143; mother of, 139–41, 162; teaching and educational administrative jobs after U.Va., 143, 144, 146–47; U.Va. experience, meaning of, 3, 145–48
Medical Center, black female CEO of, 161
Medical College of Virginia, 19
medical school. *See* School of Medicine
Medina, José, 159
Memmi, Albert, 9
Men's Leadership Project, 167
mentoring, 90–91, 132, 167, 173
Merchant, Barbara and Elizabeth (sisters of John), 57, 67, 162
Merchant, Garrett McKinley (father of John), 54–56, 62, 67, 71
Merchant, John F., 2–5, 49–82, *gallery;* black medical and engineering students, interactions with, 80; Charlottesville African American community and, 53, 72, 80, 123; choosing not to complain or dwell on negatives, 4, 60–61, 69–70, 76–77, 79, *gallery;* daughter's graduation from U.Va. law school, 81–82, 162, *gallery;* decision to stay in law school, 71–72; on desegregation experiences of university students in years following *Brown,* 5; dormitory life while in law school, 57–58, 72; encounters requiring physical resolution or threats, 73, 79–80; exhaustion and mononucleosis of, 2–3, 52, 66, 68–69, 122; family background

and dreams, 54–57, 66–67; fears of, 2, 49–51, 59–60, 72; first black law school graduate, 18, 161, *gallery;* first year in law school, 51–53, 57–64; Gregory inviting to NH summer home, 66, 163; as keynote speaker on behalf of Ridley Fund, 108; law school faculty and, 65–66; law school grades, 69–70; law school social events and, 74–76; lessons learned and building bridges, 76–80; mother of, 57, 161; playing intramural sports with other law students, 77–78; on race relations, 77; student loan for final year of law school, 70; study habits and pre-college life of, 62–63; U.Va. experience, meaning of, 3, 81, 163
Merchant, Susan (daughter of John), 81–82, 162, *gallery*
Merchant, Tabitha (niece of John), 81, 162
Meredith, James, 101
Monroe (U.Va. employee, free black in 1850s), 10–11
Monroe, James, 9, 125
"Mother of Presidents, the," state of Virginia as, 125
motivation, 33, 106, 143, 173, *gallery. See also* failure not an option
"Mr. Civil Rights of Virginia." *See* Jackson, Luther Porter
multiculturalism. *See* diversity
Murchison, Robert Clinton, 85–88

Napper, Alver W., 63
Nash, Edward, 102
National Association for the Advancement of Colored People (NAACP), 16–18; centennial commemoration, 34; on Pierce as Harvard football player, 26; Swanson's challenge to U.Va. segregated policies and, 101; Temple's participation in, 128; Turner as president of Charlottesville-Albemarle branch, 32; U.Va. chapter, 33; Virginia chapter, 29, 35

National Collegiate Athletic Association (NCAA), 26
National Institutes of Health, 154, 155
National Science Foundation's Education and Human Resources Directorate, 136
nonviolent protests. *See* civil rights movement
North Carolina Mutual Life Insurance Company, 126

OAAA. *See* Office of African-American Affairs
Obama, Barack, 65, 79
Office for Civil Rights, 35
Office of African-American Affairs/Office of Afro-American Affairs (OAAA): on black student population at U.Va., 36–38; Charlottesville black community and, 120; deans, 29, 161; "Donning of the Kente," 33, *gallery;* establishment of, 29–30; first dean (William Harris), 20, 29; GradStar Program, 173; Luther P. Jackson House, 18; on multiculturalism, 35; PCODE initiative and, 166; *Peabody Journal of Education* recognition of, 168; Peer Advisor Program, 173; publications, 25; purpose and services of, 33, 171, 172–73; as sign of progress for black students, 109, 172; "State of Race" addresses, 30, 33; STEM Enhancement Program, 173; *Still I Rise: Thirty Years of Success* (2006), 25, 33; *Visions: A Newsletter for Parents of African-American Students,* 25, 31
Office of Graduate Student Diversity Programs, 166
Office of Institutional Analysis report, 22
Office of Institutional Assessment and Studies, 23
Old Cabell Hall, 10, 132
O'Neil, Robert M., 164
"O Triple-A." *See* Office of African-American Affairs

Outreach Office, Office of Undergraduate Admissions, 166

Patterson, Robert, 10
Payne, Walter, Jr., 102
Peabody Journal of Education, 33; July 2014 issue on Office of African-American Affairs (OAAA), 168
Peterson, Gerard, 81
Phelps-Stokes Fund, 15
Picot, Rupert, Jr., 95–96, 102
Pierce, Chester, 26
Pi Lambda Phi fraternity, 131, *gallery*
Pinn, Melvin T., Jr. (cousin of Vivian), 153
Pinn, Vivian W., *gallery;* Alumni Association role, 152–53, 155, 157; Charlottesville black community, importance of support from, 156; cousin attending medical school after Vivian's graduation, 153; difficulty of returning, 149, 153–54; faculty relations with, 156; family support, importance of, 155–56; Favazza and, 116, 117, 151–52, 163; Harvard internship of, 152; interview with, 149–57; learning of earlier black medical student's unpleasant experiences at U.Va., 153; positions at NIH and Tufts University School of Medicine, 154–56; renting apartment near campus, 116, 151–52; U.Va. experience, meaning of, 117, 149–50; withholding stories of difficult times at U.Va., 155
pioneer stress, 2–3. *See also individual students*
Plato, 37
Poe, Shelli M., 159, 171
President's Commission on Diversity and Equity (PCODE), 165–67; *Embracing Diversity in Pursuit of Excellence* (report, 2004), 166
President's Commission on Slavery and the University (PCSU), 168; "Universities Confronting the Legacy of Slavery" symposium (2014), 168, *gallery*

Preston-Grimes, Patrice, 159

Price, Teresa Walker, 88, 163, 171; interview with, 119–23

Prince Edward County, VA, 58

Proctor, Samuel D., 50–51, 55, 56–57, 71, 161; *The Substance of Things Hoped For,* 56–57

public accommodations, desegregation of, 3

publications, 24–25

Puryear, Paul L., 29, 30

Quakers, 139

Quarles, Lawrence, 95–96, 97, 99, 163

quota system, 84

racism and racial relations, 32, 35; in admissions decisions, 36; at colleges and universities (generally), 1–2, 5–6, 21; continued presence of racism, 36, 109, 165; derogatory studies of blacks, 15; efforts to address, 21, 37–38, 165–68; faculty members with racist attitudes, 15, 24–25, 35, 99; first vice president and chief officer for diversity and equity, 35, 166; fraternities and, 130–31; Greenwich, CT, employment and, 54, 61, 63; as honor offense, 35; hope for improved conditions, 38, 76, 114, 148, 165, 169, 174; incidents on campus (1990s and after), 108, 164, 165; medical students encountering, 89; and "pragmatics of forgetting," 4; protected speech, racist remarks as, 37; unfair grading and, 24, 60–61, 69–70, 105–6, 146

Reconstruction, 14

Ribble, F. D. G., 65

Richmond, VA, 125, 126, 127, 162

Ricouer, Paul, 4

Ridley, Walter Nathaniel, 18–19, 101–2, 108, 160–61, *gallery*

Ridley Fund. *See* Walter Ridley Scholarship Fund

Robinson, Armstead Louis, 34

Robinson, Mildred W., 34

Rotunda, 10, 11, 39n1, 97

Royal, Frank S., 24

Runk, B. F. D., 130, 131, 133

Sabato, Larry, 135

Sacks, Peter, 6

Sampson, Ralph L., 26

School of Education. *See* Curry School of Education

School of Engineering: black professional and administrative staff, 23; first black graduate (Robert Bland), 102. *See also* Jones, Aubrey

School of Medicine, *gallery;* black professional and administrative staff, 23; dean's interaction with black medical students, 85, 88; faculty interactions with black medical students, 85–86, 88–89; first black dean (David S. Wilkes), 161; first black female graduate (Barbara S. Favazza), 114–17; first black graduate (Edward Wood), 19; Medical Academic Achievement Program (MAAP), 149; Merchant's interactions with black medical students, 80; patient interactions, racial division in, 89; Summer Medical and Dental Education Program (SMDEP), 149. *See also* Favazza, Barbara S.; Pinn, Vivian W.; Womack, William M.

Scott, Charlotte H., 22

Scott, Nathan A., Jr., 22

Scott, S. Buford, 20

Scott Stadium, 26, 132

Seasons (multicultural journal), 35

Seawell, William H., 144, 145

segregated facilities: Charlottesville, 86, 115, 122, 156; daily life in Virginia, 113–14; hospital, 52, 68–69, 89, 112; Lynchburg, VA, 84; sports and athletics, 25–26

separate but equal, 17, 19, 58, 75, 78, 80–81, 102, 125; tuition assistance to out-of-state universities for black Virginians, 17, 80. See also *Brown v. Board of Education* (1954) sexual relations between blacks and whites, 12–13

Shannon, David, 23

Sistah Circle, 44n29

slavery: Board of Visitors' statement of regret issued for slavery that helped build U.Va., 37; burial of slaves on University property, 11; faculty as slaveholders, 10, 11, 13–14, 160; fugitive slave narratives, 3; Gibbons House named for slaves William and Isabella Gibbons, *gallery;* University's historical relationship with, 9–12, 125, 168; wealth and power based on, 125; whites' willingness to talk in front of slaves, 100; women slaves, 12–13, 160

Smith, Francis, 12

Smith, William, 83

social media, 1, 5

Southall, Joseph W., 15

Spangler, C. D., 147

sports and athletics: first black athletic director (Craig K. Littlepage), 27; first black student-athletes, 26–27; football, 26, 27, 132, 141; law school intramural basketball, 77–78; leisure time activities, 25; NBA and historically black colleges, 64; scholarships for black athletes (1970s), 26; segregated facilities, 25–26

Staley, Dawn M., 26–27

Stevenson, Ian, 88, 90–91

Stokes, Fred, 21

Stuart, Alice Jackson Houston. *See* Jackson, Alice

Student Coalition (1969), 27

Student Council, 33, 35

Student Nonviolent Coordinating Committee, 128

student organizations and publications, 24–25, 28

student protests, 23–24, 25, 27, 28, 141–42. *See also* civil rights movement

Sullivan, Teresa A., 164, 168, *gallery*

Sustained Dialogue Campus Network, 166, 167

Sutton-Wallace, Pamela, 161

Swanson, Gregory Hayes, 17–18, 101–2, 160

Swanson v. Rector and Visitors of the University of Virginia (1950), 18

Task Force on Afro-American Affairs (1986), 164–65, 167; *An Audacious Faith* (report, 1987), 164–65, 166

Temple, David, Sr., 126–27

Temple, David, Jr., 125–37, *gallery;* dealing with difficult experiences, 4, 132; family and early years, 126–29; at football stadium during singing of "Dixie," 132–33; Glee Club membership, 131–32; master's degree in special education at Curry School of Education, 133, 134; as "Partnership for Excellence—Workforce Virginia 2000" director, 136; Pi Lambda Phi fraternity membership, 130–31, 132; political interests of, 127–28, 134; public service appointments and jobs held by, 133–34, 136–37; U.Va. as college choice of, 129

Thomas, John Charles, 24

Thomas, Ted, 102

Thornton (slave), 13

Tobin, Eugene, 6

Toppin, Edgar A., 27

traditionalism, 38, 97, 157, 167

Trice, James, 102, 103, 104–5, 123, *gallery*

Tufts University School of Medicine, 156

tuition assistance to out-of-state universities for black Virginians, 17, 80, 84

Turner, M. Rick, 29, 32; "State of African-American Affairs at the University of Virginia" addresses, 31

Twine, George, 71

Uncle Tom's Cabin mentality, 143

"Universities Confronting the Legacy of Slavery" symposium (2014), 168

University and Community Action for Racial Equity, 47n48
University Chapel, 12
University Library, 28, 39n1
University of Michigan, 36, 117
University of Mississippi, 101
University of Missouri, 117
University of Richmond, 19
University of Virginia (U.Va.), 19; benefits for workers and staff, 167; as Central College, 9; firsthand experiences of early African American students, 1–2, 159–60, 171–72; integrated status of, 22, 37, 130, 159; legislators as alumnae of, 126; presidential calls-to-action for inclusiveness, 164; recognition for retention and graduation rate of black students, 37, 172. *See also* African Americans at U.Va.; Grounds; *specific departments and units of the University*
University of Washington, 90–92
University Sexual Misconduct Board, 166
Upward Bound, 28
U.S. Naval Reserve, 90–91
U.S. presidents from Virginia, 125

Vaughan, Leroy, 64
Vaughan, Mo, 64
Venable Lane Burial Site Task Force, 34
Vietnam War, 90–91
Virginia Education Association, 134
Virginia General Assembly: charter of U.Va., 9; Dovell Act (1936), 17; prohibition on integrated public schools (1870), 10–11
Virginia Law Weekly, 78
Virginia Normal and Industrial Institute/Virginia Normal and Collegiate Institute (later Virginia State University), 15–16
Virginia Polytechnic Institute, 19
Virginia State College for Negroes (later Virginia State University), 16, 19
Virginia State University, 15–16, 80

Virginia Union University, 2, 16, 50, 53, 58, 64, 65
Virginia Voters League, 29

Walker, Franklin (son of Teresa Walker Price), 121, 163
Walker, Wyatt T., 64
Walker family (Charlottesville), 88, 163
Wallace, George, 59
Walls, Arthur, 97
Walter Ridley Scholarship Fund, 19, 108, 133
Warner, Mark, 136
Washington, George, 125
Washington, Joseph R., Jr., 27–28
Washington and Lee University, 19, 81
Watt, Patricia C. ("Pat"), 134
Weldon Cooper Center for Public Service (formerly Institute of Government), 30
White, Randolph L., 19
white civil rights activists (1950s and 1960s), 20
white supremacists, 15. *See also* Ku Klux Klan
Wilder, Beulah, 127
Wilder, L. Douglas, 65, 127, 134–35
Wilder, Robert, 127
Wilkes, David S., 161
Wilkins, Roy A., 27
William and Mary, College of, 81
Williams, Patricia J., 5
Willis, Amos Leroy, 20, 102–3, 120, 121, 161, *gallery*
Wilson, Larry, 22
Wilson-Puryear, Leah, 28
Womack, Fannie (mother of William), 84, 86–87, 161–62
Womack, William M., 83–93, *gallery;* Charlottesville black community and, 163; family and early years, 83–84; first year medical school experience, 85–87; grades at medical school, 87; medical school social events and, 87–88; mentoring by Dr. Stevenson, 90–91; "Monday's Child"

Womack, William M. (*continued*)
television segments, 92; mother of, 84,
86–87, 161–62; Navy service of, 91–92;
psychiatric rotation in medical school,
90; reflections on U.Va. experience,
92–93, 123; remaining years of medical
school experience, 88–89; summer jobs
at Raleigh General Hospital, 89; U.Va.
acknowledging achievements of, 4, 93;
Washington State jobs after graduation,
90–91, 92
women at U.Va.: black college applicants and
admissions, 19, 160, 161; black student-
athletes, 26–27; counter-histories of,
159–69; debt of early black graduates
to, 161; family support to black students
provided by, 162–63; first black female
faculty member (Joan C. Franks), 22;
first black female graduate (Louise

Stokes Hunter), 19; initiatives to improve
University climate for, 167; law school
students, 74; medical school students, 85,
87, 115–17, 149–57; mothers of early black
graduates, 161–62; Sistah Circle, 44n29;
slaves, 12–13, 160; Young Women Leaders
Program, 167
Wood, Edward, 19, 102, 161
Woodson, Carter G., 33, 53, 161
Woodson Institute. *See* Carter G. Woodson
Institute for African-American and
African Studies

Yancey, Charles (brother of Evelyn Jones),
119
Yancey, Dwayne, *When Hell Froze Over,* 135
Young Women Leaders Program, 167
Youth Initiatives Office (Washington, D.C.),
136